D1538448

Building a Transnational Civil Society

Also by Ingo K. Richter, Sabine Berking and Ralf Müller-Schmid

RISK SOCIETY AND THE CULTURE OF PRECAUTION (*editors*)

Also by Ingo K. Richter

DIE SIEBEN TODSÜNDEN DER BILDUNGSPOLITIK (*The Seven Deadly Sins of Educational Policy*)

Building a Transnational Civil Society

Global Issues and Global Actors

Edited by

Ingo K. Richter
Emeritus Professor of Law,
Eberhard Karls University of Tübingen, Germany

Sabine Berking
Researcher, Irmgard Coninx Foundation, Germany

and

Ralf Müller-Schmid
Editor, Deutschlandradio Kultur, Berlin

First published in 2006 by
PALGRAVE MACMILLAN
Houndmills, Basingstoke, Hampshire RG21 6XS and
175 Fifth Avenue, New York, N.Y. 10010
Companies and representatives throughout the world.

PALGRAVE MACMILLAN is the global academic imprint of the Palgrave
Macmillan division of St. Martin's Press, LLC and of Palgrave Macmillan Ltd.
Macmillan® is a registered trademark in the United States, United Kingdom
and other countries. Palgrave is a registered trademark in the European
Union and other countries.

ISBN-13: 978–1–4039–9694–7 hardback
ISBN-10: 1–4039–9694–6 hardback

This book is printed on paper suitable for recycling and made from fully
managed and sustained forest sources.

A catalogue record for this book is available from the British Library.

Library of Congress Cataloging-in-Publication Data
    Building a transnational civil society : global issues and global actors /
edited by Ingo K. Richter, Sabine Berking, Ralf Müller-Schmid.
        p. cm.
        Includes bibliographical references and index.
        ISBN 1-4039-9694-6 (cloth : alk. paper)
        1. Globalization. 2. Internationalism. 3. Cosmopolitanism.
    4. Civil society. I. Richter, Ingo. II. Berking, Sabine. III. Müller-Schmid,
    Ralf, 1967–

JZ1318.B86 2006
303.48'2—dc22   2006043554

10 9 8 7 6 5 4 3 2 1
15 14 13 12 11 10 09 08 07 06

Printed and bound in Great Britain by
Antony Rowe Ltd, Chippenham and Eastbourne

Contents

List of Figures

Foreword

This publication is based on the work of the Irmgard Coninx Foundation, Berlin, established in 2001. In cooperation with the Social Science Research Centre, Berlin and Humboldt University, the Irmgard Coninx Foundation set up the Berlin Roundtables on Transnationality to discuss current issues in international politics. As a result of the first years of research two volumes on new transnational developments are being published.

This volume deals with the question of whether a transnational civil society is possible and how far it could be a major factor in solving global and transnational conflicts. The other volume, also published by Palgrave Macmillan in 2006, is on risk policy, and discusses questions of risk prevention and precaution as well as risk communication.

The editors would like to thank Guido Albisetti (Berne), Antje Landshoff (Hamburg) and Sabine Richter-Ellermann (Berlin), members of the Board of the Irmgard Coninx Foundation. The members of the Academic Advisory Board provided invaluable support and encouragement for the endeavour of the Berlin Roundtables on Transnationality, among others Jürgen Kocka, president of the Social Science Research Centre, Berlin, Elmar Tenorth, former vice-president of Humboldt University, Berlin, Wolfgang van den Daele, Wolfgang Edelstein, Shalini Randeria, F. Schuppert and Georg Thurn.

Notes on the Contributors

Harry Bauer is a researcher in International Relations at the London School of Economics. He co-edited *International Relations at the LSE: A History of 75 Years* (2004) and is currently completing a comprehensive study on the power, practice and pathologies of private actors in global environmental politics. His main interests lie in IR theory, practice theory, contentious politics and global environmental affairs. He has worked as editor for *Millennium: Journal of International Studies*.

Dennis Dijkzeul is Professor in the Management of Humanitarian Crises at the Institute for International Law of Peace and Armed Conflict at Ruhr University, Bochum, Germany. From 2000 to 2002 he directed the Programme for Humanitarian Affairs at Columbia University's School for International and Public Affairs. He regularly consults for international organizations in Africa, Central America, Europe and the United States. His publications include *Reforming for Results in the UN System: A Study of UNOPS* (2000), *Between Force and Mercy: Military Action and Humanitarian Aid* (2004) and (with Yves Beigbeder) *Rethinking International Organizations: Pathology and Promise*.

Antonio Donini is a senior researcher at the Feinstein International Famine Center (FIFC), Tufts University. From 2002 to 2004 he was Visiting Senior Fellow at the Watson Institute for International Studies at Brown University. He has worked for 26 years in the United Nations in research, evaluation and humanitarian capacities. He is co-editor of *Nation-Building unraveled: Aid Peace and Justice in Afghanistan* (2004) and has written on the implications of the crises in Afghanistan and Iraq for the future of humanitarian action.

Susan George is Chair of the Planning Board of the Transnational Institute in Amsterdam and Vice-President of the Association for Taxation of Financial Transaction to Aid Citizens (ATTAC France). She is the author of a dozen books, the most recent of which is *Another World Is Possible If ...* (2004).

Boris Holzer is lecturer in the Department of Sociology, Ludwig Maximillian University, Munich. He is author of *Die Fabrikation von Wundern, Modernisierung, wirtscharftliche, Entwicklung und kultureller Wandel in Ostasien* (1999).

Mikhail A. Molchanov is associate professor in the Department of Political Science, St. Thomas University, Canada. His interests are the political economy and foreign policies of Russia, the Ukraine and other post-Soviet states. His most recent book is *Political Culture and National Identity in Russian-Ukranian Relations* (2002) and he is co-editor of *Ukraine's Foreign and Security Policy: Theoretical and Comparative Perspectives* (2002).

Gerhard J. Klose retired in March 2005 as a colonel in the German Army. He was Chief of the Policy and Doctrine Branch on Civil Military Co-operation (CIMC) of the Ministry of Defence in Germany. He also worked as Chief Engineer for NATO and participated in the NATO missions in Bosnia (1997) and Kosovo (2000). He is currently working as an adviser to the Germany military forces in Afghanistan.

Thomas Olesen is assistant professor in the Department of Political Science, University of Aarhus, Denmark. His research interests include social movements, solidarity and globalization. He is author of *International Zapatismo: The Construction of Solidarity in the Age of Globalization* (2004).

Susanne Soederberg is an associate professor and a Canada Research Chair in Global Political Economy in the Development Studies Programme at Queen's University, Canada. Her research interests include global political economy, corporate governance and the transnational architecture of development finance. She is author of *The Politics of the New International Financial Architecture: Imposed Leadership and the Global South* (2004), *Contesting Global Governance: Empire, Class and the New Common Sense in Managing Globalization* (2006) (with Philip G. Cerny and Georg Menz) *Internalizing Globalization: The Rise of Neoliberalism and the Decline of National Varieties of Capitalism* (2005), and *Global Governance in Question: Empire, Class and the New Common Sense in Managing North–South Relations* (2006).

Shalini Randeria is Professor of Social Anthropology at the University of Zurich. Her research interests include legal anthropology and the transformation of the nation-state, civil society, processes of globalization, anthropological demography, development studies and post-colonial theory. She is co-editor of *World on the Move: Globalization, Migration and Cultural Security* (2004) and of *Unravelling Ties: From Social Cohesion to New Practices of Connectedness* (2006).

David Rieff is Senior Fellow at The World Policy Institute at the New School, New York. He is author of *At the Point of a Gun: Democratic Dreams* *and Armed Intervention* (2002) and *A Bed for the Night: Humanitarianism in Crisis* (2002). He is a contributor to the US and British media on wars and humanitarian emergencies throughout the globe.

Dieter Rucht is Professor of Sociology and Head of the Research Group on Civil Society, Citizenship and Political Mobilization in Europe at the Social Science Research Centre, Berlin. His research interests are global social movements. He is co-editor of *Cyberprotest: New Media, Citizens and Social Movements* (2004) and of *Women's Movements Facing the Reconfigured State* (2003).

Tony Vaux is an independent consultant for humanitarian and conflict policy issues. He worked for more than 25 years for Oxfam. A global emergiences co-ordinator, he has played a key role in Oxfam's response to most of the major humanitarian crises between 1984 and 1994. He was Visiting Fellow at the Refugee Studies Centre, Oxford University between 1999 and 2000. He is author of *The Selfish Altruist: Relief Work in Famine and War* (2001).

Yuri Yevdokimov is an associate professor in the Departments of Civil Engineering and Economics at the University of New Brunswick, Canada. His research focuses on the modelling of the transportation sector and sustainable development.

Acknowledgements

The editors and publisher acknowledge the use of David Reiff, *Transnational Risks and Humanitarian Crises: The Blind Alley of Humanitarian Intervention.* © David Rieff, 2005.

The Introduction to this book was translated by Paul Knowlton; and Chapter 6, 'Critique of Capitalism in the Era of Globalization – Old Wine in New Bottles?', was translated by Robin Benson.

Introduction

Ingo K. Richter, Sabine Berking and Ralf Müller-Schmid

The subject of the present volume is twofold: on the one hand, the structural transformation of the nation-state brought about by globalization; on the other, the development of transnational civil society action. The increasing integration of markets and the emergence of an international legal system have, since end of the Cold War, markedly altered the state's governance capacities. The authors of the present volume analyse the structures and the crises of globalization processes, attempting to point out the possibilities and limits of political and civil society action at the transnational level, of a new cosmopolitan internationalism. The chapters focus in particular on economic development, social movements and the reality of the new wars.

Globalization

To this day the world political order continues to be based on a system of nation-states. Since the United Nations was founded in 1945, the number of member states has almost quadrupled from 51 founding members to a total of 191 today. All of these countries are sovereign nation-states. Since the disintegration of the European colonial empires and the breakup of the military blocs that characterized the Cold War, the world has witnessed a process of territorial disintegration that is still far from complete. This process is at the same time accompanied by an opposite, integrative development which has created global markets and global culture industries of a kind that has never been seen before.

Globalization, it seems, has become the most important frame for the organization of socio-spatial relations. The term stands for a new round of 'time-space compression', for the flow of commodities, finances, ideas and, to a lesser degree, of human labour, for a 'space of flows' rather than a 'space of places' (Castell 1996: 378). Though globalization has its roots, as Mary Kaldor states (1999: 3), in modernity itself, it was undoubtedly fuelled by the revolution in information and communications technologies in the 1980s and early 1990s and by the collapse of the communist empire that put an end to the Cold War and the division of markets it had brought about.

However, globalization as an economic process has also been accompanied by worldwide protests. The promise of freedom and wealth made possible by the mechanisms of a market economy on a global scale and the political structures of a parliamentary democracy undoubtedly nurtured the street protests of 1989 – from Berlin to Beijing. But within only a few years perceptions have changed enormously. For many people around the globe, the buzzword *globalization* has now come to connote social inequality, transnational risks, environmental catastrophes, new wars and Western hegemony, both economic and cultural, which provokes anti-Western resentment and global terrorism. The self-dynamics of the global economy and its neo-liberal theoretical base have meanwhile been branded as 'market fundamentalism' (Soros 2002), or even denounced as a new form of totalitarianism which builds its power on employees' fear of losing their jobs, on threats to offshore jobs and on unrelenting career uncertainties.

But what is globalization? If anywhere, the only place where these phenomena can be said to have been satisfactorily conceptualized is in the field of economics. In fully integrated global markets businesses can produce goods and offer services that can be bought or used by consumers without being hindered by restrictions other than those imposed by economic givens. In a liberalized capital market, capital too is fully free to move as it sees fit. Critics, however, point out that the reality is not (yet) in line with this model, that it will first be necessary to scrutinize empirically the scope of globalization by measuring both the geographic dimensions of the phenomenon and the growing densification of flows of capital and goods – just as it will be necessary to analyse the impact of globalization on the activities of national and local actors and take a close look at the infrastructures and networks that serve the ends of globalization (Hirst and Thompson 1999).

Attempts to grasp globalization, beyond economic processes, as a general social phenomenon have remained either abstract and superficial, as in McGrew's attempt to depict globalization as 'growing global interconnectedness', as a transnationality of social, political and economic activities, as an intensification of international interactions, and as a mingling of the local and the global, the internal and the external

(McGrew 1997: 6); or such attempts do little more than illustrate the shakiness of the entire conception – when e.g. the focus is placed on the development of metropolises (Sassen 1998) or the interrelations between global and local development, known as glocalization (Robertson 1995). While a conceptualization of this kind makes it possible to capture the totality of the phenomena outlined above and overcome the narrow focus on the economy, and while it may be able to illustrate the process character of the whole, the price it is forced to pay in return is that a concept so broadly formulated is in danger of losing the better part of its explanatory power.

The nation-state

The concept of the nation-state goes back to the *Acta Pacis Westphalicae* – the Peace Treaty of Westphalia of 1648 – which ended the Thirty Years' War in Central Europe. This is why the system of sovereign nation-states is referred to as the 'Westphalian system'. The Peace Treaty of Westphalia overcame the universal claim to power made by emperor and/or pope, enforced peace between Catholics and Protestants, and grounded the sovereignty of the territorial state – both its internal sovereignty (supreme power) and its external sovereignty (the right to form alliances and to wage war). The idea of sovereignty had already been laid out theoretically in the writings of Jean Bodin, who, in 1583, and in the face of the religious wars tearing France apart at the time, spoke in favour of absolute state power. A good 40 years later, Hugo Grotius provided a justification for the secession of his homeland, the Netherlands, from Spain, and in 1642 the English philosopher Thomas Hobbes grounded the idea of state sovereignty in the absolute need for a 'contract' to end the state of 'war of all against all'.

This idea of sovereignty was, in other words, bound to the notion of the state, but not yet to the concept of the nation. It was Emanuel Joseph Sieyès who, in 1789, first established this link by declaring the Third Estate of the French 'Etats Généraux' to be the legitimate representation of the nation, thus grounding sovereignty on the principle of the sovereignty of the people. This was the birth of the nation-state, an idea that was to prevail in Europe in the course of the nineteenth century and throughout the world in the twentieth century. Over the course of the nineteenth century the idea of the nation-state coalesced with the idea of democracy, an idea to which Fichte, in 1807–8, had given succinct expression in his 'Addresses to the German Nation'. On the other hand, in countries that experienced a gradual transition from absolute to constitutional monarchy, e.g. in England, attention focused on the sovereignty of parliament, and in post-independence and *post-bellum* United States the focal issues were the Union and the separation of powers (Dryzek 2000).

The idea of the nation-state achieved its breakthrough after the First World War, with the treaties of Versailles, St. Germain and Sèvres, which dissolved the Habsburg Empire and Ottoman Empire by granting all peoples the right to a state of their own and by according national minorities the right to secede or the right to minority status. The breakup of the European colonial empires in the twentieth century, which began immediately after the Second World War when India declared independence, and reached its pinnacle in Africa in the 1960s, likewise involved the formation of new nation-states. In many cases, though, this development was not based on popular sovereignty and the principle of ethnic or cultural differentiation; instead, the colonial powers simply handed over power to regional – including military – elites, who were to rule within the borders of territories that had earlier been defined, more or less arbitrarily, by European colonial authorities. The breakup of the Soviet Union and Yugoslavia seem to have ushered in a final stage of the process of territorial disintegration. Yet while the system based on the nation-state has prevailed worldwide, the foundations of the nation-state – territoriality, sovereignty and cultural identity – are beginning to disintegrate. Globalization poses a challenge to the state's economic distribution mechanisms, its political and legal functions, and, in the end, to the very concept of national cultural identity as well.

The consequences of globalization

Globalization casts fundamental doubt on the possibility of resolving the *social* question. It is largely due to the development of the welfare state that Europe, and to a lesser degree the US, have been able to reap the benefits of social peace since the second half of the nineteenth century (Habermas 1998a: 67; 1998b: 100). Resolution of the social question has been viewed as a national task since the end of the nineteenth century. It was in 1845 that British Prime Minister Benjamin Disraeli described the rich and the poor as 'two nations between whom there is no intercourse and no sympathy'; and it was his intention to unite these two populations to form one British nation. Soon after, the German Chancellor, Otto von Bismarck, created in Germany a social security system based on a link between social security and earned income, a system that survives today, albeit in modified form. This development is also closely associated with the rise of national labour unions which have since represented workers' interests, struggling to achieve, through collective bargaining agreements, a balance between the interests of workers and their employers.

Globalization has now made it possible for businesses to avoid paying social security contributions, which are seen as a brake on their productivity. This is a development that is bound, ultimately, to undercut the social structure of the nation-state. Pointing to the sword of Damocles of unemployment and social degradation, and constantly threatening offshore jobs, corporations have managed push through low-wage sectors in Western industrialized countries. In developing countries and emerging markets on the other hand, employers are able to pay starvation wages, completely avoid making social security contributions and bypass safety regulations – assuming there are any in the first place. Furthermore, national governments, increasingly vying for inward investment and jobs, have been creating special economic and tax zones (e.g. export-processing zones). The infrastructure needed is created using public funds, environmental damage is externalized to the wider community; yet in the end transnational corporations pay little or nothing in taxes or social contributions. The benefits assumed to accrue from such zones remain highly questionable (Klein 2000).

It is becoming increasingly evident that the Beveridge system of basic social security provided in the form of government services and transfers is conceivable only within the framework of the nation-state, because the system is financed through national tax revenues. A transnational social security system based on international agreements appears unthinkable, despite some faint-hearted attempts in Europe to adopt such a system, based on supranational agreements.

Even though we do not necessarily have to share Samuel Huntington's thesis of the 'clash of civilizations', it does point to a general phenomenon: the worldwide diffusion of global markets, Western consumer goods and Western consumer habits – a development that is often referred to as 'McDonaldization' – not only does not prevent people from identifying with their own traditional cultural givens, it can even serve to reinforce this identification. This situation poses a growing dilemma for the governments of nation-states. While they are neither able nor willing to prevent the global production and distribution of cultural goods and services, they are under growing pressure to defend the cultural identity and political unity of their countries. European countries, for instance, have attempted to promote national film production or to establish quotas for national film production, and are unwilling to abandon their national radio stations to a glut of US-style pop music. On the other hand, non-Western cultural forms and artifacts are being 'globalized' through migration and transmigration, through the worldwide formation of diaspora communities, and by developments in the mass media. Bollywood and ethno-pop are just two examples. The emergence of such hybrid cultures raises questions about the content and nature of national cultures and value systems in the age of globalization.

The impact of globalization is most clearly manifest in the field of *political* decision-making. Since the French Revolution the nation-state, popular sovereignty and democracy have been closely interwoven. We can speak meaningfully of 'politics', Ulrich Beck writes, only if the sovereign political state's monopoly on decision-making power is seen as resting in the whole of a unified society. Sovereignty, Beck notes, borrowing from Carl Schmitt, rests with whoever has the power to declare a state of emergency (Beck 1998: 151). Is globalization jeopardizing the systems of political representation in place in nation-states? Can Western states, pointing to human rights violations, intervene in other states, with or without a UN mandate?

There is no doubt that this field also includes the question of 'citizenship', which in its very essence is bound to the nation-state. Migration and transmigration today are giving rise to hybrid forms of loyalty, e.g. in cases where diaspora communities exert crucial influence on elections in their countries of origin, or when a population that lacks the 'right' citizenship is excluded from the process of political decision-making. Examples include the nearly three million Turkish immigrant workers and their offspring living in Germany or the more than one million Russians who are forced to live as stateless persons in the new Baltic EU states and are therefore citizens neither of their own country nor of the EU. And while German Turks have the right to vote in Turkey, and can exercise that right only there, the Baltic Russians have absolutely no right to vote at all – neither in a state nor at the level of the EU. The situation is more or less the same for millions of illegal immigrants all over the world. The erosion of citizenship and the right to vote can thus be said to be undercutting the very political legitimacy of the nation-state.

The question of the legitimacy of political power is also assuming growing importance at the international level. The international organizations themselves possess no immediate democratic legitimacy of their own, for it is governments, not parliaments, or indeed even peoples, who are represented at the UN and in other international organizations. In other words, we can speak here at best of indirect democratic legitimacy.

The UN specialized agencies, including the World Bank and International Monetary Fund, have no democratic legitimacy whatsoever; indeed, they are no more and no less than international financial bureaucracies (Imber 1997: 215). It would be wrongheaded to see in the international organizations something of the order of a new 'world state'. After all, international means 'between nations'; and what this means in effect is that these organizations not only presuppose the existence of the nation-state, but in fact serve to safeguard and bolster it (Archer 1995).

The discussion centres on the League of Nations, which was founded in the wake of the First World War, and the United Nations, which was conceived during course of the Second Word War. Against the background of the many wars fought between nation-states in the nineteenth century and the exaggerated form assumed by the nation-state in nationalism, and, finally, in view of the rise of fascism and National Socialism, the idea was that strong international organizations would assume the task of preventing war and keeping the peace. The consensus is now that neither the League of Nations nor the United Nations has lived up to the task, even though the UN Charter guarantees the existence and self-determination of its members and bans any outside intervention that has not been approved by the Security Council.

Yet the seemingly guaranteed existence and equality of all UN member states have been undermined by various developments in international relations. The UN's balance had already been markedly skewed by the creation of and the functions exercised by the Security Council as well as by the permanent status of certain members and the veto power they wield. What emerged during the Cold War, under the threat of nuclear annihilation, was a bipolar world order defined by ideology, one that virtually hamstrung the UN system for decades on end (Aron 1962; Kennedy 1987). Once the Cold War ended, the US assumed the role of a new hegemon, a development that has induced some observers to speak of a new 'empire' (Hardt and Negri 2000: 8). For the most part, the US has a negative stance toward the agreements forged by the United Nations and its follow-up institutions. On the other hand, the United Nations itself has developed from a collective military security institution into an international agency endowed with legal, economic, social and cultural powers, some of which are exercised by UN sub-organizations, but some of which are in the hands of UN special agencies, such as the International Monetary Fund and World Bank. These institutions, and in particular their investment and development policies, have profound impacts on the development of many countries. However, this growing interdependence has thus far not eroded the worldwide system of sovereign nation-states; quite to the contrary, it may well have saved the nation-state, at least for the time being (Imber 1997: 218 for the UN; Milward 1992: 42 for Europe).

At present, international non-governmental organizations (INGOs) lack formal democratic legitimacy; they simply claim legitimacy for themselves, pointing out that they are fighting for a just cause (Dryzek 2000: 129). All this has led to unmistakable and insistent demands for democratization of the international organizations and for the formation of a transnational civil society (Imber 1997: 222).

So what future is predicted for the nation-state in the age of growing transnational and global interdependence? Following the often declared demise of the nation-state, authors of many different hues agree that the state will continue to fulfil certain important functions (Habermas 1998b: 156; Etzioni 2004: 115; Hardt and Negri 2004: 354), especially economic governance functions. Paul Hirst and Grahame Thompson (1999), who generally caution against overuse of the term globalization, expect that the state will assume three key functions: the creation of a distributive compromise in an attempt to balance differing economic interests; efforts to secure such a compromise on the basis of social consensus; and reallocation of tax revenues. Phil Cerny (1990) assumes that the state will continue to be responsible for the provision of social infrastructure, for education, for certain collective goods (e.g. internal and external security) and for the formation and preservation of a collective identity. If we rule out the possibility of a world state, postulating instead the emergence of a transnational action space whose concrete form remains completely open, then we must assume that the latter's only possible source of democratic organization and legitimacy is the nation-state (Habermas 1998b: 156). However, in a context of this kind the concept of national sovereignty will acquire a fundamentally different meaning (McGrew 1997: 235), and the international organizations will have to be reformed accordingly (Imber 1997: 222; Etzioni 2004: 201; Stiglitz 2004: 206). However, this cannot be restricted to a structural reform of the UN of the kind presently under consideration. Whether the international organizations will be able even remotely to fulfil the expectations placed in them is and remains a matter of contention.

Transnational civil society

The development of the concept of *transnationality* is not the first attempt ever made to break though the boundaries set by the practice of using the nation to justify political power. The classic approach may be seen in the international law concept of *inter*nationality. However, internationality presupposes the nation; after all, it refers to the relations *between* nations. The concept transnationality goes much further; it means in effect abandoning the concept of the nation. Yet 'trans' means, first and foremost, nothing more than 'beyond', and 'transnational' must therefore be understood to mean 'beyond the national'. The word means something negative, something open, without attributing any concrete content to 'beyond'. Unlike globalization, the concern here is the organization of spheres of political influence and power potentials. Given the openness of the concept, it is not possible to make an unequivocal statement on what or whose sovereignty is at issue, i.e. who is to exercise power. Transnationality must thus be seen as referring to the scope of political action and power structures beyond the nation.

However, crossing the boundaries set by the nation-state and its sovereignty does not necessarily imply an attempt to justify any worldwide, global rule, or any 'global sovereignty' or world state.

So what does civil society mean, and how is it able to exercise its functions at the global level? Since the 1970s civil rights and environmentalist movements have been seen as the central actors of civil society action – worldwide. In the early 1960s a human rights organization, Amnesty International, set out to respond to human rights violations worldwide. At that time, attention was focused on the communist countries. The Prague Spring of 1968 can be seen as the onset of a phase of collapse of the empire of communist power, a process that was to continue for over 20 years. In 1980 shipyard workers rose up in Gdansk, and in the autumn of 1989 demonstrations in East German cities led to the rapid succession of events known as the 'velvet revolutions'. The developments in the former Eastern bloc countries demonstrated to an astonished world the scope of action open to civil society potentials, which, oblivious to borders and largely by peaceful means, succeeded in toppling an empire. At roughly the same time, an increasingly influential environmentalist movement began to take shape in the Western democracies, and, represented by protest and watchdog organizations like Greenpeace, was soon able to call attention to its concerns at the international level as well. In the 1980s, anti-nuclear activists pointed vehemently to the dangers posed by an energy policy geared to unlimited growth, and opponents of Cold War nuclear armament and the Reagan Administration's 'Star Wars' programme organized to conduct protest marches in the framework of an international peace movement.

Almost two decades earlier in the US, the civil rights movement had succeeded, in an alliance of churches, labour unions and human rights activists, in bringing an end to politically sanctioned racial discrimination. Following their example, women, homosexuals and ethnic minorities began to fight for an end to discrimination and a reconciliation of interests. This too was achieved on the basis of the broad engagement of civil society. In Latin America proponents of liberation theology were calling for social justice and an end to political oppression. Since the end of the Second World War, both the US and Europe have experienced the emergence of numerous relief organizations that have since gone on to operate globally in crisis regions. These organizations include Oxfam (founded in 1942), Médecins sans Frontières (founded 1971) and the German Cap Anamur (founded 1979). Finally, spectacular pop concerts – like the 1984 Band Aid concert organized by Sir Bob Geldof – have shaken the world public awake by calling attention to famine disasters in Africa and for a sense of global responsibility for the sufferings of the post-colonial world. The fundamental question now is concerned with the relationship between civil society and the state in democracy.

The representative democracy typical of Western industrialized societies has nearly everywhere taken on the form of a parliamentary system in which popular sovereignty is exercised through elections, in which the popular will is articulated by and through political parties. Elected parliamentarians represent all of the people, which must be understood to include the totality of social organizations. True, there are in democratic societies numerous organizations of this kind, including interest groups and social movements; but there are also reciprocal relationships between these groups and the political parties, and this means that such organizations will attempt to gain political influence, and that the political parties will seek to integrate these organizations. In democracy both the concept of the political system and the concept of governance extend to the totality of all forms of political power in institutions, political parties and associations, and thus also in civil society.

However, in the course of the history of Western democracies the civil society foundation of democracy has been pushed to the background. Democratic self-determination has been largely reduced to representation, and the arrangements agreed upon cast in the form of constitutions, which sought to set freedom in chains. Still, again and again, there have been efforts to restore to democratic self-determination the civil society connotation it originally had, to revive self-determination beyond representation, and to stress the free, libertarian character of constitutions.

But what kind of state is it that these movements oppose? Is it the liberal, democratic, constitutional state which guarantees and protects the very freedom of association and assembly enjoyed by these movements?

Viewed historically, the conception is a child of the early nineteenth century. In Germany no revolution or gradual transition from monarchy to republic materialized, as it did in France or England – political developments were defined through a prism that set state and society in opposition to one another. The state remained monarchic and autocratic, in later years growing increasingly capitalistic and imperialistic. Civil society was, by comparison, the refuge of civil liberty, culture and education, public spirit, discussion, cooperation, tolerance. A democratic public sphere emerged under the helmet of the monarchic state. Yet this public sphere changed in the course of the twentieth century, one reason being that the state overwhelmed society, integrating its forms of organization and procedure, another, more important one being the development of political parties, the so-called social partners, and the media (Habermas 1989). The so-called neo-Marxist movement of the 1970s viewed the state as an agency of capital (late capitalism) which, based on the social compromises achieved with the labour movement and the social security provided by the welfare state, had succeeded in integrating the working class into the state and thus neutralizing it (O'Connor 1973; Offe 1984).

Viewed from this perspective, protest movements and social movements appeared to be something like a 'rebirth of a democratic public sphere' in which those affected, the disenfranchised and exploited, could voice their true interests – an option that was not given by their right to vote. These movements pointed publicly to problems that really existed. They struggled for transparency and public discussion, and insisted on and exacted solutions and reforms that the state and political parties would never have achieved on their own, due to existing economic power relations. This was, in other words, true civil society, one that raised claims to democratic self-determination – a democracy that it accused the constitutional state of lacking. True, this state found itself in a precarious situation, because on the one hand the movements, making use of their basic democratic rights, were pointing insistently to problems that really existed, and, on the other, because they were mobilizing forces and adopting forms of action that might endanger the stability of the political system. In this situation the state opted for a two-pronged strategy of inclusion and exclusion (Dryzek 2000: 85, 103), seeking to integrate these movements and embark on a course of reforms, while at the same time doing its best to suppress them and deprive them of the air they needed to breath.

Today, the aim of a transnational civil society must be to solve worldwide problems that are not accessible to solution by nation-states or the international organizations and also to confer on the international organizations a democratic legitimacy that they do not yet possess. Problem-solving capacity and self-determination are the criteria that must be used to judge the ideas that are being proposed in connection with efforts to concretize the notions of a transnational civil society.

Pluralist approaches – international non-governmental organizations

The ongoing discussion on the position of NGOs in state and society has in the meantime been extended to international politics, with INGOs now seen as assuming at the international level the role that NGOs have played at the national level. The term 'non-governmental' tells the whole story: these organizations are *non*-governmental, *not* part of government, a fact they clearly emphasize. They justify their existence and work with reference to their criticism of the political system, both the national and the international. This criticism is levelled at the parliamentary system with its political parties and its bureaucracy, but also at the inability of the political system to come to effective terms with important world problems, in particular with the power of international corporations, with environmental degradation, with population growth, with poverty and hunger in the world, to name just a few. Even though NGOs/INGOs do not see themselves as part of government, they are part of the public sphere and they take on responsibility for public tasks. Some observers even go as far as to claim that NGOs/INGOs are better equipped to deal with these tasks than governments, that they are, in effect, the 'actual government'. This is how the fascinating idea of 'governance without government' came about (Etzioni 2004: 153).

But who are these INGOs? How do you become an INGO? The social movements are undoubtedly NGOs. But associations are too, and they include interest organizations of the so-called social partners, employers and employees, but also not-for-profit organizations – e.g. regional and folklore associations, friends-of-the-opera clubs and animal protection associations. But what about religious and ethnic organizations? The American NAACP is certainly an NGO, as was the ANC in Apartheid South Africa. Is the Catholic Church not the world's largest INGO? And then there are the humanitarian organizations, in particular the Red Cross and its parallel organizations (e.g. the Red Crescent), Médecins sans Frontières, Save the Children, CARE, Oxfam and numerous others. And the media? Are the media not INGOs? CNN? Or the *New York Times*? Al Jazeera or Reuters? While there have been attempts to classify and analyse the subject matter (e.g. Clark 1991), there are no entry restrictions for INGOs, nor are there any criteria for selection or recognition. If there are any registration procedures, the selection criteria are very rough in nature.

Looked at in historical terms, NGOs/INGOs can be traced to three sources:

1. *Corporativism* – which came about as a critical response to the party-dominated parliaments in Europe's autocracies at the beginning of the twentieth century. The idea was that parliaments should not be elected, in particular not on the basis of political parties, but should be made up of representatives of associations: business associations, family organizations, scientific associations, and so on. The Spanish Cortes under Franco and the Italian Fasci under Mussolini were constituted in this way. But there were also mixed types, with one chamber of parliament being elected, the other constituted by associations.

2. *Humanitarianism* – disregarding for the moment forms of relief and support of the kind typically provided by the Church, or communal and labor union organizations, some of which have roots reaching far back in history, we can pinpoint the Red Cross, which was founded in 1864 and has since been embedded in the international organizations on the basis of international treaties, as the origin of today's humanitarian organizations. New humanitarian organizations emerged in the wake of the two world wars. Like CARE in particular, they were devoted to mitigating the suffering caused by war. Finally, beginning in the mid-twentieth century, a great number of organizations were founded that were dedicated to charitable (humanitarian or religious) purposes, e.g. organizations like Oxfam or Caritas (see Vaux in the present volume).

3. *Social activism* – the social protest movements of the 1970s gave birth to the so-called social movements, which took on more or less effective and durable forms of organization. For this reason they too can be referred to as NGOs/INGOs (see Oleson and Rucht in the present volume).

While the organizations that grew out of points 2 and 3 above are still with us, the form of organization in 1 above has vanished – but not without leaving behind the association structure on which it was based. Indeed, it can be said that at both the national and the international level associations continue to play a central role in politics. This is why, in this connection, we speak today of neo-corporativism.

The actual corporativist idea – i.e. replacing the party system with a system of associations – having vanished, there are now two typical models of NGO/INGO participation, both of which presuppose the existence of the state and parliamentary democracy: an organizational and a procedural variant. In the first NGOs/INGOs form bodies that are invited to participate in the work of government; we need think here only of the EU's European Economic and Social Committee (EESC). In the second these organizations become involved in politics by organizing protests and conferences, participating in hearings, concluding contracts with governments, planning and conducting rescue actions, conducting media campaigns, forming parties – the field of their possible involvement in politics is at once broad and highly contradictory (Dryzek 2000: 57). While the first form is the vehicle of choice of firmly established associations, the second is the field of the social activists (Wapner 1996; Köhler 1998).

Inclusion of NGOs/INGOs offers major advantages for the political system of parliamentary democracy. These organizations are either in possession of expertise or are able to mobilize it; they work to get the people affected by politics involved in decision-making; they push to open up the political system *vis-à-vis* society, but without destabilizing the former; they neutralize protest potential; they help to legitimize the political system; they lend a hand in implementing political decisions; and they provide a social early-warning system for possible misdirected developments in society. But the participation of NGOs/INGOs can also entail negative impacts for the political system. Selection of the organizations to be involved in political decision-making processes is always difficult and never without contradictions; the procedures governing participation are not in keeping with traditionally accepted democratic practice; the legitimacy of the participating organizations is questionable; participation takes time and causes frictional losses; there are often doubts as to the reliability of the participating organizations; and NGO/INGO participation itself causes shifts in the balance of the political system.

Some observers and analysts see in the involvement of INGOs in international politics the quintessence of international civil society (McGrew 1997: 12; Shaw 1997: 12; Dryzek 2000: 135). Indeed, there is no reason to doubt the transnationality of the involvement of INGOs. And it would be hard to overestimate their problem-solving capacities; today, many world problems are no longer accessible to solutions without INGO involvement (for two entirely different perspectives, see George and Klose in the present volume). The World Social Forum can for this reason rightly be seen as the centre of thinking and reflection about the future of the world, one in which productive solutions are sought and found, and one that is not confined to protests. But what about the quality of civil society? How do things stand with self-determination? Who determines what him- or herself? If an organization's representatives are elected, we may perhaps assume that that they look after the interests of their members. But whose interests does the environmental NGO Robin Wood represent, or Human Rights Watch? The interests of forests and the interests of those deprived of their human rights, no doubt, for the latter have no way to determine their own affairs. Looked at soberly, we see that the issue concerned here is not self-determination but action in the interest of the common good; but there is no democratic legitimacy for this action in the interest of the common good – except perhaps the legitimacy conferred by doing good. The legal basis of the work of NGOs/INGOs is also doubtful. Certainly, the Red Cross works in a legitimized international framework, but most similar organizations do not. They have created their own legitimacy, and they can point at best to the recognition of their own membership, and sometimes that of governments, as a basis for it. If we are to assess the undoubted merits of INGOs in the process of building a transnational civil society correctly, we will have to look elsewhere for a basis to start from.

Institutional approaches – community

The thrust of pluralist approaches is, broadly speaking, to strengthen social forces within states and in the international community, and to do so at the expense of state power or the dominance of the international organizations. There is, however – as we have seen – good reason to doubt whether a realization of pluralist approaches in the framework of a transnational society appears suited to serve the purpose advancing democratic self-determination and bolstering problem-solving capacities. Indeed, there are observers who see the principal cause of all international problems in weak statehood and who therefore call for efforts to strengthen the state – not necessarily with a view to adding to its tasks but in the name of improved efficiency – 'strength, not scope', as Francis Fukuyama put it (2004: 7). According to Fukuyama, the strength of the state must be sought, on the one hand, in strengthened organizational and political designs, and, on the other, in an enhanced legitimacy base and in cultural and structural factors. However, commitment to democratic institutions and procedures alone is not sufficient to ground the strength of statehood; the actual concern is the norms, values and culture informing statehood. It is the latter that, for Fukuyama, account for the real strength of states, and they, rooted in democratic self-determination and in possession of the problem-solving capacities needed to get the job done, can thus be seen as the true civil society (Fukuyama 2004: 39, 41).

Since the 1980s political philosophy has been the scene of a controversy between liberalism and communitarianism on how best to shape the community – a debate that has thus far left few traces in politics. The so-called communitarians have attacked alleged liberalist positions, asserting that the liberalism predominant in Western nations poses a danger to the future of the West, while the community spirit prevalent in other cultures holds out far more promise for the future. The communitarians claim to have the concepts needed to build a global civil society, noting that attempts to impose Western liberalism throughout the world are doomed to failure. This was a very fundamental debate on the key elements and makeup of community (MacIntyre 1981; Sandel 1982; Walzer 1983; Taylor 1985; etc., versus Rawls 1971; Dworkin 1977, etc.). The discussion focused on individual rights vs. the common good; the individual vs. the community; the personal vs. the social. Viewed in philosophical terms, the issue was whether the self chooses its own goals or whether these goals are given and choice is determined by social background. Viewed in political-historical terms, the issue revolved around the controversy over whether society is formed by the individual and the state, or whether a multiplicity of intermediary institutions serves to mediate between state and individual. These institutions include the family, neighbourhood, community, church, associations, and so on. Amitai Etzioni has revived this controversy, using it to ground his conception of a transnational society (2004: 161).

But it is still unclear whether communitarianism is actually calling for a different constitution, other institutions and procedures, or whether its aim is in effect to infuse the old institutions with a new spirit. Etzioni has called for a new, balanced relationship between autonomy and sociality in international organization, invoking shared values, in order to go on, concretely, to outline an enlarged transnational civil society. His conception is predicated on the continuing existence of the nation-state, calls for reform of the international organizations, and he emphasizes, in addition to national and international organizations, the transnational communitarian organizations that Etzioni sees developing out of today's INGOs – according a special role to professional and humanitarian organizations.

If we look into this concept with a view to the role it could play in creating a transnational civil society, we are forced to assume that while the arrangements are clear enough – after all, the idea of the community implies that the rules governing community are given for individuals – the measure of self-determination involved remains open. Despite Etzioni's call for a balanced relationship between autonomy and sociality, we have no choice but to assume that the community dimension will dominate. One interesting aspect, though, is that the organizational model for transnational civil society is predicated not on the organization of the state and the international community along the lines of civil society, but on the need for civil society organizations which supplement the nation-state and international organizations. In other words, in the end there is no reason to expect from this concept any thrust in the direction of strengthening and consolidating statehood.

Communicative approaches – deliberation

In democracy too – at least according to the traditional notion of democracy – the validity of laws rests on a majority will that has emerged on the basis of elections and voting in the framework of a concrete procedure. Voting and decisions are the foundation. Even if a law is wrong, it is seen as valid owing to the legitimacy conferred on it by voting and decision-making. It is, though, possible to set against a legitimacy of this kind an alternative approach based not on voting but on deliberation. Since no one is in possession of the truth, we can take the will of the majority for the truth, even though we know that the majority is not tantamount to truth; or we can declare the outcome of a process of deliberation to be the truth and accept the law that it gives rise to. In the ideal case the outcome of a process of this kind is consensus; but that will inevitably be the exception. Or we can design choice-related decisions on the basis of the model of rational choice, and do so in such a way that the outcome is binding. Or we can shape the discourse in such a way as to ensure that all those involved will accept the outcome. In any event, those who organize discourses expect this to mean that the quality of outcomes will improve, at least compared with majority decisions with their more or less arbitrary character. The quality of decisions can be further enhanced if experts are involved in the deliberations and the media publicly organize relevant discourses.

The history of political thought has known many relevant models, a good number of which are referred to in this connection: the Socratic dialogue, the *Forum Romanum*, the medieval disputation, the Italian law faculties of the early modern age, the diets of the Holy Roman Empire, the founding fathers of the United States, the eighteenth- and nineteenth-century debating societies of the European middle classes. Differ as they may, their public character, open exchange of arguments and adherence to set procedures and rules governing recognition were designed to ensure that the outcome served to solve problems, and that it came closest to the truth.

We could also write the history of parliamentarism as a history of deliberation. The constitutional deliberations of the late eighteenth and in particular the nineteenth centuries were marked by the rationality of their discourses and the openness of their argumentation; parliaments were the central locus of the public exchange of ideas (Dryzek 2000: 14). Today's parliament, rationalized and shaped by political parties, is an achievement of the early twentieth century. Even today parliamentarism has its 'great moments' in cases where the major issues of the age are addressed on the floor of parliament; but these are rare cases. Under the influence of the audiovisual media in particular, the formation of public opinion has shifted outside parliaments and has become a public sphere in its own right. Those involved in shaping this new public sphere, under the watchful eye of what has come to be known as moderators, include (in addition to politicians) scientists, economists, labour union officials, clerics, artists and certain publicists and journalists. This mediaization of the formation of public opinion has been both exalted as democratization and denounced as manipulation.

We find in the scholarly literature two principal analytical approaches devoted to the development of public deliberation: Habermasian discourse theory and the Beckian theory of reflexive modernization. Habermas has analysed the *Structural Transformation of the Public Sphere* (1989), developed a *Theory of Communicative Action* (1984, 1987), and, in *Between Facts and Norms* (1996), applied his discourse theory to democracy and the validity of law. His model of communicative rationality, which he sets in opposition to what is known as instrumental rationality, describes the conditions under which decisions that may claim truth can come about through discourses. Here the legitimacy of democratic decisions and the validity of law are traced back to such discourses. It is, however, necessary to create the conditions required for such discourses; Habermas uses the concept of the ideal speech situation to outline these conditions, noting that they must find expression in certain procedural rules. The approach has now found broad international resonance, including in the Anglo-Saxon world (Barber 1984; Dryzek 1990; Bohmann 1996), and while it has been further developed and modified, even reformulated for application to post-national and transnational contexts (Habermas 1998b: 156; Dryzek 2002: 115), its fundamental concern continues to be the call for deliberative democracy.

It was in 1976, in his conception of the 'Risk Society', that Ulrich Beck first developed a distinction between a first and a second age of modernity (Beck 1992). Since then, together with a number of colleagues and associates, he has further developed the approach into a theory of 'reflexive modernization' (Beck et al. 2004). While the first, the actual age of modernity, was marked by standardization, institutionalization, rationalization and a growing differentiation of role systems, the second modernity is characterized by deterritorialization and transmigration, de-traditionalization and multi-perspectivity, uncertainties and risks, multilingualism and value plurality, and a plurality of identities and futures. People are forced to reconfigure their pasts and their future perspectives, to rework, weave, combine; in short: to reflect them (Beck et al. 2004). This is a discursive process, one, though, that forces us to arrive at decisions, and this is the reason why Beck chose to give his collection on the topic the title *Deterritorialization and Decision* (Beck et al. 2004).

Deliberative democracy is not organizational in nature, it is procedural democracy. Does it contribute to creating a transnational civil society? There is a good number of examples of transnational discourses: the *Lex Mercatoria* and the Law of the Sea are two examples from international law for outcomes of century-long processes of negotiation and experience. Today efforts to restrict whaling and to preserve the earth's ozone layer are the subject of ongoing international negotiations. There is a good number of principles that have been established on the basis of transnational deliberations, including the principle of sustainable development or gender mainstreaming. There are also consensuses on a framework, though they are, in essence, restricted to specifying the preconditions under which discussions and negotiations may be regarded as outcomes of deliberative democracy, e.g. political equality, exclusion of the use of force and open-endedness (Dryzek 2000: 166). But what about the issue of self-determination? Looking at the way that discourses are conceived theoretically, there can be no doubt that the processes involved are self-determined. But do discourse constraints not tend to even out differences of opinion? Is there not a consensus constraint? How are people to be enabled to participate in such discourses? In the end are not education and possession of assets the factors that determine participation and success? As indispensable as deliberative elements may be in the creation of a transnational civil society, attempts to translate the concept into reality may still be highly questionable and riddled with pitfalls and risks. Still, it is indisputable that deliberation is the most important element involved in international problem-solving.

Building a transnational civil society

On the one hand, a transnational civil society is expected to help solve problems that are beyond the reach of the sovereign nation-state or the international community as constituted in the United Nations. On the other, a transnational civil society is expected to confer, through self-determination, democratic legitimacy on the international community that the latter still lacks today.

Now, the pluralist approaches show very clearly that today it is INGOs in particular that have a transnational problem-solving capacity which by far eclipses that of the international organizations. Today international economic, financial, social and cultural developments are simply inconceivable without the involvement of INGOs, as is evidenced in particular by the contributions to the present volume by Soederberg, Holzer, Dijkzeul, Rucht and Oleson. On the other hand, while INGOs claim to be strengthening democracy, there are doubts as to their own democratic legitimacy. While the present contributions by Soederberg, Holzer, Dijkzeul and Rucht point unmistakably to deficits in the democratic legitimacy of 'the other side', criticism of and resistance to undemocratically exercised power does not in itself constitute democratic legitimacy, for this would require transnational civil society to give itself democratic structures. It must be seen as paradoxical that those with a focus on human rights who have set their sights on promoting democracy tend more, in fact, to serve technocratic progress than democracy.

The institutional approaches, on the other hand, may very well serve to strengthen the democratic legitimacy of a transnational civil society, at least if we are thinking here not of formal democracy but of the norms, values and cultures that are required to confer substance and durability on democracy. On the other hand, we will not be inclined to place inflated expectations in the ability of these approaches to bolster problem-solving capacities, for they tend first and foremost to add to the complexity of existing structures. The contributions to the present volume that are devoted to institutional approaches – in particular, those by George, Soederberg, Klose, Vaux and Donini – clearly highlight the problem-solving capacity inherent in institutional approaches.

Presumably, however, it will take the integration of both pluralist and institutional approaches into the model of a deliberative democracy organized by the sciences and the media to do justice to the claims raised for a transnational civil society. Only if we ignore calls for a world state organized along parliamentary lines and disburden ourselves of the illusion of a worldwide social grassroots-democratic movement will we be able to say that a transnational civil society does indeed have a chance of coming to terms with transnational problems and at the same time of living up to the standards of democratic legitimacy. Under these conditions, though, democratic legitimacy can mean no more and no less than that the problems facing the world, analysed by science and articulated by the media, will prove accessible to discussion and decision. Based on a variety of examples, the chapters presented in the present volume point to possible approaches to translating this claim into reality.

Susan George outlines some of the global risks stemming from untrammelled neo-liberal policies and the ongoing worldwide integration of markets. Viewed from her perspective, these risks are not only growing, but globalization and the corporations and institutions that propagate it, including the world's neo-liberal governments, led by the US, are in a sense the focus of the disease that must now be contained. Be it the environment, social insecurity or the risks posed by genetically modified foods, George argues for legislation and regulations that will reduce the global market to a human(e) dimension. While civil society can provide for publicity and set out moral imperatives, it cannot itself solve the problems, for it lacks the material resources necessary to do so.

Boris Holzer examines the subtle relationship between society and modern corporate business. In particular he devotes his chapter to the new dimensions of corporate powers and their potential adversary: transnational civil society. This term, he points out, is conveniently used for what is actually an assemblage of diverse, and sometimes even conflicting, interests and expectations. Nevertheless, inferring their legitimacy from the broad conviction that they are seen as representing a wider public interest – in contrast to corporate interests – they have gained considerable influence, especially in the areas of human and minority rights and environmental policy. But, the author notes, the particular strength of transnational civil society groups, the absence of an encompassing formal authority, is also their main weakness.

The problems of transnational debt are the focus of *Susanne Soederberg*'s chapter. Despite the neo-liberal logic according to which liberalized capital flows create wealth and economic growth, examples show that the opposite holds true for emerging markets and weak economies. This development may lead, as the case of Argentina clearly shows, to growing risks, instability and bankruptcy. On the other side, the main beneficiaries are global financial actors, based mainly in

Wall Street. Soederberg also describes how the plan for a Sovereign Debt Restructuring Mechanism developed by the IMF was effectively quashed by interest groups of the major creditors and the US Treasury Department.

Mikhail Molchanov and *Yuri Yevdokimov* use the case of the recently opened Baku–Ceyhan oil pipeline to highlight the fatal but successful interactions between transnational corporations, the political interests of Western industrialized countries and a 'cunning' state like Azerbaijan. On the other hand, the pipeline constitutes the first challenge in the region for an internationally backed and locally organized protest movement of civil society groups against environmental degradation.

Shalini Randeria delineates the dilemmas of civil society actors engaged in rendering accountable international institutions and cunning states that capitalize on their perceived weakness in an era of globalization. Using empirical material from India, she shows the state to be an active agent in shaping the selective domestication of international norms and policies. Her fine-grained ethnography of two World Bank-funded projects in India and of the Inspection Panel at the Bank offers a nuanced analysis of the pragmatic, issue-based alliances among the Bank, different levels of state administration and various NGOs. She argues that not only is the Bank a structurally schizophrenic institution pursuing contradictory policies, but also that the state is not a monolithic entity with unified intentions. But civil society is equally heterogeneous with human rights and environmental NGOs deeply divided on issues of displacement and disenfranchisement of poor communities.

Dieter Rucht seeks to distinguish between new critical groups and forms of criticism of globalization, including moderate NGO reformism, radical reformers of transnational mass movements and the anti-system critique articulated by left-wing radicals. While the first two currents of protest emphasize the concept of civil society as a corrective aimed at globalization and the state, left-wing radicals denounce the concept as a 'myth', interpreting civil society in negative terms as part and parcel of the bourgeois establishment, a fig leaf for the real cleavages in society. What is needed at present for a more fundamental critique of society is not only integration of – or at least combined efforts on the part of – radical and reform-minded groups in the face of social injustices, but also a new critical theory of society – beyond a discourse restricted to relatively small circles.

Thomas Oleson's chapter focuses on a non-European form of radical democracy and civil society organization: the Zapatistas in Mexico, the first indigenous protest movement which managed, in the 1990s, to attract worldwide attention by making use of modern communications technologies including the Internet. They have their own understanding of democracy, which they describe as 'ruling by obeying'. Rooted in traditional indigenous community life, this concept calls for a closer relationship between those who govern and the governed. Oleson also outlines how this concept has influenced social movements elsewhere.

Harry Bauer explores another aspect of emerging transnational civil society: formal and informal collaboration between environmental NGOs (ENGOs) and private corporations. There is no doubt that environmental issues have become a cornerstone of the activities of civil society groups and that they have gained wide acceptance among the general population. Retail goods labelled as produced in ecologically sustainable ways are widely marketed in cooperation with corporations and ENGOs, as the example of the Forest Stewardship Council (FSC) clearly demonstrates. Even though the future of green alliances remains unclear, these alliances may turn out to be a much needed link in global environmental governance.

Global crisis governance and new wars are the third field analysed in the present volume. Here the question is whether and to what extent the international community is in a position to prevent suffering and prosecute human rights violations and mass murder. What grim results may stem from abuse of humanitarianism for political purposes? And should we not stop using the vocabulary of humanitarianism to cover political interests? What role can the UN, the military and humanitarian organizations play – and are they playing it?

David Rieff voices scepticism about the possibilities and limits of global governance with respect to crisis intervention and war. Whether we advocate a new transnational order or the old Westphalian view of the sovereign state, for Rieff commitment to justice and suppression of disorder are out of the question. But how can human rights, indeed international law, be guaranteed? Can the UN and its agencies – the UNHCR or WHO – make all wrongs right? Is cosmopolitan internationalism – the view that it is possible to govern the world – sentimental, self-regarding, blind, ahistorical? Should we not, after all, stop calling any and every crisis a humanitarian disaster and start using a political vocabulary again? Instead of blaming the UN for crises it might perhaps have been able to prevent, we should start focusing on the tasks an international organization is able to fulfil today. Global peace may be – indeed is – a fine notion, but it is also a utopian one.

The profound new influence of Western governments on humanitarian operations is the key problem on which *Tony Vaux* focuses, and not only from the perspective of aid workers. Even though far more funds became available after the end of the Cold War, and again after 9/11, there is a strong tendency to distort humanitarianism to bring it closer in alignment with Western security concerns. The result is a concentration of humanitarian activities in a limited number of areas, a shift from development aid to short-term disaster relief, an almost total marginalization of local voices from the affected countries. Recent humanitarian developments appear to point to the limits of any civil society engagement. One crucial factor in this regard is the ever closer cooperation observed between armed forces and aid agencies.

Gerhard Klose, a retired colonel of the German *Bundeswehr*, outlines this development from the perspective of superior power. The armed forces of Western countries will, Klose notes, increasingly be used for operations referred to as humanitarian interventions, operations that primarily serve political purposes – i.e. are linked to security concerns and the desire to enlarge the political and economic influence. Humanitarianism is becoming a political strategy, so-called 'integrated missions' are designed to 'win hearts and minds' as a first stepping stone to gaining more influence. The traditional actors of humanitarian aid are, as Klose points out, no longer able to take for granted a legal situation in which their work is supported by taxpayers' money. Humanitarian operations now are increasingly required to be embedded in military contexts and approved by the military, otherwise humanitarian organizations are forced to rely solely on donor money. While this certainly looks like a grim overview of international developments, it does convey, quite clearly, a snapshot of new power relations and perceptions.

Antonio Donini rejects this view of humanitarian aid as an extended arm of politics. In view of this concept, the universalistic claims of Western humanitarians ring hollow at best. Recent developments with respect to humanitarian interventions and the War on Terror have destroyed the long-term trust in and respect for relief work. Aid workers has no choice but to rely on local forces, tribal communities, civil society groups – no matter how they differ from generally accepted Western patterns. This may require a departure from top-down, supply- and externally-driven approaches.

Dennis Dijkzeul has for many years been engaged in field research in the war-torn Republic of Congo. Here no Western political interests have halted the ongoing disintegration of the country, the selling off of natural resources by corrupt warlords and the suffering this entails for the civilian population. Dijkzeul explains the breakdown of the Congolese state and examines the various responses of the humanitarian agencies still active in this area. Despite a situation of almost nonexistent civil society structures, he sees among the major threats to any peaceful recovery the problems posed by identity politics (Caldor 1999: 76) among those excluded from global markets and the fatal practice of labelling minority groups. On the other hand, international relief agencies have little or no knowledge of local circumstances. In all likelihood their role is about to become even more peripheral than they themselves realize.

What picture emerges from these studies? There are civil society processes underway both beyond the nation-state and within the framework defined by it. As economy and culture grow increasingly integrated at the global level, civil society will itself be subject to a process of integrative development. At the same time, there are signs that politics is returning to society, that global tasks are being viewed with a new realism, that there is a growing tendency 'to bring the state back in'.

References

Archer, C. (1995) *International Organisations*, 2nd edn. (London: Allen and Unwin).

Aron, R. (1962) *Paix et guerre entre les nations* (Paris: Calmann-Levy).

Barber, B. (1984) *Strong Democracy: Participatory Politics for a New Age* (Berkeley, CA: University of California Press).

Beck, U. (1992) *Risk Society: Towards a New Modernity* (London: Sage).

Beck, U. (ed.) (1998) *Politik der Globalisierung* (Frankfurt: Suhrkamp).

Beck, U., Bonß, W. and Lau, Ch. (2004) Entgrenzung erzwingt Entscheidungen: Was ist neu an der Theorie reflexiver Modernisierung? in U. Beck and Ch. Lau, *Entgrenzung und Entscheidung. Was ist neu an der Theorie Reflexiver Modernisierung?* (Frankfurt: Suhrkamp), pp. 13–64.

Bohman, J. (1996) *Deliberation: Pluralism, Complexity and Democracy* (Cambridge, MA: MIT Press).

Castell, M. (1996) *The Rise of the Network Society* (Oxford: Blackwell).

Cerny, P. (1990) *The Changing Architecture of Political Structure, Agency, and the Future of the State* (New York: Sage).

Clark, J. (1991) *Democratizing Development: The Role of Voluntary Organisations* (London: Earthscan Publications).

Dryzek, J. (1990) *Discursive Democracy: Politics, Policy and Political Science* (New York: Cambridge University Press).

Dryzek, J. (2002) *Deliberative Democracy and Beyond: Liberals, Critics, Contestations* (Oxford: Oxford University Press).

Dworkin, R. (1977) *Taking Rights Seriously* (Cambridge, MA: Harvard University Press).

Etzioni, A. (2004) *From Empire to Community* (London: Palgrave Macmillan).

Fukuyama, F. (2004) *State Building: Governance and World Order in the Twenty-First Century* (London: Profile Books).

Habermas, J. (1984) *The Theory of Communicative Action I: Reason and the Rationalization of Society* (Boston, MA: Beacon Press).

Habermas, J. (1987) *The Theory of Communitative Action II: Lifeworld and System* (Boston, MA: Beacon Press).

Habermas, J. (1989) *Structural Transformation of the Public Sphere: An Inquiry into a Category of Bourgeois Society* (Cambridge, MA: MIT Press).

Habermas, J. (1996) *Between Facts and Norms: Contributions to a Discourse Theory of Law and Democracy* (Cambridge, MA: MIT Press).

Habermas, J. (1998a) Jenseits des Nationalstaats? Bemerkungen zu Folgeproblemen der Globalisierung, in U. Beck, *Politik der Globalisierung* (Frankfurt: Suhrkamp), pp. 67–84.

Habermas, J. (1998b) Die Postnationale Konstellation und die Zukunft der Demokratie, in J. Habermas, *Die Postnationale Konstellation: Politische Essays* (Frankfurt: Suhrkamp), pp. 91–169.

Hardt, M. and Negri, A. (2000) *Empire* (Cambridge, MA: Harvard University Press).

Hardt, M. and Negri, A. (2004) *Multitude* (New York: Penguin Books).

Hirst, P. and Thompson, G. (1999) *Globalization in Question: The International Economy and the Possibilities of Governance* (Cambridge: Polity Press).

Huntington, S. (1996) *The Clash of Civilizations* (New York: Simon and Schuster).

Imber, M. (1997) Geo-Governance without Democracy? Reforming the UN System, in A. McGrew (ed.) *The Transformation of Democracy?* (Cambridge: Polity Press), pp. 201–230.

Kaldor, M. (1999) *New and Old Wars* (Stanford, CA: Stanford University Press).

Kennedy, P. (1987) *The Rise and Fall of the Great Powers* (New York: Random House).

Klein, N. (2000) *No Logo. Taking Aim at the Brand Bullies* (New York: Picador).

Köhler, M. (1998) From the National to the Cosmopolitan Public Sphere, in D. Archibugi, D. Held and M. Köhler (eds.) *Re-Imagining Political Community: Studies in Cosmopolitan Democracy* (Cambridge: Polity Press), pp. 231–251.

MacIntyre, A. (1981) *After Virtue: A Study in Moral Theory* (London: Duckworth).

McGrew, A. (1997) Globalization and Territorial Democracy: An Introduction, in A. McGrew (ed.) *The Transformation of Democracy?* (Cambridge: Polity Press), pp. 1–24.

Milward, A. (1992) *The European Rescue of the Nation Sate* (London: Routledge).

O'Connor, J. (1973) *The Fiscal Crisis of the State* (New York: St. Martin's Press).

Offe, C. (1984) *Contradictions of the Welfare State* (Cambridge, MA: MIT Press).

Rawls, J. (1971) *A Theory of Justice* (London: Oxford University Press).

Robertson, R. (1995) Glocalization: Time-Space and Homogeneity–Heterogeneity, in M. Featherstone et al. (eds.) *Global Modernities* (London: Sage), pp. 25–44.

Sandel, M. (1982) *Liberalism and the Limits of Justice* (Cambridge: Cambridge University Press).

Sassen, S. (1998) *Globalization and its Discontents: Essays on the New Mobility of People and Money* (New York: New Press).

Shaw, M. (1997) *Civil Society and Media in Global Crises: Representing Distant Violence* (London: Frances Pinter).

Stiglitz, J. (2004) *Globalization and its Discontents* (New York: Penguin Books).

Soros, G. (2005) *On Globalization* (New York: Public Affairs).

Taylor, C. (1985) *Philosophy and the Human Sciences: Philosophical Papers 2* (Cambridge: Cambridge University Press).

Walzer, M. (1983) *Spheres of Justice: A Defence of Pluralism and Equality* (Oxford: Blackwell).

Wapner, P. (1996) *Environmental Activism and World Civic Politics* (Albany, NY: State University of New York Press).

Part I

The Political Economy of a Transnational Civil Society

1

Transnational Risks: A New Challenge for Global Civil Society

Susan George

All technologies are risky. Let me borrow from the French architect and philosopher Paul Virilio, who looks at every technology developed as a certain source of risk. For him, the accident is built in: if you invent the aeroplane, you simultaneously invent the crash; the computer implies catastrophic loss of information; nuclear fission means Chernobyl and Three Mile Island, and so on. Although Virilio himself doesn't take the concept this far, I would add that *crime* is also built in and can be traced all the way back to Stone Age technologies. Any instrument that can be used as a bludgeon or honed to a sharp point carries with it the risk of murder, just as the propagator of computer viruses is coextensive with the information society and the hijacker is aviation's version of the pirate.

The inevitability of built-in risk of accident and crime is the principal reason we need the state. In my view, no one has yet persuasively refuted the logic of Thomas Hobbes, who recognized in the seventeenth century that, left in a 'state of nature', which is the 'war of all against all', men would cry out for protection and willingly accept even the most oppressive state, the Leviathan, because they simply cannot live with such constant and all-pervading levels of risk.

It strikes me that in the early twenty-first century, particularly since 11 September 2001, we are once more experiencing something like the fear Hobbes attributed to his imagined pre-state creatures. We, too, are crying out for protection. This is most clear in the United States where, under the Bush administration, Americans have surrendered basic constitutional freedoms in the hope of being protected from future attack. But as Benjamin Franklin said, 'Those who renounce liberty for security deserve neither'.

Terrorist attacks and global warming are indicators that we have indeed entered the era of *transnational* risk. Does this mean we must take Hobbes' logic a step further, that we must necessarily establish a *transnational* state as well, or perish? Although my position on this question may seem contradictory, I do not think a transnational state is the answer, at least not yet. Nor do I believe that the private sector can be entrusted with the prevention of global risks. I will return to these points.

First, however, I would like to step back and argue that contemporary capitalism (also known as 'globalization' or 'neo-liberalism') is not merely increasing the risks we face as individuals, as members of a given community and as a species, but also lies at their very heart. Let me stress that I am not referring to risk as it is commonly associated with capitalism; I am not referring to the classic economic model in which capitalism and risk-taking are inextricably joined and the hope of material reward is the motor of the system. Innovation occurs because people are willing to gamble. No one can set up a business or even buy securities on the stock market without taking a risk. Christopher Columbus would undoubtedly not have risked sailing westward without the incentive of discovering riches as well as a new trade route to the Indies. According to a recent article in the *New York Times*, Boeing became great because its leaders were passionate about aviation and ready to bet the company on a new concept like the 747, but it is now governed by a Board interested only in financial results (and thereby, paradoxically, are placing the company at risk). Capitalism in this sense is based on risk freely accepted, on gambles, on taking chances. Our word *hazard* derives from the Arabic *al zahr*, which means dice.

So, rather than expand on capitalist risk in this classic sense, I want to look at the numerous new risks imposed on people whose lives and well-being increasingly depend on someone else's throw of the dice. They have little or no choice in the matter; they are victims of capitalist globalization's frenetic search for profit, its disregard for nature and for human beings and its drive to transform all human activities into marketable commodities. The resulting individual and collective risks are imposed, not freely accepted. The transformative power of transnational capital – what Joseph Schumpeter (1942, 1975) called 'creative destruction' – has grown exponentially over the past two decades, particularly since the end of the Cold War. For most people, however, it has destroyed far more than it has created. Risk-taking has, in this sense, become compulsory.

The neo-liberal programme, also known as the Washington Consensus, is not just economic; it has become the supreme arbiter of political decision-making as well. This programme pushes privatization, deregulation and increased corporate control over labour and the environment. Governments and international institutions have allied with transnational corporations and financial market operators to impose the Holy Trinity of capitalist freedoms: freedom of investment, freedom of capital movements, freedom of trade in goods, services, agricultural commodities and intellectual property. The private sector is not merely allowed but is *expected* to make social and political decisions as well as economic ones. Hardcore neo-liberalism is naturally most advanced in the United States, but is rapidly gaining ground even in countries which had taken the welfare state furthest, like France and Germany. This extreme right-wing worldview stands in stark contrast to the first 30–40 years of the post-Second World War period when everyone was some stripe of Christian or Social Democrat, a Keynesian or a Marxist. The construction of more just societies, based on solidarity, then seemed the only natural and honourable path. The goal of these societies was to protect citizens against illness, unemployment, disability, old age and the like.

What is the connection between the present, corporate-led, neo-liberal intellectual hegemony and heightened risk? Whenever and wherever social protection and the welfare state are dismantled, as they must be according to Washington Consensus doctrine, millions of poor Americans, including people working at two jobs, are forced, in the richest country on earth, to live exposed to lack of health care, homelessness and accidents. The problem for poor people in poor countries is naturally much worse, as the statistics clearly demonstrate.

Evidence showing the growth of inequalities over the past 20 years, both within and among countries, has become overwhelming. Anyone who has opened a newspaper in the past few years presumably knows about the increase in hunger, the number of people living on less than the equivalent of a dollar a day, the collapse of health and education systems, the spread of AIDS and so on.

I dislike the expression 'social safety-nets' because, like fish, most people who fall into such nets are unlikely to escape them and will remain trapped in poverty. But even those meagre nets are becoming frayed. In the North, the goals of the neo-liberal programme are to roll back the gains of social and labour movements made over the past 100 years, to cut state and public services to the bone and to make individuals responsible for their own fate, no matter what the circumstances. Private transportation, private education, private health care, insurance, etc. are the norm.

In the South, The World Bank and the International Monetary Fund, working hand in hand with the US Treasury, have imposed structural adjustment packages in over 100 indebted countries, making risk-provoking neo-liberal doctrine the rule. For years, people like me denounced the human consequences of these austerity programmes but to no avail; now the criticism is also coming from people at the core of the system like Joseph Stiglitz, former head of President Clinton's Council of Economic Advisors and former Chief Economist of the World Bank; as well as the present Chief Economist of the Bank, François Bourguignon. Neo-liberal goals also directly contradict the principles enshrined in the Universal Declaration of Human Rights, but we will leave these risk-exposed people aside now, even though there are billions of them, and ask how mass poverty in both rich and poor countries can exist when, in the aggregate, the world has never been richer than it is today.

The role of the media in relation to risk should be examined more closely in this context. Most of the media have been exceptionally complacent with regard to the capacity of right-wing foundations' protégés to dominate editorial pages, critical reviews, bestseller lists, radio and television chat shows and in a general way to set the terms of the entire social, economic and political debate. Although most glaring in the United States, this ideological bias is not confined to the American corporate-owned media. More and more, the media everywhere refuse genuine dissent and even exclude objective reporting on sensitive subjects. The citizens' movement is attempting to establish alternative media to cover its own activities which the mainstream won't touch, and here the Internet is a useful tool, but these are no substitute for lively debate in mass media with a mass audience.

If neo-liberalism exposes individuals to heightened risk, what about the collective risks society faces? Here too one can point to globalized free market capitalism as the culprit.

As soon as reduction of greenhouse gases was even mooted in the United States, a powerful coalition of energy, mining and automotive transnational corporations formed a lobby with the environmentally-friendly name 'Global Climate Coalition'. They lobbied fiercely over a decade for limiting action to 'voluntary' measures to reduce greenhouse gases. When I looked at their website recently, I discovered that the Coalition had been 'deactivated' because all its goals had been met by the Bush administration's policies. Who can argue that transnational capital reduces transnational risks?

Or take the example of the production and dissemination of Genetically Manipulated Organisms (GMOs). Although scientifically speaking one can't swear that GM foods are potentially harmful, scientific evidence and practical experience show that the GM plants themselves pose real dangers to the environment when grown outside the laboratory. They cannot be confined to where they are planted, they interact in unpredictable ways with other flora and fauna and, once cultivated in natural surroundings, cannot be recalled. Whatever genetic pollution they cause is irreversible. Some have called the proliferation of GMOs a biological Hiroshima.

Yet we're told that 'You can't stop scientific progress', or that being against GMOs is to be 'anti-scientific' – as if our research laboratories were full of idealistic scientists seeking truth instead of technicians working for large corporations seeking only their own profits and power. My research on the GMOs approved for cultivation over the past decade by the US Department of Agriculture revealed that half were owned by Monsanto. Eighty per cent of these authorized varieties were controlled by three giant firms, while over 90 per cent were patented by the top five companies. GMOs are sold to farmers as part of a package of inputs and are developed to be herbicide-tolerant or to produce their own insecticides. The scientists who create them proceed as if Darwin had never existed. They ignore the obvious fact that weeds and insects will develop resistance and require larger and larger doses of chemicals for effective control.

Leaving aside the potential health risks, isn't it risky enough to plant these irreversible environmental contaminants and allow our food chain to be controlled by a few giant corporations? Neo-liberals don't think so, even if the public does. The United States, claiming its agricultural exporters are losing over $300 million a year, is suing the European Union for imposing a moratorium and establishing labelling and traceability laws on GMO imports. The Dispute Resolution Body of the WTO will hear the case and, since the WTO does not recognize the precautionary principle, the US is likely to win, just as it did in the case of the EU refusal to import hormone treated beef.

Capital-intensive agricultural production cannot wait for nature's timetable and wants animals to mature faster. The result is mad cows and Creuzfeldt-Jacob disease for humans or excessive, resistance-creating use of antibiotics in animal feed. Chemicals used in both agricultural and industrial production are clearly correlated with the incidence of cancer. Epidemiological studies of the Texas–Mexico border in the *maquiladora* manufacturing zone show that cancer rates there are the highest in both countries. Depleted uranium used in munitions during the Gulf War, and the Bosnian or Kosovo conflicts, has caused birth defects of epidemic proportions. Statistically speaking, people – again mostly the poor – are far more likely to suffer illness and death due to such environmental factors.

Transnational capital wants freedom of trade and multilateral or regional trade agreements like NAFTA, negotiated under pressure from business interests, have displaced millions of small farmers and reduced food security for them, their families and their countries. Mexico, for example, under pressure from the United States, embraced foreign investors and opened its borders. Not only has its small farming sector been decimated by cheap imports of US subsidized corn, but the *maquiladora* factories are closing and manufacturing is moving to China. In the first eight months of 2003 alone, more than 370 factories closed, causing job losses in the tens of thousands.

Transnational capital also wants freedom of capital movements and the IMF has made sure that indebted countries – well over 100 of them – respect this wish. The consequences have been one devastating financial crisis after another. To take only the past decade, beginning with Mexico in 1994, IMF policies have encouraged speculation and its bail-outs have rewarded the speculators rather than the governments, much less the populations, of the affected countries. Speculators have realized huge profits, while local businesses have failed in droves, leaving thousands of employees jobless. Joseph Stiglitz has clearly explained how the game works. Typically, a powerful speculator or consortium will take out a huge loan in, say, Thai *baht* from a Thai bank. With the borrowed currency, they buy dollars. The massive quantity of *baht* sold all at once in order to purchase the dollars causes the Thai currency to lose value precipitously. Now the speculator can pay back his loan to the Thai bank in devalued *baht*. The remaining dollars are his to enjoy. This is a form of legal embezzlement, approved and abetted by the IMF which has also systematically made post-crisis, billion dollar loans to these governments. The money was immediately sucked out of the country by foreign banks and local elites.

Because governments like that of Thailand have signed structural adjustment agreements with the Fund, they are powerless to close their borders to outflows of capital. During the Asian financial crisis of 1997–98, only Malaysia and China, which did not have structural adjustment programmes, were able to prevent capital outflows. They overcame the crisis with relative ease despite the destabilization of the entire region.

But the action of the Fund doesn't stop with wrecking the currency and siphoning public money into private hands. Next, it insists that the Thai (or other) Central Bank jack up interest rates in order, they say, to 'control inflation'. Indebted companies, unable to reimburse their creditors at the new rates, without enough cash flow to pay their suppliers, quickly go bankrupt. When enough companies are bankrupt, the banks themselves start to go under. Then, as the *International Herald Tribune* put it, American and Japanese transnational corporations arrive and 'snap up' the bankrupted companies at a fraction of their real value. The IMF repeated the process in Russia, Brazil, Turkey and Argentina. Argentina was the Fund's shining example, doing everything it was told. Its reward is renewed hunger, unemployment rates of 40 per cent and a haemorrhaging of hard currency, while debts increase (see Soederberg in this volume).

Risks for ordinary people, who had nothing whatever to do with provoking the crisis, are naturally compounded. In Mexico, 28,000 small businesses failed and ordiinary Mexicans are worse off now than they were in the early 1970s. Well over half the population live below the official poverty line. In Indonesia, 30,000 bank employees lost their jobs in a single week. In Korea, workers who could no longer feed their families committed what came to be called 'IMF suicides', sometimes taking their families with them into death.

Do the social sciences also play a part in collective transnational risk? I would submit that the IMF and its accomplice in structural adjustment, the World Bank, are populated with thousands of 'social scientists', mostly economists. But are these people really 'scientists'? Not if a scientist is someone who formulates a hypothesis, tests it and throws it out if it doesn't work. Neo-liberal social 'scientists', on the other hand, continue to work on the basis of the same hypothesis no matter how many times it can be shown that these hypotheses do not 'work' for millions of people in the afflicted countries. If a bridge collapses, the engineers who made the calculations are responsible and are called to account. If an economy, an entire society, collapses, the IMF policymakers are never held to account; indeed they are free to pursue exactly the same failed policies for years on end. Perhaps the clue is that these policies *do* in fact 'work' for foreign banks and speculators, and transfer vast amounts of wealth from South to North, from the poor to the rich.

One could go on giving examples of how neo-liberalism multiplies individual and collective risk but it's time to ask whether civil society can in fact effectively confront this problem. The challenges are huge and the mere fact that civil society is invoked in this context shows that somewhere, someone else – notably the state and our international institutions – has abdicated responsibility. It shouldn't be up to civil society to protect the entire planet and its inhabitants from the harmful impact of world capitalism, but this is implicitly the task it has been assigned, and one which, to a large degree, it has accepted.

As someone who has for several decades tried to expose and fight these global risks, allow me to submit that one can get a little tired of finding no help whatsoever in high places. I suggest that civil society shouldn't have to do this job single-handed; that we need laws and enforceable rules, not the never-ending struggle to confront first this danger, then that one. The risk for transnational civil society is to become the 'Sisyphus society', eternally obliged to start again, because corporations and financial markets do as they please and governments govern on their behalf.

We – that is, North American and European civil society – won one fight against transnational capital's interests when, in 1998, we defeated the Multilateral Agreement on Investment (MAI). This neo-liberal treaty was being negotiated in secret at the OECD and would have given all powers to corporations, none to citizens, none to governments. But at the beginning, even when we carefully explained the danger to them, the media wouldn't touch the subject, telling us it was 'too complicated, too technical'; that the public wouldn't understand and wouldn't want to know about it. In France, through a hastily assembled coalition of civil society organizations from many different sectors, we managed to educate enough people and parliamentarians, who had never heard of the MAI, and we finally made it a hot topic, hot enough for France to withdraw and cause the negotiations to collapse. But my point is that we shouldn't have been *obliged* to do this in the first place. Governments should never have become involved in such blatantly pro-corporate negotiations and kept their own parliaments in the dark.

Furthermore, 'civil society' almost always has to work for nothing, on tiny, self-raised budgets and the people who participate in these campaigns have to give their time on a voluntary basis while facing adversaries who can spend millions. It's a miracle civil society ever wins anything. Seattle and Cancun may also prove to be steps on the way to dismantling a hugely unfair world trading system

A major problem for civil society is the total absence of democratic process and machinery above the individual state level. One has virtually no hope of influencing EU policy, except through individual member states. It's hopeless to try to change the World Bank, the IMF or the WTO directly. Why are people sometimes found demonstrating in the streets? One reason is that they have nowhere else to go.

I asked earlier whether we need a transnational state in order to confront transnational risk. Even if such a state were possible, it would not be desirable because it would be made up of, and serve, exactly the same interests as those against which we are now obliged to struggle. There is an invisible transnational government anyway; a visible one would only make matters worse.

Dissent from the dominant ideology and good ideas for new initiatives are always ridiculed at the beginning. Dissenters have a lot to lose and most people cannot afford to lose too much. Dissenters also have to become accustomed to being ignored. But I am encouraged that, despite the drawbacks, the pitfalls, the huge forces arrayed against us, we are still moving forward and the global justice movement is growing. Our opponents may have the money and the power, but we have the numbers, the ideas and the moral claim on justice and democracy.

References

Ehrenreich, Barbara (2001) *Nickel and Dimed: On (Not) Getting By In America* (New York, Metropolitan Books).

Schumpeter, Joseph A. ([1942] 1975) *From Capitalism, Socialism and Democracy* (New York: Harper).

Virilio, Paul and Sylvère Lotringer (1983) *Pure War*, trans. Mark Polizzotti (New York: Semiotext(e)).

2
Corporate Power and Transnational Civil Society

Boris Holzer

The relationship between society and the modern business corporation is an ambivalent one. On the one hand, large corporations produce and deliver the goods and services that many consumers worldwide apparently desire. On the other, that does not mean that corporations and their decisions are universally appreciated. Rather, one can hardly deny that no other institution has been 'so consistently unpopular as has the large corporation' (Kristol 1975: 126). In the wake of the globalization of business, this attitude appears to have spread across the world. Today, there is a McDonald's or a Nike dealership in every corner of the world. But chances are that not too far away one will also meet an anti-corporate activist voicing concern about environmental degradation, workers' exploitation and cultural imperialism. Criticism of that sort is neither rare nor confined to political activists. Academics and politicians too have shown an increasing interest in transnational corporations and regularly conclude that transnational corporations (TNCs) undermine the sovereignty of elected governments and that their activities have undesired consequences for the host countries.

The emergence of a world economy has been inextricably bound up with the rise of transnational corporations (Dicken 1998; Dunning 1993; Sklair 1995). From the very beginning – and long before 'globalization' became a buzzword – the global corporation has been under scrutiny as an 'emerging power' (Barber 1968) and a threat to the sovereignty of the nation-state (Vernon 1973). In a world society increasingly marked by transnational economic and cultural linkages, TNCs have undoubtedly acquired an important position as the producers and distributors of goods and services. They have long transcended a role of mere economic units and have become an important cultural and – according to some critical observers – even political force (Barnet and Müller 1974; Sklair 2002).

Although TNCs are subject to regulation by the nation-state, their transnational reach appears to endow them with a superior position: their investment decisions and employment policies can be crucial to the economic well-being of whole regions. In order to secure economic growth and political stability, nation-states have to enter a global competition for investment. In such a competition, the parameters of regulation, representing potential costs for business, are one of the bargaining resources. Transnational business can use its mobility as a lever to negotiate a favourable deal. Accordingly, the fear that TNCs will be able to shape the global political agenda to their advantage is widespread (Martin and Schumann 1997). Large corporations exert significant influence through their decisions. There is nothing peculiar about transnational corporations in this respect: the power of business has always been regarded as a problematic if manageable consequence of the market economy for democratic political systems (Lindblom 1977). Globalization appears to diminish further the capacity of territorially based politics to rein in and control increasingly footloose capital. Yet that does not mean that corporations will 'rule the world', as Korten (1995) fears. At least, their rule is far from uncontested. Not only do nation-states retain significant means of regulating business practice, but there are other limits to the exercise of corporate power. Business is constrained not only by legal rules and political decisions, but also by social standards. A company that violates those standards may neither be prosecuted nor be liable to a fine, but may quickly find itself in the limelight and suffer the loss of customer support. As I will argue in this chapter, the question of corporate power must therefore be approached from a perspective that does not simply pit it against necessarily deficient forms of state power, but also takes into account the considerable authority of non-state actors such as NGOs and advocacy groups.

Dimensions of corporate power

If civil society activism is the answer, what precisely is the question? How does globalization affect the relationship between business and society, and why does it shift the balance of power in favour of corporations? There are a couple of different answers to this question. The first is a straightforward extrapolation of earlier arguments about corporate power. It concerns the size and resources of corporations. Every organization is 'powerful' in the sense that it can use its hierarchy of command to summon and direct the contributions of a large number of individuals. By opening up opportunities for action not accessible to any individual, a large organization may thus be regarded as considerably more powerful than an individual actor or a spontaneous group of actors. If we follow Bertrand Russell (1986) and assume that power amounts to 'the production of intended effects', corporations are indeed powerful collective actors. But how powerful are they? The mere size in terms of members is not a very accurate indicator of a corporation's capacities. Employees without tools and departments without budgets would hardly count as signs of power. Since corporations need to pay wages, buy machines and trade commodities, their financial resources are a more meaningful indicator. If corporation A has more revenues than corporation B, it can use them for a variety of purposes in the future. Consequently, a frequently cited piece of evidence for the power of large corporations is the tremendous amount of money that they move. That allows us not only to compare TNCs among themselves (as in the famous Global Fortune 500 index), but also to rank both states and corporations according to their financial resources. On the basis of such a comparison of corporate sales and country gross domestic products (GDPs) one discovers that, for instance, of the 100 largest 'economies' in the world, 51 are corporations and only 49 are countries (Anderson and Cavanagh 1996; 2000).

The fact that TNCs rank higher than many countries – especially less developed ones – in such a list is often regarded as a sign of their 'privileged position' in global governance (McGrew 2000: 148). Yet the straightforward nature of such a conclusion is misleading. Even from the perspective of a resource-based concept of power neither GDP nor revenues are suitable indicators because they are not resources that are at a decision-maker's disposal. After all, a government cannot 'spend' GDP, part of which still remains in private hands. A more sophisticated ranking of financial resources therefore compares government budgets and gross corporate revenues (Gray 1999). The result shows that only seven national governments outrank the richest corporations and that the top 100 are now comprised of 66 corporations and 34 governments. However, a slightly different method of comparison may result in a rather divergent picture. If we grant that revenues are not a good indicator of the spending power of corporations and thus use value added instead (and again GDP as an indicator of state power), no TNC gets into the top 40 of the largest economies (Held and McGrew 2002: 44). The problem with such rankings is not only that their results obviously vary greatly according to the method of measurement. More importantly, it appears that even a seemingly simple assessment of financial resources cannot provide a conclusive answer to the question of corporate power. The assumption that money equals power does not take us very far. It is unclear to what extent a translation from financial into political 'capital' is possible. The different results obtained by different methods of ranking states and TNCs indicate that there is no linear transitive order that would allow us to deduce a power differential of, say, 100 per cent between some entity possessing US$100 million and another one with US$200 million. In other words, on whatever basis we rank corporations and countries with regard to their financial resources, such an approach can at most give an indication of their degree of economic power. That may be a rough approximation to a corporation's actual ability to exert influence on others. After all, money cannot just buy tools and manpower, it may also facilitate access to the corridors of state power.[1] Yet as an indicator of corporate power including its more subtle cultural and political dimensions and ramifications (cf. Epstein 1973; 1974) economic wealth remains ambiguous at best.

We therefore have to consider another answer to the question of corporate power. Instead of focusing on individual actors and their resources, it adopts a relational perspective. That means regarding power as an attribute of social relationships, not of individual (or corporate) actors. For Max Weber – and for many theorists today – the essence of power lies in the opportunity to assert and carry out one's will in a social relationship even against resistance (Weber 1980: 28). Such an inclusive definition of power leaves open what the 'chance' is based on. It may be wealth but also charisma, persuasiveness or sheer physical dominance. At any rate, it is important to keep in mind that the power subject's assessment of that chance is decisive – and not the judgement of scientific or other observers (Wrong 1995: 8). Seemingly objective indicators of physical strength or economic wealth are meaningful to the extent that the power subject's evaluation is obvious enough, but they can be misleading if not. The most conspicuous aspect of the relational power of corporations certainly is the superior bargaining position of mobile capital *vis-à-vis* the nation-state (Strange 1996; Tarzi 2000). The respective power of TNCs flows from their position within a web of competitive relations. It is based on the exit options of mobile capital and may appropriately be called a form of 'transnational power of withdrawal' (Beck 1998; 2002: 95ff.). Unlike power relations between states, it is not based on the threat of invasion but rather on the threat of emigration: the potential exit of capital bears consequences that the local or national political decision-makers will be held accountable for. It can therefore be employed as a (more or less credible) threat.

To the extent that corporations have the option of relocating their operations and may thus inflict losses of both tax payments and jobs on a country, they can exert power in bilateral negotiations. The globalization of capital has increased corporations' exit options, although it would be wrong to regard global capital as entirely footloose. TNCs still need to be based somewhere; scenarios of a complete 'corporate takeover' (Monbiot 2000; Hertz 2001) appear to be exaggerated, at least if we take into account that nation-states enter the bargaining process with valuable assets of their own. The operations of TNCs depend on access to territory – which by and large still remains under the control of individual nation-states. To the extent that transnational corporations and their demand for access to territory grow, the governments which control access might even be strengthened. The increase of transnational activities thus does not only challenge the nation-state but also reinforces it: 'It increases the demand for the resource which the nation-state alone controls: territorial access' (Huntington 1973: 355). When this argument was made, it was beyond doubt that nation-states have control over the access to their territory. One should not exaggerate the changes, but certainly this assumption now has to be treated with caution. It is all too obvious that the increase in trans-border flows has diminished the extent of control by nation-states, e.g. regarding labour migration in the European Union. In other areas states have simply been rendered less important, e.g. regarding e-commerce and other information-driven activities (Sassen 1995).[2] In sum, the relational power of TNCs concerning their bargaining with nation-states has been reinforced through the mobility of capital despite countervailing trends such an increased demand for access to territory.

This development is underpinned by a third aspect of corporate power that is often referred to as structural power. Our definition of power as one's ability to carry out one's will even against resistance puts too much emphasis on the actual conflict of objectives between power-holder and subject. For power should not be understood in terms of manifest intentions alone. Following Weber's lead we often too readily restrict power to the intentions of individuals (or corporations, for that matter) through which a 'will' is formed and then explicitly 'asserted'. However, power does not always take the form of obvious and intentional acts but may also occur in the form of 'non-decisions', e.g. when power-holders are able to 'set the agenda' to make it unnecessary to actually enforce anything (Bachrach and Baratz 1962; Lukes 1974). Power may be exercised without any noticeable resistance to it. This is particularly true in those situations in which the threats, i.e. the potential damages faced by the uncooperative power subject, are not directly 'negative sanctions'. We usually conceive of power in terms of a constellation that allows the power-holder to sanction the power subject in the case of nonconformity. For instance, the sanction may take the form of some negatively evaluated action such as physical or social punishment. The 'punishment' administered by corporations *vis-à-vis* states, however, is regularly not only more subtle – it is often not a negative one at all. Rather, corporations offer positive incentives, such as investments or, alternatively, threaten to withdraw them. The negative sanction in this case is based on a complicated conversion: it is the threat of withdrawing an established and expected positive reward. If people are accustomed to receiving certain benefits, e.g. wages or other regular payments, to lose them becomes a threat – and their potential withdrawal therefore turns into a negative sanction (Luhmann 1987: 120). Since corporations are in a privileged position to dispose of benefits such as jobs and tax credits, they wield structural power to the extent that others either depend or at least count on those benefits. In this regard, structural power builds on and amplifies both resource-based and relational forms of power. Wealthy corporations have more 'benefits' to distribute; and the more mobile they are, the higher the chances that they can use the potential withdrawal of benefits to their own advantage.

The public exposure of corporations

The assessment of the resource-based, relational and structural dimensions of power shows that highly mobile and wealthy organizations such as TNCs are indeed powerful. It would be wrong, however, to stop the analysis at this point. For corporate power is not exercised in a social vacuum. There are other than purely state-imposed limitations to corporate decision-making. In addition to being subject to national regulation, corporations have to take into account the more informal normative expectations of advocacy groups, social movements and other sectors of civil society. That holds true for the national as well as the transnational realm. Large corporations are subject to a high degree of 'public exposure'. Business decisions affect a wider public and touch on public interests; they are also afflicted by measures taken in the name of public interest (Dyllick 1989). Especially in areas bearing a potential environmental impact, such as the chemicals industry, the public has grown wary of the side-effects and long-term consequences of decisions. Therefore, the traditional concept of business decisions as essentially private, made by or on behalf of the owners of a company, which liberals such as Milton Friedman (1970) adamantly advocate, no longer holds. Rather, these decisions are increasingly becoming public due to their alleged impact on others. The larger the company, the more likely it is to have such an impact. Therefore, the 'price of successful economic growth for a company is that it gains increased public visibility. It is thus more subject to public scrutiny and public criticism than a small company' (Willetts 1998: 225).

That said, the public exposure of corporations gains new relevance with regard to the question of transnational regulation. Conflicts between TNCs and social movements in the field of environmental protection and human rights have called attention to the role of a transnational civil society for the monitoring and 'civil regulation' of business (Bendell 2000). The significance of a transnational civil society is associated with the lack of transnational regulation in the stateless world polity. Filling the gap between a highly developed transnational economy and a rudimentary 'world politics', protest movements engage in transnational 'sub-politics' that supplement and transgress the boundaries of formal state politics (Beck 1996). With regard to those sub-political actors, the power of corporations needs to be reconsidered. For advocacy groups and social movement organizations often are as transnational as their corporate counterparts; they are also much less dependent on corporate-distributed benefits than nation-states. Certainly, they do not remotely match any TNC's financial resources. But when it comes to direct confrontation, they have proved capable of making up for this deficit by attacking the Achilles' heel of the modern corporation: its brand and reputation. TNCs are likely to be easy targets on the grounds of their public image. They often assume top positions in individual markets and seek to foster their reputation through extensive as well as expensive advertising campaigns.

Anti-corporate protest groups, environmental social movement organizations and human rights advocacy networks have in several instances succeeded in challenging transnational corporations. One of the first TNCs to feel the power of transnational protest actions was the Swiss food giant Nestlé. The controversy surrounding its marketing of infant formula products, i.e. of substitutes for the breastfeeding of babies in the Third World, brought the activities of TNCs into the limelight. Succumbing to a transnational boycott orchestrated by the International Nestlé Boycott Committee (INBC), Nestlé signed an agreement with NGOs, pledging to implement the WHO/UNICEF 'International Code of Marketing of Breast-milk Substitutes' in 1984. The Nestlé case is a prime example of successful campaigning against a transnational company (Sethi and Post 1979; Gerber 1990). Other companies with recent experiences with transnational protest groups include BP, Nike and

McDonald's (Klein 2000). More recently, some highly publicized events contributed to the impression that civil society actors have sufficient power to challenge the economic and political establishment as such. For example, the 'Battle of Seattle' in which a broad coalition of protest groups, trade unions and transnational NGOs laid siege to the WTO's negotiations in Seattle has been discussed as one instance of civil society resistance against corporate-driven globalization (Smith 2002). The same goes for the successful campaign against the negotiations about a Multilateral Agreement on Investment (MAI), which were stopped as a result of multifaceted movement pressure on national governments (Klein 2000: 443; Sklair 2002: 164ff.).

A popular and enduring tale of anti-corporate protest concerns the controversy between the Royal Dutch/Shell Group and Greenpeace over the redundant Brent Spar oil buoy in 1995. It is an example of a very direct confrontation between a company and particular protest group. The storage buoy Brent Spar, located in the North Sea, was due to be sunk in the Atlantic by its operator, Shell Expro (UK). This was opposed by Greenpeace activists who orchestrated a major publicity campaign throughout Europe and seized the platform to prevent the deep-sea disposal. Shell's petrol sales fell by 20–30 per cent, in particular in Germany, where protesters even launched violent attacks on Shell petrol stations. In addition to the consumer boycott, more and more European politicians voiced concern over Shell's plans during the run-up to the North Sea conference in Bergen. After repeated occupations of the platform and internal disputes between the Dutch, British and German Shell companies, Shell finally agreed not to dispose of the platform at sea.

Shell's cave-in was due in part to the sheer professionalism of Greenpeace in broadcasting its message. The pressure group pursued the campaign with almost 'military precision', according to one Shell manager (cited in Paine and Moldoveanu 1999: 1).Video footage of the events on the platform was made available to TV networks, and the Internet was used to disseminate up-to-date information. Greenpeace's methods were not only professional in using modern communications technologies but also in casting itself as the underdog. Ironically, the success of the Brent Spar campaign depended on the fact that initially it seemed unlikely to succeed, if only for the apparent imbalance of power between the oil giant and the environmentalists. Brent Spar was portrayed as a David and Goliath contest. The weaker party used indirect levers to prevail against its much more powerful opponent (Tsoukas 1999). In cases like this, the sympathies of the public are much more likely to be with the weaker party. Accordingly, one of the most widespread criticism of Shell was that the company was arrogant – it did what no one else could do, at least not what the 'man on the street' would be allowed to do, for instance simply dumping waste at the sea.[3]

Ultimately, all companies depend on public acceptance of their operations. Public expectations add another, more informal dimension to the legal restrictions on the exercise of corporate power.[4] Yet from the viewpoint of transnational corporations societal demands appear increasingly contradictory and elusive. The globalization of communications systems has exacerbated this problem because activities in one locale are now scrutinized by a transnational public representing various value systems. For the implementation of decisions this may lead to problems, as Phil Watts of Shell International observed:

> Communications technology has created a global goldfish bowl. All multinational companies operate in front of a hugely diverse world-wide audience. ... [S]ince the ethical, social, cultural and economic priorities which underlie their demands are ... often local and personal, those demands will differ, will often conflict, and may be irreconcilable. (Watts 1998: 24)

If we take non-state actors into account, the 'diffusion of power' (Strange 1996) in the transnational realm not only means that corporations gain bargaining power *vis-à-vis* state governments, it also endows NGOs such as Greenpeace with the authority to challenge the legitimacy of decisions. For transnational NGOs, the lack of global legal or political authority creates the space to establish themselves as 'non-state authorities'. If cross-border legal standards do not exist or are insufficiently institutionalized, NGOs can act as spokespersons and define standards of appropriateness. Successful anti-corporate protest builds on the fact that in world society the legality of operations may be insufficient to ensure legitimacy. Thus a central axiom of the relationship between business and the state is called into question: the nation-state's capacity to transform one into the other. For instance, the legal character of the Brent Spar disposal was not disputed. The operation complied not only with British but also with international law. Initially, none of the affected states objected to it. What Shell could not ensure was acceptance by the (transnational) public. Led by Greenpeace, it ultimately challenged the legitimacy of the proposal to dump irrespective of its legality. The crucial and troubling point for corporations is that the legality of their operations may be insufficient to ensure their legitimacy. In legal terms the acceptability of a decision may be clear, even in different national contexts. Yet broader standards of what is acceptable and what is not are always contested and vary from place to place. To the extent that such standards are voiced by advocacy groups, TNCs cannot benefit from the legitimacy which legal regulation should confer on their decisions. Public discourse can then play a decisive role in conflict situations and civil society actors shape that discourse considerably.

Transnational civil society as a 'counter-movement'

A range of contemporary observers regard transnational social movement organizations, global mass media and local grass-roots movements as a potential counterweight to the one-sidedness of corporate globalization (Chin and Mittelman 1997; Sklair 1998). The myriad of transnational, informal political networks is summarily described as a 'transnational civil society' whose civility is seen in its representing a counter-balance to the predominantly economic nature of globalization. Against the backdrop of an impending 'corporate planet', the forces of transnational civil society are thought to provide a necessary, public-spirited counter-balance (Karliner 1997). Civil society, it seems, has to fill in for the lack of market regulation on a transnational level. Thus civil society activism becomes a counter-movement (Polanyi 1957), i.e. a movement that seeks to redress the balance between market forces and politics (Chin and Mittelman 1997; Mittelman 2000). As a reaction to economic globalization, which is perceived as a form of 'globalization from the top', civil society actors aim to promote a more democratic 'globalization from below' (Falk 1995). The resulting concept of civil society owes much to de Tocqueville, who was among the first theorists to conceive of civil society as a defensive counterbalance to the modern state and as a locus for 'the constructive actions of altruistic concern' of freely associated citizens (Whaites 1996: 241). De Tocqueville thought that civil society's associations offered the opportunity 'to pursue great undertakings in common' (de Tocqueville 1951: 122). Civil society is deemed capable of acting as a counterbalance against particular interests, namely those of economic and political elites.

Using the concept of civil society in this context is not unproblematic, however. The history of the idea of civil society dates back to the time of the Greek *polis*, where the concept was originally designed to grasp the nature of a pre-modern, urban community. In the transition to a modern, highly complex and differentiated society the idea of civil society has undergone important conceptual shifts. Most importantly, it is no longer intended to denote the encompassing system of society. Rather, it is now part of a distinction within society – that between civil society and the state (Luhmann 1987). Following Hegel, civil society is conceived of as a means of social integration 'above the individual yet below the state' (Wapner 1996: 4).[5] Civil society has thus become the counterpart to the administrative state bureaucracy. Against the bureaucratic structure of the state apparatus, the modern notion of civil society emphasizes civil society's potential for self-organization. While the state provides the national community with a formal-juridical framework, civil society assumes a central role in struggles over the legitimate social order. Since the modern democratic state draws its legitimacy from representing a self-governed political community, it also depends on civil society to provide this legitimacy. The distinction between state and civil society is thus paradoxical – the state is not simply 'the other side' of civil society but also the formal expression of its political identity. This makes it difficult to uphold a simple opposition of the state and civil society.[6]

Against this backdrop, it is hardly surprising that the term 'transnational civil society' is not primarily used with reference to and in distinction to the state. Following de Tocqueville's focus on voluntary associations, the emergence of a transnational civil society is usually related to the border-spanning activities of social movements and NGOs, especially in the fields of ecology and human rights (cf. Princen and Finger 1994). Those activist groups are described as agents of a transnational (if not global) civil society and an emerging transnational public sphere (Beck 1996; Lipschutz 1996; Dryzek 1999). The globalization of social movement activities has not been confined to the late twentieth century. As Boli and Thomas (1999) demonstrate in their reconstruction of the growth of transnational NGOs, there has been a continuous expansion of both organizational structures and activities across the globe for more than 100 years. The number of transnational NGOs has grown enormously during that period, with an especially pronounced growth since the 1970s. Currently, there are about 20,000 transnational NGOs concerned with a wide range of issues (Willetts 1998: 200).[7] According to one estimate, 27 per cent of these organizations are concerned with human rights issues, 14 per cent with the environment, and 10 per cent with women's rights (Smith 1997: 46).

Whether this development has been facilitated by economic globalization, which in many ways established the channels of communication and transport thence utilized by social movements, is undisputed. Among the globalization processes in various domains, economic globalization has certainly made the most significant progress so far. However, even if other globalizing tendencies depend on those achievements, their logic should not be ignored. After all, both the economic and other globalizing processes relied on the structures which enabled global communication, be it early means of transport or modern telecommunication. If one takes these long-term developments of society as the underlying trend of globalization, one may summarize that 'the processes that have produced a globalized economy have also produced a globalized civil society' (Willetts 1998: 208).

Yet merely pointing out the growth of the transnational civil society sector does not explain why civil society groups have been successful in making claims against both governments and corporations. Obviously, representatives of civil society command considerable legitimacy *vis-à-vis* corporations because they are deemed to represent a wider public interest. In contrast to TNCs and their 'egoistic' economic motivation, NGOs and advocacy groups are regarded as disinterested representatives of civil society. They can thus profit from the general distrust of any form of raw, unbridled self-interest in modern society (Meyer and Jepperson 2000). Although the pursuit of profit is by no means a dubious or discredited endeavour *per se*, it is expected to be moderated to remain compatible with and controlled by social norms. The formally enforceable framework of such norms is provided by legal regulation. Although laws may not set out precisely what is acceptable and what is not in a society and that entirely legal actions may nevertheless elicit protest, this problem is amplified by globalization which leads many processes to break out from the political and legal constraints of the nation-state: If people (or protest groups) feel affected by the attendant border-crossing consequences, they cannot be mollified by the prospect that a political process could change the situation; in the absence of a world government, there is no formal political process to deal with such problems. Therefore, the basis of power in such conflicts is not so much the state apparatus as the informal influence provided by the moralization and mobilization of public discourse.

In the absence of an encompassing formal authority, public normative disputes over transnational issues have to be settled against the backdrop of a 'broad world polity of shared rules and models' (Meyer 2000: 236). These rules cannot be enforced from above since authority in the world polity is fragmented. Instead they must be constructed from below. The political system of nation-states constitutes an established if fragmented authority framework in the world polity. And even in a stateless world polity the sovereign national sub-units maintain formal legal authority within their borders. But at the same time, transnational organizations can exercise their own kind of authority, a form of 'rational-voluntaristic' authority as opposed to the 'legal-rational authority' of nation-states (Boli 1999: 277–87). Both TNCs and environmental protest groups seek to benefit from rational-voluntaristic authority. Whilst TNCs enact the cultural script of rational progress and economic growth, environmental pressure groups draw on notions of environmental life quality and act as the disinterested advocates of nature. However, corporations cannot benefit as much from the legitimacy provided by this broad cultural script as NGOs. Only the latter appear as representatives of an 'enlightened' form of self-interest rather than a 'naked' or 'raw' one. Within the framework of modern world culture, NGOs can therefore claim the moral high ground. Since the support of other 'moral observers' in the public sphere is important for both corporations (to maintain reputation) and NGOs (to secure commitment), the normative infrastructure of world culture turns out to be more favourable to the claims and activities of NGOs (Boli, Elliott and Bieri 2003).

The public resonance of the claims of NGOs is the pivotal point in scenarios of a kind of 'civil regulation' (Bendell 2000) that could supplement and even partly replace state regulation at the transnational level. It should be noted, however, that this strength of civil society is also its main weakness. For reliance on mobilized public opinion makes it almost impossible to develop and pursue policies systematically. As Lippmann put it, 'the force of public opinion is partisan, spasmodic, simple-minded and external' (1925: 151). Since the influence of NGOs and social movement organizations (in contrast to state governments) is not based on a generalized form of support, they depend on the volatile and unpredictable attention span of the public. That makes it difficult to carry anti-corporate campaigning – successful as it may be in each instance – much beyond the 'anti' and to turn it into a more constructive political force in global politics. Coordinating efforts have so far been limited to specific issue areas such as environmental protection or labour standards. Furthermore, some interesting but still limited developments towards more comprehensive policies have taken place under the umbrella of the World Social Forum (WSF). Yet we should bear in mind that if we speak of a transnational civil society, we use a convenient and deceptive shorthand for what is actually an assemblage of diverse, even conflicting interests and expectations. That is no argument against civil society's capacity to keep corporations at arm's length, at least occasionally. Civil society actors command a great deal of legitimacy in the global realm. They derive their legitimacy and influence from their articulation of broadly shared rules and standards that transnational corporations, despite their power, find difficult to ignore. Even if we should not expect civil society activism to result in a form of regulation that is both comprehensive and consistent, its contribution to the globalization of basic environmental and labour standards remains significant.

Notes

1. Lobbying activities of corporations are well documented and researched, but their efficacy is difficult to assess. See Grenzke (1989) for an account of corporate-sponsored 'political action committees'.
2. From a different perspective, the regulatory power of nation-states is threatened by information asymmetries. TNCs can tap their worldwide knowledge, while governments are confined to their own domain. This is reflected in the statement of one CEO who admits: 'We would not knowingly break the rules anywhere. We always employ one set of experts to tell us what they are, and another set to tell us how to get round them' (cited in Tugendhat 1973: 163).
3. 'How can you tell 90 million Germans religiously to sort their rubbish and not expect them to cry foul when they see a global company fly-tipping its rubbish into the sea, or have a government committed to integrating ecology into all policy areas without people beginning to take personal responsibility?' (*The Guardian*, 'Agenda benders', 22 June 1995).
4. 'Organizations in modern societies are public not only in the sense that their structures, processes and ideologies are open to observation, but also in their ultimate dependence on public acceptance, i.e. of positioning themselves in relation to the perceptions and policies of society at large' (Brunsson 1989: 216). See Millstein and Katsh (2003) for an overview of direct and indirect forms of regulation.
5. For a more comprehensive review of theories of civil society, see Cohen and Arato (1992).
6. Logically speaking, the *excluded* is *included* on both sides of the distinction, thus turning the clear-cut opposition into what Hofstadter (1979) calls a 'tangled hierarchy'.
7. Since these figures are based on UN estimates, they usually include a number of NGOs which are commonly not considered as social movements, e.g. business and science associations and standardization bodies. However, the figures give a rough impression of the growth of transnational civic activities.

References

Anderson, Sarah and John Cavanagh (1996) Corporate Empires, *Multinational Monitor* 17(12); http://multinationalmonitor.org/hyper/mm1296.08.html.
—— (2000) Top 200: The Rise of Corporate Global Power, *Multinational Monitor* (Washington, DC: Insititute for Policy Studies); http://www.ips-dc.org/.
Bachrach, Peter and Morton S. Baratz (1962) Two Faces of Power, *American Political Science Review*, 56: 947–952.

Barber, Arthur (1968) Emerging New Power: The World Corporation, *War/Peace Report*, VIII: 7ff.

Barnet, Richard J. and Ronald E. Müller (1974) *Global Reach: The Power of the Multinational Corporations* (New York: Simon & Schuster).

Beck, Ulrich (1996) World Risk Society as Cosmopolitan Society? Ecological Questions in a Framework of Manufactured Uncertainties, *Theory, Culture & Society*, 13: 1–32.

—— (1998) Wie wird Demokratie im Zeitalter der Globalisierung möglich? in Ulrich Beck (ed.) *Politik der Globalisierung* (Frankfurt am Main: Suhrkamp), pp. 7–66.

—— (2002) *Macht und Gegenmacht im globalen Zeitalter. Neue weltpolitische Ökonomie* (Frankfurt am Main: Suhrkamp).

Bendell, Jem (2000) Civil Regulation. A New Form of Democratic Governance for the Global Economy? in Jem Bendell (ed.) *Terms for Endearment: Business, NGOs and Sustainable Development* (Sheffield: Greenleaf), pp. 239–255.

Boli, John (1999) Conclusion: World Authority Structures and Legitimations, in John Boli and George M. Thomas (eds.) *Constructing World Culture: International Nongovernmental Organizations since 1875* (Stanford, CA: Stanford University Press), pp. 267–300.

Boli, John, Michael A. Elliott and Franziska Bieri (2003) Globalization, in George Ritzer (ed.) *Handbook of Social Problems: A Comparative International Perspective* (London: Sage).

Boli, John, and George M. Thomas (1999) INGOs and the Organization of World Culture, in John Boli and George M. Thomas (eds.) *Constructing World Culture: International Nongovernmental Organizations since 1875* (Stanford, CA: Stanford University Press) pp. 13–49.

Brunsson, Nils (1989) *The Organization of Hypocrisy. Talk, Decisions and Actions in Organizations* (Chichester: John Wiley & Sons).

Chin, Christine B. N. and James H. Mittelman (1997) Conceptualising Resistance to Globalisation, *New Political Economy*, 2: 25–37.

Cohen, Jean K. and Andrew Arato (1992) *Civil Society and Political Theory* (Cambridge, MA and London: MIT Press).

de Tocqueville, Alexis ([1840] 1951) *De la démocratie en Amérique*, vol. II (*Oeuvres complètes*, tome 1b) (Paris: Gallimard).

Dicken, Peter (1998) *Global Shift: Transforming the World Economy* (London: Paul Chapman).

Dryzek, John S. (1999) Transnational Democracy, *Journal of Political Philosophy*, 7: 30–51.

Dunning, John H. (1993) *The Globalization of Business* (New York: Routledge).

Dyllick, Thomas (1989) *Management der Umweltbeziehungen. Öffentliche Auseinandersetzungen als Herausforderung* (Wiesbaden: Gabler).

Epstein, Edwin M. (1973) Dimensions of Corporate Power, part 1, *California Management Review*, 16: 9–23.

—— (1974) Dimensions of Corporate Power, part 2, *California Management Review*, 16: 32–47.

Falk, Richard A. (1995) *On Humane Governance: Toward a New Global Politics* (Cambridge: Polity Press).

Friedman, Milton (1970) The Social Responsibility of Business is to Increase its Profits, *New York Times Magazine*, pp. 32–33, 122, 124, 126.

Gerber, Jurg (1990) Enforced Self-regulation in the Infant Formula Industry: A Radical Extension of an 'Impractical' Proposal, *Social Justice*, 17: 98–112.

Gray, Charles (1999) Corporate Goliaths, *Multinational Monitor*, 20(6); http://multinationalmonitor.org/mm1999/99june/economics.html.

Grenzke, Janet M. (1989) PACs and the Congressional Supermarket: The Currency is Complex, *American Journal of Political Science*, 33: 1–24.

Held, David and Anthony McGrew (2002) *Globalization/Anti-Globalization* (Cambridge: Polity).

Hertz, Noreena (2001) *The Silent Takeover: Global Capitalism and the Death of Democracy* (London: Heinemann).

Hofstadter, Douglas R. (1979) *Gödel, Escher, Bach: An Eternal Golden Braid* (New York: Basic Books).

Huntington, Samuel P. (1973) Transnational Organizations in World Politics, *World Politics*, 25: 333–368.

Karliner, Joshua (1997) *The Corporate Planet. Ecology and Politics in the Age of Globalization* (San Francisco: Sierra Club Books).

Klein, Naomi (2000) *No Logo* (London: HarperCollins).

Korten, David C. (1995) *When Corporations Rule the World* (West Hartford, CT: Kumarian Press).

Kristol, Irving (1975) On Corporate Capitalism in America, *The Public Interest*, 41: 124–141.

Lindblom, Charles E. (1977) *Politics and Markets. The World's Political-Economic Systems* (New York: Basic Books).

Lippmann, Walter (1925) *The Phantom Public* (New York: Macmillan).

Lipschutz, Ronnie D. (1996) *Global Civil Society and Global Environmental Governance: The Politics of Nature from Place to Planet* (Albany, NY: State University of New York Press).

Luhmann, Niklas (1987) Staat und Politik. Zur Semantik der Selbstbeschreibung politischer Systeme, in *Soziologische Aufklärung* 4 (Opladen: Westdeutscher Verlag), pp. 74–103.

Lukes, Steven (1974) *Power: A Radical View* (London: Macmillan).

Martin, Hans-Peter and Harald Schumann (1997) *The Global Trap. Globalization and the Assault on Prosperity and Democracy* (London and New York: Zed Books).

McGrew, Anthony (2000) Power Shift: From National Government to Global Governance? in David Held (ed.) *A Globalizing World? Culture, Economics, Politics* (London and New York: Routledge), pp. 127–166.

Meyer, John W. (2000) Globalization: Sources and Effects on National States and Societies, *International Sociology*, 15: 233–248.

Meyer, John W. and Ronald L. Jepperson (2000) The 'Actors' of Modern Society: The Cultural Construction of Social Agency, *Sociological Theory*, 18: 100–120.

Millstein, Ira M. and Salem M. Katsh (2003) *The Limits of Corporate Power: Existing Constraints on the Exercise of Corporate Discretion* (Washington, DC: Beard Books).

Mittelman, James H. (2000) *The Globalization Syndrome: Transformation and Resistance* (Princeton, NJ: Princeton University Press).

Monbiot, George (2000) *Captive State: The Corporate Takeover of Britain* (London: Macmillan).

Paine, Lynn Sharpe and Mihnea Moldoveanu (1999) *Royal Dutch/Shell in Transition (A)* (Boston, MA: Harvard Business School).

Polanyi, Karl ([1944] 1957) *The Great Transformation: The Political and Economic Origins of Our Time* (Boston, MA: Beacon Press).

Princen, Thomas and Matthias Finger (1994) *Environmental NGOs and World Politics: Linking the Local and the Global* (London: Routledge).

Russell, Bertrand (1986) The Forms of Power, in Steven Lukes (ed.) *Power* (Oxford: Blackwell), pp. 19–21.

Sassen, Saskia (1995) *Losing Control? Sovereignty in an Age of Globalization* (New York: Columbia University Press).

Sethi, S. Prakash and James E. Post (1979) Public Consequences of Private Action: The Marketing of Infant Formula in Less Developed Countries, *California Management Review*, 21: 35–48.

Sklair, Leslie (1995) *Sociology of the Global System* (London: Harvester Wheatsheaf and Prentice Hall).

—— (1998) Social Movements and Global Capitalism, in Fredric Jameson and Masao Miyoshi (eds.) *The Cultures of Globalization* (Durham, NC and London: Duke University Press), pp. 291–311.

—— (2002) The Transnational Capitalist Class and Global Politics: Deconstructing the Corporate–State Connection, *International Political Science Review*, 23: 159–174.

Smith, Jackie (1997) Characteristics of the Modern Transnational Social Movement Sector, in Jackie G. Smith, Charles Chatfield, and Ron Pagnucco (eds.) *Transnational Social Movements and Global Politics: Solidarity beyond the State* (Syracuse, NY: Syracuse University Press), pp. 42–58.

—— (2002) Globalizing Resistance: the Battle of Seattle and the Future of Social Movements, in Jackie Smith and Hank Johnston (eds.) *Globalization and Resistance. Transnational Dimensions of Social Movements* (Lanham, MD: Rowman & Littlefield), pp. 207–227.

Strange, Susan (1996) *The Retreat of the State. The Diffusion of Power in the World Economy* (Cambridge: Cambridge University Press).

Tarzi, Shah M. (2000) Third World Governments and Multinational Corporations: Dynamics of Host's Bargaining Power', in Jeffrey A. Frieden and David A. Lake (eds.) *International Political Economy: Perspectives on Global Power and Wealth* (London and New York: Routledge), pp. 156–166.

Tsoukas, Haridimos (1999) David and Goliath in the Risk Society: Making Sense of the Conflict between Shell and Greenpeace in the North Sea, *Organization*, 6: 499–528.

Tugendhat, Christopher (1973) *The Multinationals* (Harmondsworth: Penguin Books).

Vernon, R. (1973) *Sovereignty at Bay* (Harmondsworth: Penguin Books).

Wapner, Paul (1996) *Environmental Activism and World Civic Politics* (Albany, NY: State University of New York Press).

Watts, Philip (1998) The International Petroleum Industry: Economic Actor or Social Activist? in John V. Mitchell (ed.) *Companies in a World of Conflict: NGOs, Sanctions and Corporate Responsibility* (London: Royal Institute of International Affairs/Earthscan), pp. 23–31.

Weber, Max ([1921–2] 1980) *Wirtschaft und Gesellschaft. Grundriß der verstehenden Soziologie* (Tübingen: J. C. B. Mohr (Paul Siebeck)).

Whaites, Alan (1996) Let's Get Civil Society Straight: NGOs and Political Theory, *Development in Practice*, 6: 240–244.

Willetts, Peter (1998) Political Globalization and the Impact of NGOs upon Transnational Companies, in John V. Mitchell (ed.) *Companies in a World of Conflict: NGOs, Sanctions and Corporate Responsibility* (London: Royal Institute of International Affairs/Earthscan), pp. 195–226.

Wrong, Dennis H. (1995) *Power: Its Forms, Bases and Uses* (Brunswick, NJ: Transaction Books).

3
The Governance of Transnational Debt: The Role of the International Monetary Fund[1]

Susanne Soederberg

Introduction

Despite an excess of high-level discussions and agreements dedicated to strengthening the international financial architecture, neither governments nor markets are nearer to solving the problems of transnational debt (cf. Soederberg 2004a; cf. IMF 1997). Transnational debt refers to 'all the forms of debt across frontiers: all the liabilities incurred, and claims established, between institutions or individuals under one political jurisdiction' (Strange 1998a: 91–2). In November 2001, in response to the mounting economic problems in Argentina, and its apparently imminent and largest default in history, the IMF's First Deputy Managing Director, Anne Krueger, proposed a new approach to dealing with sovereign debt: the Sovereign Debt Restructuring Mechanism (SDRM) (Eichengreen 2002a and b). The motivation behind this plan was to provide better incentives for debtors and creditors to agree on prompt, orderly and predictable restructuring of unsustainable debt (IMF 2003). Specifically, SDRM 'would allow a country to come to the IMF (or, Fund) and request a temporary standstill on the repayment of its debts, during which time it would negotiate a rescheduling or restructuring with its creditors' (given the Fund's consent) (IMF 2001). Since Krueger introduced SDRM, the restructuring framework has come under sustained attack from a diverse set of interests, including international creditors, non-governmental organizations (NGOs) and the US Treasury Secretary. Not surprisingly, the new bankruptcy procedure for insolvent governments was not supported by the Fund's International Monetary and Financial Committee (IMFC) – a body responsible for advising, and reporting to, the Board of Governors – at the Annual Meeting of the World Bank and IMF in April 2003.

However, the lack of support for SDRM does not mean that this policy is not worthy of critical reflection. There are at least three reasons why it is important to investigate SDRM. First, an analysis of the issues and problems involved in managing transnational debt thus far aids our understanding of why the IMF and the US government have been balking over the financing of debt restructuring *vis-à-vis* Argentina. Second, the official debates surrounding SDRM, most notably between the IMF and the US Treasury Department, significantly shape future policy directions of managing transnational debt since they reflect the more discriminating and neo-conservative approach to multilateral assistance of the second Bush administration (2001–present) under which aid is provided only to countries with solid fundamentals and the size of aid packages is limited (Eichengreen 2001b; cf. Soederberg 2004a, especially chapter 6; 2004b). And, third, while SDRM was struck down, the IMFC did support none the less a set of reforms restricting the Fund's rescue lending to crisis-hit countries and encouraging a more active role for the majority of creditors caught up in sovereign bankruptcy.

So far, the literature on SDRM has been dominated by heavily economistic and technical analyses (Akyüz 2002; Cooper 2002; Eichengreen 2002a). The upshot has been that more critical questions, such as who benefits – and why – from the risk inherent in an international financial structure dominated by free capital mobility and lax (public) regulatory structures have not been addressed. I fill this void by exploring a largely neglected dimension of the SDRM debates, namely, the detrimental effects of constructing an imperative of capital account liberalization in the international economy, and, relatedly, the growing reliance of emerging market economies, like Argentina, on private, short-term capital inflows to sustain government spending. My primary objective is to analyse the international discussion triggered by the Argentine case regarding the means to deal with risk associated with sovereign default. As such, the focus of the discussion is not on Argentina *per se*, but on the significance of SDRM *vis-à-vis* the assumption that open capital accounts are vital to achieving economic growth in the South, a central tenet of the neo-liberal-led Washington Consensus. In doing so, I argue that the official debates surrounding SDRM and subsequent, market-based solution to future sovereign defaults ('collection action clauses') amplify, as opposed to mitigate, financial risk by recreating the disciplinary power of transnational lenders *vis-à-vis* governments of middle-income countries.

This chapter is divided into four main sections. Section two examines the shifting landscape of the global development finance over the past decade and the significance, as well as mounting contradictions, of the imperative of free capital mobility. Section three explores the official debates surrounding SDRM in order to demonstrate how the disciplinary power of transnational financial capitals were further strengthened *vis-à-vis* governments of middle-income countries. And finally, section four concludes by suggesting that the tensions between two opposing understandings of risk – financial risk versus social risk – continue to characterize the attempts to govern transnational debt in the new millennium (Soederberg and Taylor 2004).

Amplifying risk through financial liberalization

Changes in global financial flows and development finance

Financial flows have undergone at least three structural changes since the early 1990s (Griffith-Jones 1996; Strange 1998b; World Bank 2003). The first distinguishing feature has been the sheer size of the capital flows. Between 1992 and 1993, for example, capital inflows reached an annual average of around $62 billion in Latin America, compared with 1983–90 when net capital inflows averaged only $10 billion a year. Second, official development finance, especially its largest component, bilateral aid, has lagged behind private flows (Ocampo 2001). Because of this, governments of emerging markets have grown more dependent on international financial players to fill their public and private coffers. According to the Executive Secretary of the UN Economic Commission for Latin America and the Caribbean (ECLAC), José Antonio Ocampo, the majority of capital flows to the middle-income countries are not only more short-term (one year or less) than they were in the 1980s, but also these countries receive the highest concentration of the most volatile flows (Ocampo 2000; ECLAC 2002). The increased disembedding of (highly esoteric) financial instruments from the real economy through technological innovation and liberalization processes constitutes the third change in financial flows. Although not divorced from the productive sphere, the steady intensification of financialization has meant that growth rates of turnover of financial assets are many times higher than the growth of any indicator of 'real' activity (Altvater 2002). In other words, finance is no longer a means of facilitating the exchange of goods and services but has become an end in itself, largely feeding void left by the trade and budget deficits (cf. World Bank 2004).

The upshot of these changes has been the creation of a highly complex and incredibly volatile form of transnational debt, including a plethora of private and public creditors and debtors, spanning national boundaries. As Strange notes, this form of debt includes assets claimed by foreign shareholders in enterprises in another country, inter-bank loans across frontiers, bonds issued to non-nationals by governments and other institutions and firms, as well as credits or guarantees extended by states or multilateral organizations like the IMF and World Bank or the regional development banks in Asia, the Western Hemisphere or Africa (1998a: 91–2).[2]

The logic of free capital mobility

Instead of creating a new set of regulations commensurate to the changes in capital flows and the increase in power of transnational creditors in the South, institutions tied to the Washington Consensus, such as the IMF, began to emphasize – in the form of conditionalities – the need for debtor countries to commit to capital account liberalization in order to achieve 'economic progress' (cf. D'Arista and Griffith-Jones 2001). Or, in the words of the former Chief Economist of the World Bank, Joseph Stiglitz, 'while [the new directive] may have been quiet, it was hardly subtle: from serving global economic interests to serving the interests of global finance. Capital market liberalization may not have contributed to global economic stability, but it did open up vast new markets for Wall Street' (2002: 207).

As I have argued elsewhere (Soederberg 2004a), the core logic surrounding Washington's push for capital account liberalization rests on the basic assumption that international financial markets are not only inherently rational in nature, but also lead to mutual gain. Liberalized capital flows, for instance, are thought to create greater welfare benefits because foreign savings supplement the domestic resource base. As a result, this leads to a larger capital stock and places the economy on a potentially higher growth path. Free trade in capital, through international borrowing and lending, actually helps lower the costs of the inter-temporal misalignments that periodically arise between the patterns of production and consumption. Put plainly, capital inflows permit national economies to pay for imports in the present with exports in the future. Another benefit from financial liberalization is believed to be that the sharing and diversification of risks that otherwise would not be possible become feasible (Guitán 1997: 22; Felix 2002). Critically, since capital markets are inherently rational, they will enter those countries that demonstrate sound regulatory practices such as balanced budgets, low inflation, market liberalization and stable exchange rates. According to this line of reasoning, markets act as a disciplinary force that can punish profligate governments through investment strikes and capital flight (Gill and Law 1993). It is interesting to note that the inherent rationality of financial participants lies at the base of SDRM, particularly in its concern for avoiding any moral hazard in future IMF bailouts. Is this conventional wisdom correct or just convenient?

It is worth highlighting that the assumption that market actors are inherently rational is not uncontested. David Felix suggests that this position does not have general backing from more basic theorizing about the stability of competitive market economies. Rather, the theorizing indicates that liberated financial markets are inherently prone to destabilizing dynamics that can also destabilize aggregate production, trade, and employment in such economies (Felix 2002; cf. Haley 1999; Patomäki 2001). Indeed, an argument could be made that the institutional investors are drawn to middle-income countries because of the higher risks involved, as the latter bring higher returns. In contrast, however, the debtor nations, at least the lower echelons of society, do not benefit in the same way from higher volatility (ECLAC 2002). As I argued (2004a), the greatest beneficiary of an international financial system based on the principle of free capital mobility is the American political economy (Gowan 1999).

We now turn our attention to the political effects of the adherence to open capital accounts in the emerging markets.

Emerging markets and global financial flows

The Herculean task of signalling creditworthiness to global financial players by adhering to the conventional wisdom of the Washington Consensus and placating domestic social strife has proved to be increasingly difficult for governments of middle-income countries. In particular, the tension between the principle of national self-determination and the neo-liberal principle of capital account liberalization – as part and parcel of the neo-liberal package of reforms – has contributed to a legitimacy crisis in many emerging markets. The changing nature of capital flows to emerging market economies has had important political ramifications for governments of debtor countries, or what I refer to as a policy paradox. Ilene Grabel identifies at least two negative and mutually reinforcing effects that financial flows have on national policy formation in the emerging markets: 1) the imposition of constraints on policy autonomy; and 2) the creation of greater vulnerability to the economy to risk, financial volatility, and crisis (1996).

To attract capital inflows, most of which stem from highly mobile sources of foreign capital (mostly from G7 countries), governments of emerging markets must send positive signals to investors about their credibility and market-friendliness, such as degrees of capital mobility, labour and production costs, and political stability (Maxfield 1996). Thus the need to signal creditworthiness to global financial markets has not only limited the scope of policy autonomy of states in emerging markets, but has generated stark tension between the accountability of policymakers to the needs of transnational capital as opposed to those people it governs (Gill and Law 1993; Soederberg 2004a). To attract this crucial source of public financing, governments are pressured to enter into a 'pact with the devil' whereby market credibility assumes a central position in policymaking in such areas as exchange and interest rates as well as through tight fiscal policies. The latter can begin to conflict or even take precedence over other domestic concerns, especially the needs of subordinate segments of the population, such as the rural poor (Soederberg and Taylor 2004; and see George in this volume).[3]

A corollary to this is the growing structural power of transnational financial capitals, such as institutional investors (macro-hedge, pension and mutual funds) *vis-à-vis* the states in the South. Geoffrey Underhill notes that the growth in capital volatility and mobility acts to constrain the policymaking autonomy of elected governments, particularly with regard to exchange rate and monetary policy, but also with fiscal (taxation) and social policies. For Underhill, these tensions have resulted in a substantial 'legitimacy deficit', further exacerbated by the need to adjust to the pressures imposed on them by 'global restructuring' (1997: 19). This tension assumes a distinct expression in the South, particularly in countries like Argentina. For instance, Haley suggests that investors are attracted to those countries that rapidly implement and maintain intense neo-liberal reforms (privatization, liberalization) while simultaneously controlling political opposition to these measures. Put another way, these investors will find liberal democracy not only unnecessary, but also perhaps contrary to their interests (1999; and see Holzer in this volume). Thus, and especially during times of crisis when capital is most needed, governments of Third World countries need to signal their creditworthiness by demonstrating political stability. These conditions can readily lead to increased forms of coercion and other expressions of authoritarianism aimed at quelling overt manifestations of class conflict in order to attract and maintain capital inflows. The limits placed on policy autonomy and the growing priority given to transnational finance in terms of neo-liberal policies can increasingly constrain political space for the articulation of subordinate voices.[4]

Debating the governance of transnational debt

The biggest threat to creditors has always been default. Strange observes that after the 1980 debt crisis the ruling classes of many developing countries decided to neither trade nor borrow from the global economy, thereby 'doing their best to be self-sufficient, autonomous and, as some argued, free' (1994: 112). She notes that '[a]nxiety to keep the debtors inside the financial structure despite their difficulties was all the greater if the debtor country was large, was a substantial importer of Western goods and was host to a large number of Western transnational corporations – none of whom were anxious to cope with a decoupled debtor country' (ibid.).

During the spring 2002 meetings of the IMF and World Bank in Washington, DC, the G7 Finance Ministers and the IMF's monetary and finance committee endorsed a twin-track approach to improving procedures for dealing with sovereign bankruptcies. It is important to highlight that what the G7 ministers received, however, was a watered-down version of what was originally proposed by the IMF's Deputy Managing Director, Anne Krueger, in November 2001. Broadly, Krueger's original proposal suggests a 'sovereign debt restructuring mechanism' (SDRM-1), which would entail a new international legal framework based on the features of domestic bankruptcy proceedings in the private sector. This was essentially aimed at creating a binding set of laws through which crisis-stricken countries could halt panics and keep investors from pulling their money out of the nation – so buying time for political leaders to work out debts in an orderly fashion – much like Chapter 11 of US bankruptcy law (Soederberg and Taylor 2004; Soederberg 2006). In doing so, the IMF ignored the insistence of high-profile NGOs such as Jubilee 2000 to base the restructuring of sovereign debt on Chapter 9 of the US legal code, which applies to governmental organisations like municipalities. Unlike Chapter 11, which applies to corporations, Chapter 9 contains more humane and democratic ways of dealing with insolvency. For example, 'a municipality is not expected to stop providing basic social services essential to health, safety and welfare of its inhabitants in order to pay its creditors'; for another, 'people affected by the plan have the opportunity to voice their arguments, be they employees of the municipality or "special taxpayers" – i.e., special in the sense that they are expected to pay more. Taxpayers have the right to be heard in all matters relating in a Chapter 9 case, and to object to the confirmation of the plan' (Pettifor et al. 2001: 22).

Under the proposed SDRM-1, the IMF would play a central role by determining which countries would be eligible to participate in SDRM and by ensuring that member countries adhere to the procedures laid out by the SDRM framework. SDRM-1 described a process in which countries in crisis would call a halt to debt payments as they negotiated with private sector lenders under the jurisdiction of a new international judicial panel. During these negotiations, the IMF would serve to protect the debtor country from litigation. The conditions of repayment after a country declared bankruptcy would be negotiated among the creditors by super-majority – a situation in which 60–75 per cent of the creditors agree to the terms of restructuring, which would then be binding for the rest (and, of course, the debtor country). The proposed role of the IMF would be to oversee voting and adjudicate disputes in this process. According to Krueger, the role of the IMF would be vital to the success of such a system (IMF 2001). For SDRM-1 to be realized, however, the IMF's Articles of Agreement would have had to be subject to reform. For any such change to occur, the US, which wields veto power, has to agree with these changes (see George in this volume).

However, the US government did not agree with the conditions set out in SDRM-1. (It should be noted that powerful financial interests, such as the Emerging Markets Traders' Association and the Securities Industry Association, also rejected the SDRM proposal.)[5] After heavy criticism from the Treasury Undersecretary, Krueger revised her proposal (SDRM-2) to enhance the role and power of creditors. Essentially, SDRM-2 was more in line with Taylor's insistence on a decentralized, market-based approach based on a broader use of 'collection action clauses' (CACs) in bonds issued by sovereign governments' provisions. CACs entail provisions that allow a super-majority of bondholders to approve a process that is believed to make it easier to restructure debt by allowing a majority of creditors to impose a deal. A super-majority of creditors is deemed important as it overcomes the problem of 'collection action', which occurs when individual creditors consider that their interests are best served by preventing what is termed a 'grab race', in which creditors try to get the best deal possible from the debtor government in order to enforce their claim as quickly as possible. This grab race is believed to hinder other creditors and thus may lead them in capturing the limited assets available (Boorman 2002).

It is this feature of SDRM-2 that was touted during the World Bank IMF annual meetings in April 2003, at which the IMFC welcomed the inclusion of CACs by several countries, most recently Mexico, in international sovereign bond issues. The IMFC also welcomed the announcement that, by June 2003, EU countries issuing bonds under foreign jurisdictions would include CACs. In fact, the IMFC went on to state that it looked forward to the inclusion of CACs in international bond issues becoming standard market practice, and called on the IMF to promote the voluntary inclusion of CACs in the context of its surveillance practices. Obviously this ensures that countries adhere to neo-liberal policies set out in the Washington Consensus (IMF 2003).

Krueger's modified SDRM-2 effectively reduced the amount of control the IMF had over how the standstill (a temporary suspension of payments) would work, or even how debts would be restructured. A caveat is in order here. Despite the fact that the role of the IMF is minimized, it should be recalled that the ability of the Fund to provide a 'seal of approval', and thereby signal the creditworthiness of a debtor nation to its international creditors, makes the Fund an integral and coercive feature not only in the negotiation of debt but also the reproduction of the status of private financial markets. Moreover, embracing the notion that a near-default on sovereign debt may be worked out through legal frameworks and an IMF-centred international agreement, plays an important role in both normalizing and disciplining the power of transnational capital over sovereign states (IMF 2003). In doing so, the Fund also serves to put forward a particular version of reality that stands in contrast to contesting views, most notably the many voices who have been calling for debt cancellation over the past few decades.[6]

It should be underlined that SDRM-2 was neither transparent, nor inclusive. The only ostensibly independent forum attached to SDRM-2 process was the proposed Sovereign Debt Dispute Resolution Forum (SDDRF). According to Krueger, SDDRF was to be set up as 'a legal body whose functions would be to register claims and resolve disputes [and] would be independent of the Fund and its Executive Board, in parallel with approaches used in other organizations' (IMF 2003). Nevertheless, it should be noted that the powers of SDDRF were limited in two ways. First, although the IMF had stated that SDDRF should be independent of the Fund, it had also highlighted that it would retain a veto over SDDRF decisions. Second, SDRM-2 did not include citizen participation in the resolution processes of financial crises (see Scholte in this volume). On the one hand, SDRM-2 favoured a *laissez-faire* approach, allowing market participants more power in the default procedures. This approach was clearly designed to increase the coercive power of transnational capital over debtor countries. Private financial institutions, led by their association, the Institute of International Finance, played a tactical game of supporting collective action clauses in the apparent hope of killing the plan for a judicial mechanism that would in effect reduce their power (*Financial Times* 2002a). On the other hand, as is clear from its response to the Meltzer Commission mentioned earlier, the Treasury did not want the IMF to assume a life of its own, nor does it want to see the creation of a new and truly global financial institution that could oversee such processes, as this could entail the threat of moving toward a multilateral as opposed to unilateral forms of norm-creating and decision-making processes.[7]

It should also be highlighted that the official debates on the SDRM have excluded developing countries. In fact, until the Annual Meeting of the IMF and World Bank in early Autumn 2002 (including the G7 Finance Ministers), official discussions surrounding sovereign debt default took place exclusively between the Fund and the US Treasury. Given the importance of this issue to industrialized countries, acting on behalf of the interests of transnational capitals who have supplied the credit to emerging markets, the SDRM was not raised for discussion at the UN Financing for Development Conference at Monterrey, Mexico in March 2002, despite the so-called inclusionary and democratic nature of the innovative gathering, involving civil society organizations, the IMF, the World Bank, the World Trade Organization, the G7 countries and the developing world (Soederberg 2004a). Indeed, a fair, independent and transparent process for negotiating debt restructuring would prove fatal to the disciplinary effects involved in sovereign bankruptcy. Neither the debtor country nor its citizens should have a voice in the negotiations. An act of exclusion, as many Argentines know too well, is necessary to bring together 'like-minded' groups and individuals to the table.

SDRM is also reserved for what the IMF deems as 'important' emerging market economies, and thus is not applied across the board to all classes of debtors, such as the Highly Indebted Poor Countries (HIPCs) (Greenhill 2001). More importantly, the debates surrounding SDRM seem to normalize sovereign debt default which is a reality for Argentina, and may equally become one for Uruguay and perhaps Brazil, with countless more to follow. Indeed, the fact that international policymakers are seriously debating the issue portends that default is to be a regular occurrence in the world economy. Relatedly, another feature of the debate that is neglected is that sovereign debt default runs contrary to the neo-liberal logic that unfettered market freedom leads to economic viability and prosperity for the South. Indeed, the very fact that sovereign debt default is even occurring doesn't seem to be problematized in the SDRM debates.

Conclusion

The debates on the SDRM do little to further the interests of stability and social justice in countries like Argentina, but instead seek to strengthen the power of international creditors *vis-à-vis* sovereign states. Indeed, despite their differences, there exists a significant concurrence between the IMF and US Treasury Secretary with regard to two overlapping areas of debt restructuring. First, there is a growing consensus within the Bush administration and the IMF that the way forward is through 'selective bailouts'. The latter reflects the Bush administration's position that crisis management needs to be complemented by crisis prevention (US Department of Treasury 2002). Second, and relatedly, the key to preventing crises is to remove what economists consider the moral hazard problem. For Krueger and Taylor, the existing system of crisis resolution relies too heavily on bailout loans, which in turn create and sustain moral hazard. Moral hazard stipulates that awareness that the IMF will bail out countries in the event of a financial crisis makes the crisis more likely for two reasons. On the one hand, creditors are more willing to lend to high-risk debtor nations; on the other, the presence of the IMF weakens pressure on governments to pursue policies – such as fiscal restraint and prudent financial supervision and regulation – that could help prevent crises (Lane and Philips 2001; cf. Mussa 2002).

The difficulty with the solutions proposed by the SDRM debates is that continued adherence by the ruling classes in the South to neo-liberal tenets have become increasingly difficult to pursue, especially given the narrowing social basis for the neo-liberal project in the wake of ever-widening income inequality and less and less accountability of governments to civil society. Drawing on 2002 data from the ECLAC, Emir Sader points out that the number of people living below the poverty threshold in Latin America increased from 120 million in 1980 to 214 million in 2001 (43 per cent of the population), with 92.8 million (18.6 per cent) living in destitution (2003; Rock 2002).

In all, the SDRM debates seem to reflect the general characteristic of how crisis-hit countries have been dealt with by the IMF over the past two decades. Three features come to mind. First and foremost, financial liberalization is posited as a desirable policy because, like trade liberalization, it leads to economic growth and stability. Second, bad policies pursued by debtor nations, not the actions of the IMF or those of banks or speculators, are seen as the root of the crisis (Schuler 2002). Third, and related to this neoclassical assumption, it is believed that debtor countries should be exposed more directly to the exigencies of transnational finance so that they may be forced to undertake market-based solutions to their current economic and political problems. What the SDRM debates – and the subsequent refusal of the IMFC to implement the framework proposed by Krueger – highlight is not only Strange's prescient remark that while 'the evolution of that system has changed the nature of the debt problem ... neither governments nor markets are any nearer a final solution to the question of how to manage transnational debt than they were in the 1980s' (Strange 1998a: 91), but also, the differentiated, and even conflictual, meanings of 'risk' continue to aggravate the problem (Soederberg and Taylor 2004).

Notes

1. For a detailed discussion on transnational debt, see my *Global Governance in Question: Empire, Class and the New Common Sense in Managing North–South Relations* (London: Pluto Press/Ann Arbor: University of Michigan Press, 2006).
2. For example, Argentina's total debt in 1999 was comprised of the following sources: IMF credit (3 per cent), multilateral credit (10 per cent), bilateral (4 per cent), short-term debt (21 per cent), private creditors (62 per cent) (e.g. US institutional investors, European and Japanese retail investors) (Pettifor et al. 2001: 19).
3. Despite the attempts by the Argentine government to adhere to market-led restructuring demanded by the IMF, poverty rates increased dramatically after the 1990s. In fact, according to official figures, 57.5 per cent of Argentines now live on or below the poverty line (Petras and Veltmeyer 2003; Patroni 2003).
4. In recent years, a number of factories (*fabricas ocupadas*) across Argentina have been taken over and run by their workers. Eager to protect the virtues of private property and reinforce the perception that Argentina possesses a disciplined and inexpensive workforce, the state has responded to this and other forms of popular organization (*los piqueteros*) with increasing violence and repression (Carerra and Cotarelo 2003; Dinerstein 2003a and b; Rock 2002). While this strategy may temporarily soothe the jittery nerves of Argentina's international creditors, the upshot of growing state-led oppression will only be to increase, as opposed to mitigate, the ongoing legitimacy crisis of the state *vis-à-vis* civil society organizations.
5. See, for example, *Emerging Market Traders Association (EMTA) Survey: Third Quarter 2002 Emerging Markets Debt Trading US$ 670 Billion.* http://www.emta.org/ndevelop/pr3q02.pdf [Accessed 15 November 2003]. See also Securities Industry Association, *Leading Financial Industry Associations Propose Market-Based Approach to Sovereign Debt Restructuring and Note Inherent*

Flaws With IMF's Proposal, http://www.emta.org/ndevelop/pr3q02.pdf
    [Accessed 3 June 2003].
6. Jubilee 2000, South Centre, Debt Relief International, AFL-CIO, and the Mercy
    Foundation.
7. See *Financial Times* (2002b); *Washington Post* (2002); *The Economist* (2002: 67).

References

Akyüz, Yilmaz (2002) *Reforming the Global Financial Architecture: Issues and
    Proposals* (London: Zed Books).
Altvater, E. (2002) The Growth Obsession, in L. Panitch and C. Leys (eds.) *Socialist
    Register* (London: Merlin Press), pp. 73–92.
D'Arista, J. and S. Griffith-Jones (2001) The Boom of Portfolio Flows to 'Emerging
    Markets' and its Regulatory Duplications, in S. Griffith-Jones, M. F. Montes and
    A. Natsution (eds.) *Short-term Capital Flows and Economic Crises* (Oxford: Oxford
    University Press), pp. 112–134.
Boorman, J. (2002) Sovereign Debt Restructuring: Where Stands the Debate?
    Speech delivered at a conference co-sponsored by the CATO Institute and *The
    Economist*. New York, 17 October. Available at http://www.imf.org/external/
    np/speeches/2002/101702.htm.
Carerra N. I. and M. C. Cotarelo (2003) Social Struggles in Present Day Argentina,
    Bulletin of Latin American Research, 22 (2): 201–213.
Cooper, R. (2002) Chapter 11 for Countries? *Foreign Affairs*, 81(4): 90–104.
Dinerstein, A. (2003a) The Battle of Buenos Aires: Crises, Insurrection and the
    Reinvention of Politics in Argentina, *Historical Materialism* 10(4): 5–38.
Dinerstein, A.(2003b) ¡Que se Vayan Todos! Popular Insurrection and the Asambleas
    Barriales in Argentina, *Bulletin of Latin American Research*, 22(2): 187–200.
ECLAC (2002) *Globalization and Development* (Santiago: ECLAC).
Economist (2002) Economics Focus: Sovereign Bankruptcies, 6 April.
Eichengreen, B. (2002a) *Financial Crises and What to Do about Them* (Oxford:
    Oxford University Press).
Eichengreen, B. (2002b) Crisis Prevention and Management: Any New Lessons
    from Argentina and Turkey? Background paper for the World Bank's Global
    Development Finance 2002 (Washington, DC: World Bank).
Felix, D. (2002) The Economic Case against Free Capital Mobility, in L. E. Armijo
    (ed.) *Debating the Global Financial Architecture* (Albany, NY: State University of
    New York Press), pp. 126–158.
Financial Times (2002a) G7 'Breakthrough' on Debt Default. 28 September.
Financial Times (2002b) US Scorns IMF Plan for Bankrupt Governments, 6 April.
Gill S. and D. Law (1993) Global Hegemony and the Structural Power of Capital,
    in S. Gill (ed.) *Gramsci, Historical Materialism and International Relations*
    (Cambridge: Cambridge University Press), pp. 93–124.
Gowan, P. (1999) *The Global Gamble: Washington's Faustian Bid for World
    Dominance* (London: Verso).
Grabel, I. (1996) Marketing the Third World: The Contradictions of Portfolio
    Investment in the Global Economy, *World Development*, 24(11): 1761–1776.
Greenhill, R. (2001) IMF Meetings Give Go-ahead for Bankruptcy Plan – but on
    Whose Terms? Jubilee 2000 UK, 1 October. Available at http://www.
    jubilee2000uk.org/analysis/articles/imf011002.htm.

Griffith-Jones, S. (1996) International Capital Flows to Latin America, in Victor Bulmer-Thomas (ed.) *The New Economic Model in Latin America and its Impact on Income Distribution and Poverty* (London: Macmillan), pp. 127–143.

Guitán, M. (1997) Reality and the Logic of Capital Flow Liberalization, in C. P. Ries and R. J. Sweeney (eds.) *Capital Controls in Emerging Economies* (Boulder, CO: Westview Press), pp. 189–244.

Haley, M. (1999) Emerging Market Makers: The Power of Institutional Investors, in L. E. Armijo (ed.) *Financial Globalization and Democracy in Emerging Markets* (London: Macmillan), pp. 74–90.

Henwood, D. (1998) *Wall Street: How it Works and for Whom* (London: Verso).

IMF (1997) IMF Builds on Initiatives to Meet Challenges of Globalization, *IMF Survey* (Washington, DC: IMF).

IMF (2001) A New Approach to Sovereign Debt Restructuring. Address by Anne Krueger, First Deputy Managing Director, International Monetary Fund. Delivered at the National Economists' Club Annual Members' Dinner, American Enterprise Institute Washington, DC. Available at: www.imf.org/external/np/speeches/2001/112601.htm.

IMF (2003) Proposals for a Sovereign Debt Restructuring Mechanism (SDRM): A Factsheet. Available at www.imf.org/external/np/exr/facts/sdrm.htm.

Lane, T. and S. Philips (2001) IMF Financing and Moral Hazard, *Financing & Development*, 28(2). Available at http://www.imf.org/external/pubs/ft/fandd/2001/06/lane.htm.

Maxfield, S. (1996) *Gatekeepers of Growth: The International Political Economy of Central Banking in Developing Countries* (Princeton, NJ: Princeton University Press), pp. 34–51.

Mussa, M. (2002) *Argentina and the Fund: From Triumph to Tragedy* (Washington, DC: Institute for International Economics).

Ocampo, J. A. (2000) A Broad Agenda for International Financial Reform, in J. A. Ocampo, S. Zamagni, R. Ffrench-Davis and C. Pietrobelli (eds.) *Financial Globalization and the Emerging Economies* (Santiago: ECLAC), pp. 41–62.

Ocampo, J. A. (2001) A Broad Agenda for International Financial Reform. Paper presented at the American Economic Association Annual Meeting, New Orleans, January. Mimeo.

Patomäki, H. (2001) *Democratising Globalisation: The Leverage of the Tobin Tax* (London: Zed Books).

Patroni, V. (2003) Disciplining Labour, Producing Poverty: Neoliberal Structural Reform and Political Conflict in Argentina. Paper presented at the Empire, Neoliberalism, and Resistance Symposium. Department of Political Science, York University, Toronto, 3–4 November. Mimeo.

Pettifor Ann, L. Cisneros and A.O. Gaona (2001) *It Takes Two to Tango: Creditor Co-responsibility for Argentina's Crisis – and the Need for Independent Resolution* (London: Jubilee Plus).

Petras, J. and H. Veltmeyer (2003) *System in Crisis: The Dynamics of Free Market Capitalism* (London: Zed Books).

Rock, David (2002) Racking Argentina, *New Left Review*, 17: 55–86.

Sader, Emir (2003) Can the Leaders Leave Neoliberalism Behind? *Le Monde Diplomatique* (February), http://mondediplo.com/2003/02/12latinleft [Accessed 20 February 2003].

Schuler, K. (2002) Fixing Argentina, *Policy Analysis*, 445, 16 July.

Soederberg, S. (2004a) *The Politics of the New International Financial Architecture: Reimposing Neoliberal Domination in the Global South* (London and New York: Zed Books).

Soederberg, S. (2004b) American Empire and Excluded States: The Bush Administration's Millennium Challenge Account and the Shift toward Pre-emptive Development, *Third World Quarterly*, 25(2): 297–302.

Soederberg, S. (2006) *Global Governance in Question: Empire Class and the New Common Sense in Managing Globalization* (London: Pluto/Ann Arbor: University of Michigan).

Soederberg, S. and M. Taylor (2004) The New Latin American Debt Crisis and its Implications for Social Policy: Lessons Drawn from the Argentine Case. Commissioned by the Canadian Foundation of the Americas (FOCAL). 2004. Ottawa, Canada. Available at www.focal.ca/images/pdf/debt_crisis.pdf.

Stiglitz, Joseph (2002) *Globalization and its Discontents* (New York: W. W. Norton).

Strange, S. (1998a) New World of Debt, *New Left Review* 1 (230) (July–August): 91–114.

Strange, S. (1998b) *Mad Money* (Manchester: Manchester Press).

Underhill, G. R. D. (1997) Private Markets and Public Responsibility in a Global System: Conflict and Co-operation in Transnational Banking and Securities Regulation, in G. R. D. Underhill (ed.) *The New World Order in International Finance* (London: Macmillan), pp. 17–24.

US Department of Treasury (2002) Promoting Global Growth, Statement of Treasury Secretary Paul H. O'Neill at the International Monetary and Financial Committee Meeting (Washington, DC: US Treasury Secretary).

Washington Post (2002) IMF Scales down 'Bankruptcy' Plan, 2 April.

Weisbrot, Mark and Dean Baker (2002) *Paying the Bills in Brazil: Does the IMF's Math Add Up?* (Washington, DC: Center for Economic and Policy Research), 25 September. Available at http://www.cepr.net/Brazil-debt-final.pdf.

World Bank (2003) *Global Development Finance* (Washington, DC: World Bank).

World Bank (2004) *Global Development Finance* (Washington, DC: World Bank).

4
Sustainable Development of the Caspian Sea Energy Resources: The Role of Civil Society

Mikhail A. Molchanov with Yuri Yevdokimov

Introduction

The Central Asian Caspian region is drawing increasing attention from nation-states, transnational corporations, international institutions and other actors interested in the exploration and development of its oil and gas resources. Non-governmental organizations (NGOs) in the region and their counterparts abroad have expressed concern over industrial practices that exact a heavy toll on the environment and put pressure on local labour and other vulnerable groups in such countries as Georgia and Azerbaijan. These advocacy efforts focus on the idea of sustainable development of the region.

Construction of the Baku–Ceyhan pipeline, which connects the oil fields of the Caspian littoral state of Azerbaijan with a seaport in southern Turkey, is one case in point. International environmental groups and civil rights organizations have protested against the public financing of the project which, in their view, fails to address the legitimate concerns of the Azeri, Georgian and Turkish constituencies directly affected by the construction and exploitation of the pipeline.

The debate revealed issues of cross-national significance. The exploration and development of oil and gas deposits can be realized in a variety of ways, some of which promote economic growth and sustainability, while others sacrifice the latter to the former. Emerging economies need international investments, just as corporations need access to resources to propel further economic growth. However, economic growth as such is meaningless if society at large does not enjoy its benefits, while bearing the brunt of environmental and social risks. Sustainable development can be achieved only on the basis of international cooperation that brings together business, governments and civil society actors capable of articulating interests and demands on behalf of the nation. While corporations and governments tend to be preoccupied with the bottom line, civil society focuses on long-term benefits for the community.

As developing states jockey for international investments, the burden of social responsibility, which market actors are unwilling to shoulder, is also increasingly being shed by states. Globalization and the retreat of the state are prompting civil society actors to claim certain rights of representation and advocacy historically exercised by governments. Environmental protection and social inclusion, community values and traditional ways of life, ethnic identities and threatened occupations are all issue areas in which the state is supposed to play a key role, but unfortunately fails to do so, particularly in less developed countries. These same areas have never been of primary concern to business. International civic groups have little choice but to step in and ensure that the public interest is served. Ideally, these efforts may lead to the creation of a new international governance structure that will promote sustainable development and social stability. Conversely, the continuing transfer of state functions into the private realm may further erode already weakened governments and destabilize societies.

Transnational corporations, oil politics and the environment

The Central Asia-Caspian region is among the richest in the world in terms of energy resources, which surpass those of the US and Western Europe. It is estimated that by 2010 oil wells of the Caspian Sea littoral may be pumping between 2.4 and 5.9 million barrels a day, exceeding the production capacity of South America's largest oil producer, Venezuela (Caspian Sea Region Country Analysis Brief 2004). Natural endowments make the region strategically important. Caspian oil, in spite of its relatively high sulphur content, is of sufficiently good quality, lies within close reach of the established international trade routes and belongs for the most part to poor, commodity-exporting countries. The US Department of Energy estimates that the region has nearly 33 billion barrels of proven oil reserves and close to 220 billion barrels of oil in potential reserves. More cautious estimates give a figure of 40–50 billion barrels, still not a negligible quantity (Eytchison 2003).

Caspian natural gas is considered among the potentially crucial sources of energy supply for India, China and Europe. These reserves are estimated at 243–248 trillion cubic feet, which is broadly comparable to total North American reserves (Hill and Spector 2001).

Most countries of the region have undergone rapid deindustrialization as part of 'market reform' packages. Privatization and the auctioning off of nationalized industries have dispossessed millions while enriching post-Communist rulers and their business associates. The dismantling of economic sectors oriented towards domestic consumption has left energy exports as the only viable source of national income. As industrial production more than halved in 1991–95, domestic demand for locally produced hydrocarbons went into a tailspin. The severing of their former ties to Russia deprived Azerbaijan, Georgia and Kazakhstan of the industrial capacities required to develop their oil and gas fields. Economic downturn stalled transitions to democracy and entrenched authoritarianism and financial dependency throughout the region. As national budgets dwindled, post-Communist regimes turned to international investors (Karagiannis 2002).

However, an upsurge in investments has not translated into immediate public benefits. By and large, energy exploration and development are proceeding haphazardly and without due regard to the environment or the needs of society at large. Industrial activities threaten the natural habitat of many species of birds, fish and marine animals. Among those most threatened are the Caspian beluga and other species of sturgeon, which have been listed as endangered in several Red Data Books and under the provisions of the US Endangered Species Act. Once these species are extinct there can be no replacement, since 90 per cent of their world population is to be found only in the Caspian Sea area. Oil extraction pollutes the sea and contributes to sturgeon extinction, which alone costs states in the region at least $6 billion in trade forgone annually (Golubchikov 2002: 91).

The human habitat suffers too, since the oil industry claims vast swathes of the Caspian Sea board and agricultural land. Both the social and environmental sustainability of the region are at risk. Capital stock requires urgent modernization. Labour productivity is low, and the living standards in all countries of the region are currently below their respective 1990 levels. Excessive emphasis on a monoculture oil economy is threatening traditional businesses and established lifestyles, annihilating industrial diversity and severely affecting agriculture in both oil-producing and oil-transporting states. While NGOs advocate broad international consultations and tripartite cooperation in the development of the region's energy sector between the governments, transnational corporations and civil society actors, such consultations have never been a priority.

The interests of the transnational corporations (TNCs) involved in the Caspian frequently diverge, as do the interests of their 'home' states. Russia supports oil transportation through the Baku–Novorossiisk pipeline which it controls, while Washington and London are backing alternative energy transportation routes. The idea of a US-led development of the Caspian energy resources is part and parcel of the Bush–Cheney National Energy Strategy, which has been 'founded on the understanding that diversity of supply means security of supply' (Kretzmann 2003: 13). China, currently the world's third largest oil consumer, is wary of the US plans, and has acquired stakes in oil production in Kazakhstan, Russia and Azerbaijan (Luft 2004). China supports construction of a new oil pipeline from Kazakhstan via Kyrgyzstan to the Chinese province of Xinjiang, with a view that the pipeline will eventually extend all the way to Shanghai (Sieff 2004). Russia is behind the plans for another pipeline that will connect Bulgaria's Black Sea coast to the Aegean port of Alexandropoulos in Greece.

Such Western firms as British Petroleum, Amoco, Chevron Texaco, ExxonMobil and others have invested an estimated $50 billion in oil and gas exploration here, predominantly in Azerbaijan and Kazakhstan. In Azerbaijan alone, foreign direct investment (FDI) rose 16-fold, from $330 million in 1995 to $5,354 million in 2002. Annual FDI flows to Azerbaijan shot up from $227 million to $1,392 million in just one year, and increased a further 70 per cent the year after. The US, Great Britain and Norway accounted for 57 per cent of the total FDI stock, with more than 70 per cent of all FDI inflows going to the oil and gas industry. By 2004, Azerbaijan had soared to the head of the UNCTAD Inward FDI Performance Index, having received $4,769 million foreign direct investment in one year only. The cumulative FDI inward stock reached $13,408 million. Most of this money came in the form of equity purchases. As GDP growth became fully dependent on foreign investors, 30 foreign affiliate companies with links to some of the largest transnational corporations in the world shared most of the Azeri economy amonst themselves (UNCTAD 2035: 21, annexes).

Following their 1998 merger, BP and Amoco have dramatically extended their operations in the Caspian Sea littoral. The two had also become key lobbyists for American oil interests in the area and became directly engaged in local politics. Amoco executives were instrumental in securing the approval of a controversial state visit of the late Azeri dictator Heidar Aliev to Washington in August 1997. The state visit culminated in the signing of a new Amoco oil exploration deal. The following year, the company's interests in Azerbaijan were further expanded with a 25 per cent stake in the oil exploration consortium led by the Azeri state company SOCAR. Amicable relations between the company and the Azeri government continued after Aliev's death, with the succession to the presidency of his son and former SOCAR's vice-president Ilham. By 2004, BP Amoco's interest in the ACG (Shirag) oil field in Azerbaijan exceeded 34 per cent.

To consolidate its gains, the BP-led consortium proceeded to build the $2.95 billion Baku–Tbilisi–Ceyhan (BTC) export pipeline with a planned capacity of 50 million tonnes of oil a year, or nearly 10 per cent of the total oil supplied annually by Saudi Arabia. Compared to the annual average of 6.2 million tonnes passing through the Baku–Supsa pipeline, which was built earlier, BTC represents a significant boost in exports from the region. By comparison, only about 2.5 million tonnes of Azeri oil went through the Baku–Novorossiisk pipeline in 2004, a reflection of Russia's relative marginalization in the political economy of Caspian oil.

Strategic interest in Caspian oil was reiterated in the official report to the US president and British prime minister, the US–UK energy dialogue. The report acknowledges that both Western countries 'have noted the huge energy potential of Russia, Central Asia, and the Caspian'. Accordingly, both governments gave strong backing to the BP-led Baku–Ceyhan project (*Guardian Weekly*, 20–26 November 2003, p. 10).

At the same time, negotiations on the status of the Caspian shelf failed to produce a mutually acceptable agreement. In January 2005, the Ministry of Foreign Affairs of the Republic of Turkmenistan issued a statement that called on other littoral states to submit to international arbitrage, preferably under the aegis of the United Nations. According to the statement, 'certain participants to the negotiations process ... neglect legitimate interests of the other states' (RIA Novosti, 26 January 2005). As official negotiations came under strain, the role of non-governmental groups directly talking to each other is becoming more prominent. The major concerns that NGOs raise are environmental protection and sustainable development. The idea of sustainable development animates various forms of civic action which both local and international NGOs undertake with regard to transnational activities in the Caspian.

International cooperation and sustainable development

The concept of sustainable development can be traced back to the 1972 Stockholm Conference on the Human Environment and the Brundtland Commission's Report in 1987. It was further developed at the UN's Earth Summit in Rio de Janeiro, in 1992. The summit strongly emphasized the links between the environment and development, and between the social and economic aspects of development. The summit's Agenda 21 called for the 'broadest public participation and the active involvement of the non-governmental organizations' in the implementation of such objectives as sustainable human development and environmentally conscious management of resources (Preamble). It encouraged international cooperation in combating poverty, changing consumption patterns, and protection and management of fragile ecosystems. The summit established that manifold challenges of environment and development represent a single package of interconnected issues and not two separate blocs of problems that can be dealt with separately, let alone played off against each other.

Most definitions of sustainable development focus on prudent resource management, fair income distribution, consistent consumption and non-declining utility (Pezzy 1992: 13–14). The World Commission on Environment and Development defines it as 'development that meets the needs of present generations without compromising the ability of future generations to meet their own needs' (WCED 1987: 43). Here, sustainable development is defined as an historical objective of humanity as a whole, a process that unites people of the world both spatially and temporally, relying for its success on globally coordinated efforts of several generations.

The World Bank's (1988: 1) approach to sustainable development emphasizes three interrelated dimensions of sustainability: 'Economic growth, the alleviation of poverty and sound environmental management are in many cases mutually consistent objectives.' If economic sustainability means ensuring non-declining consumption and utility, the social dimension of sustainability involves increased public participation in decision-making processes; implementation of community-based management systems; restoration and conservation of local environments and cultures; and enhancement of social roles and life prospects of youth, women and indigenous peoples. Taking public concerns into account in policy and business development promotes social inclusion and participation. Often, cooperation between NGOs at home and abroad proves crucial as a means to bring public concerns to the attention of decision-makers.

Following Sen's (1983) approach to poverty as 'the deprivation of capabilities', sustainability in the social sense is often viewed as development of a social environment where everyone can accumulate and develop his or her human capital to its fullest. Relating sustainable development to human freedom emphasizes the notion of social capital, i.e. productive and life-enhancing aspects of collective action, as undertaken by civil society organizations:

> Focusing on human freedoms contrasts with narrower views of development, such as identifying development with the growth in the gross national product, or with the rise in personal income, or with industrialization, or with technological advance, or with social modernization ... Viewing development in terms of expanding substantive freedoms directs attention to the ends that make development important, rather than merely to some of the means that, *inter alia*, play a prominent part in the process. (Sen 2001: 3)

The environmental dimension of sustainable development focuses on preserving the natural wealth of the planet. Frequently, environmental degradation happens, and is excused, in the name of narrowly understood 'economic development'. However, making responsible stewardship of the environmental resources second to the idea of economic growth undermines prospects for future development. Humanity's crucial dependence on these often limited and non-renewable resources must properly be understood to make possible optimal management of these resources in the future. The established patterns of economic behaviour have to be changed to promote sustainability. Raising these issues and expanding our understanding of human-caused factors affecting environmental health is the task that international actors, including international non-governmental organizations (INGOs) are often best placed to undertake.

International cooperation in the name of sustainable development is seen as a 'continuous and constructive dialogue, inspired by the need to achieve a more efficient and equitable', environmentally friendly 'world economy, keeping in view the increasing interdependence of the community of nations' (Agenda 21 1992: ch. 2). Since sustainable development includes economic, social and environmental dimensions, international economic relations should be pursued in such a way as to conform to all three sets of goals simultaneously. However, the presently prevailing understanding of globalization, which is informed by neoclassical free trade theory, focuses on the narrowly understood economic goals to the virtual exclusion of all others. In this paradigm, trade objectives may actually conflict with social and environmental goals, such as development of a robust civil society, preservation of the environment, optimal utilization of natural resources, maintenance of biodiversity, and others. This calls for a new type of international relations that do include the above-mentioned goals.

International cooperation should support sustainable development by providing an optimal balance between utilization and renewal of resources. Sustainable development depends on equitable international trade policy and prudent environmental stewardship. To no less an extent, it depends on sound economic policies and national leadership responsive to the long-term needs of society. Effective governance and public administration that foster dialogue with partners in civil society make it possible to integrate societal concerns into the decision-making process. This encourages increased democratic participation and community ownership of decisions that affect all members of society. As civil society expands its reach and influence, national actors find their counterparts abroad and establish transnational links, which feed into the development of a truly global network of civic organizations.

The role of civil society

Civil society is defined as a realm of organized, voluntary social activities and practices that lies between the individual and the state. Individual participants in these practices are 'acting collectively in a public sphere to express their interests, passions, and ideas, exchange information, achieve mutual goals, make demands on the state, and hold state officials accountable' (Diamond 1994: 5).

While most definitions of civil society separate it from the state and relate it to voluntary participation in various forms of collective action, there is less agreement on the nature of the relationship between civil society, family and the economy. Some aspects of the current debate originate in the differences between the Hegel–Marx tradition, which relates the notion of civil society to private economic interests separate from the state (and hence includes market actors in its definition of civil society) and the Locke–de Tocqueville tradition, which in its current reincarnation emphasizes associational life distinct from both the state and the market:

> [C]ivil society is obviously related to both the state and the market, but it should not be confused with either. Civil society may be seen as

that sector of social reality in which human interests that are not rooted in the family or in economic power or in state administration seek to affirm themselves and defend their rights and prerogatives. (de Santa Ana 1994: 3)

We subscribe to the latter notion for both analytic and practical purposes. Analytically, this helps distinguish between the profit-motivated activities of corporations whose power often exceeds that of a typical smaller state, and the voluntary, non-profit activities of civic associations in the so-called third sector of the economy. In practical terms, it is naïve to see corporations and civic groups alike as somehow equally concerned with such issues as global democratic deficit or environmental degradation. They are not, and cannot be, as the first often contribute to those very problems that the second are trying to address.

An activist interpretation of civil society finds it in the sphere of social and political activity that lies outside established political parties. Here, individuals, organizations, groups and non-hierarchically organized movements attempt 'to democratize the state, to re-distribute power, rather than to capture power in a traditional sense' (Kaldor 2003: 9). In doing so, they have to engage private sector actors which may act in tandem with the state, but may also respond to the articulated demands of civic movements and organizations.

In all countries of the Caspian Sea littoral, civil society is still in its infancy. In such countries as Azerbaijan, Turkmenistan or Uzbekistan, it had no real chance of developing, as authoritarian governments did their best to suppress emerging civic movements. While civil society as such has yet to be formed, its individual precursors, national and transnational NGOs, have made an appearance and established themselves as a more or less permanent feature of public life in the region. It is these individual civil society actors that we will relate to as an emergent civil society that challenges undemocratic regimes of the Caspian.

By the mid-1990s, several of these organizations had established themselves as providers of expert advice to government, promoters of best practices, environmental and human rights watchdogs. In Azerbaijan, such NGOs as the Green Movement, the Ecological Union of Azerbaijan, Ecoil, ECOS, the Ecological Society 'Ruzgar' and For Clean Caspian became engaged in the fight for environmentally conscious business practices. Ecological NGOs strive to ensure positive changes in business projects and contracts that had originally paid scant attention to the harm they cause to the environment. TNCs were forced to respond to these activities by taking the notion of corporate social responsibility more seriously. BP Amoco in particular has distinguished itself with a series of projects aimed at improving the public image of the corporation and directly contributed to local community development through a number of charitable activities.

Civil society organizations active in Kazakhstan include Green Salvation, Centre of Ecological Initiatives, INKAR, 'Kaspii Tabigati', Caspian for the 21st Century, Central Asian Fund, and others. Some contribute to the activities of a parastatal, the National Environment Centre of Sustainable Development (NECSD), and combine research activities with advocacy that ranges from the purely environmental to more complex political, economic and social issues. The Kazakh NGOs 'Globus', 'Kaspii Tabigati' and 'Caspian for the 21st Century' have monitored activities of the transnational consortium Karachaganak Petroleum Operating (KPO), which includes American, British, Italian and Russian firms. Since 2004, the international NGO Crude Accountability has lent its support to local activists by starting a discussion with the KPO sponsor International Finance Corporation (IFC) on health and safety aspects of emissions from the Karachaganak oil and gas field. Thanks to the efforts of civil society activists who protest against pollution of the North Caspian shelf, such TNCs as Offshore Kazakhstan International Oil Consortium (OKIOC) and Tengizchevroil (a subsidiary of ChevronTexaco) have been forced to begin a dialogue with the public (Solyanik 2001).

In Georgia, the main issue has been construction of the BTC pipeline. In 2003, several Georgian NGOs were joined by the INGOs Institute for MultiTrack Diplomacy (USA) and the CEE Bankwatch Network to protest against the international financing of the construction project. Arguing that no public money should be used for 'human rights abuse, corruption and environmental destruction', activists asked the EBRD to withdraw its support from the construction consortium. Protesters argued that the project 'conflicts with Georgian law and fails to include concrete plans for reducing poverty and increasing democracy in Georgia' (Falcor.org 2003).

The Georgian association Green Alternative continued these protests by launching a legal action against the BP-led consortium and the government's alleged capitulation before foreign interests. The group maintained that Georgian citizens were not provided with adequate information, nor adequately involved in the decision-making process. It has also charged that the government pressed ahead with construction after being pressured to do so by the consortium. Activists revealed that the Georgian Environment Minister at the time, Nino Chkhobadze, complained to BP's chief executive, Lord Browne, that 'BP representatives are asking the Georgian government to violate its own environmental legislation'

(*News Central Asia*, 27 June 2003). In spite of that, the minister approved the construction, which directly threatens the Borjomi–Kharagauli National Park and the Borjomi mineral water industry, just a few days later.

In their struggle for a clean environment, social equity and sustainable development, Caspian NGOs draw on the expertise and resources of a number of INGOs and civil society actors in the West. Activities of the Green Alternative in particular have found wide support among Western environmental groups, leading to the acceptance of the NGO's demands for fair compensation to the people who had lost their land to the pipeline. The leader of the Georgian group, Manana Kochladze, was awarded a Goldman Environmental Prize in 2004 at a ceremony in the US.

Environmentalists and human rights activists in the West reacted to the BTC controversy with complaints to their own governments which focused on British Petroleum and its consortium partners' alleged violation of the OECD's Guidelines for Multinational Enterprises. Companies implementing the BTC project, according to the deposition submitted by INGOs, have neglected the OECD-stipulated obligations that call on companies to 'contribute to sustainable development and to refrain from seeking or accepting exemptions from environmental, health, safety, labour, taxation, and other legislation'. INGOs, which include Cornerhouse, FERN, Friends of the Earth, Germanwatch, BUND, and Campagna per la Riforma della Banca Mondiale, have also cited concerns on a lack of community consultation (Groups file claim 2003).

Concerted efforts of international civil society activists have brought positive changes to BP's practices in the region. These now include building and equipping schools in the neighbourhoods traversed by the pipeline, funding scholarships for Georgian students, implementing various community investment programmes and providing grants to support social and economic projects of related nature. In December 2004, BP published its first Sustainability Report for Azerbaijan, reporting that the BTC consortium 'has undertaken an extensive stakeholder consultation process that has led to many design and construction modifications and has helped shape sustainability initiatives including community and environmental investments' (BP Azerbaijan 2004: 13).

The continuing engagement of both domestic and international NGOs is motivated by their concerns over the pipeline's impact on nature and people's civil rights. NGO causes range from protection of the environment to foreign debt to the legality of the development agreements to corruption and human rights abuse by the national governments. It increasingly appears that these issues form a single package which has to be dealt with as such. Piecemeal solutions will not work.

To give but a few examples, corruption is bred and exacerbated in no small part thanks to the large sums of money, some of it 'soft', that foreign investors bring into the country. Development assistance, if misused, may well complicate the problem of foreign debt (Stiglitz 2002: 84, 89–132). Environmental protection relies on the TNCs' respect for national laws, but weak and admittedly corrupt governments are poor protectors of the law. Protests by concerned citizens are frequently suppressed by investment-greedy governments, which stall the development of civil society, further authoritarianism and contribute to human rights abuses.

Because of the transnational nature of these issues, unfinished democratic transitions and underdevelopment of civil society, neither Azeris nor Georgians are well equipped to solve these problems on their own. While Ilham Aliyev's regime in Azerbaijan at times appears even harsher than his late father's dictatorship, Saakashvili's Georgia still suffers from ethnic separatism, disunity and casual oppression of minorities, problems with the judicial system and human rights protection. It continues to harbour Chechen terrorists, albeit unintentionally. According to the Country Reports on Terrorism released by the US Department of State in April 2005, 'Georgia is still used to a limited degree as a terrorist transit state'. These and other features mean that Georgia, even if not quite a failed state, is definitely a state and nation in the making. In both countries, the early shoots of a civil society are represented mostly by a few NGOs which can hardly achieve much without continuing support from the outside.

Activists in the region rely on the help and support of their counterparts abroad, INGOs headquartered in Great Britain, the US, France, Russia, Italy, Norway and other countries with direct and indirect interests and stakes in the area. They also rely on the help of such organizations as the UN Secretariat Department of Economic and Social Affairs' NGO Section. An informal regional network of NGOs under the aegis of the UN (UN-NGO-IRENE) was established in April 2002. The UN Economic and Social Council (ECOSOC) has granted consultative status to several leading NGOs in Azerbaijan and elsewhere in the region. In November 2004, two of these secured support from the United Nations System in Azerbaijan and the Government of Azerbaijan to launch a High Level Consultation and Capacity Building program for Azerbaijan and the Caspian region. The NGO Section/ECOSOC of the UN DESA is involved in the activities of the UN-NGO Informal Regional Network in Azerbaijan as an external partner.

External coordination is necessary to support local NGOs both financially and via the transfer of know-how, exchange of best practices, and the like. It is also needed because some of the key issues these NGOs are trying to address arise out of the activities of transnational companies, which increasingly define economic developments in the region. The elusive 'nationality' of the transnationals involved in gas and oil exploration in the Caspian provides clues for civil society activists who establish cross-national links with their partners abroad, in the transnationals' 'home' countries. As Klein (2001: 84) has observed, 'around the world, activists are piggy-backing on the ready-made infrastructures supplied by global corporations', which 'thanks to the sheer imperialist ambition of the corporate project at this moment in history' act as catalysts for transnational and 'cross-sector organizing – among workers, environmentalists, consumers, even prisoners, who may all have different relationships to one multinational'.

The BTC pipeline under public scrutiny

The efforts of international civil society are bringing positive changes to the Caspian region. Under the influence of the 'third sector' campaigns that traverse national boundaries, transnationals started taking the notion of corporate social responsibility more seriously. Faced with public criticism, BP has responded with a series of corporate documents that address sustainability and social protection issues associated with the pipeline project. BP's own consultant admitted that 'the project broke resettlement guidelines and local laws and violated international standards on no fewer than 173 counts' (International Centre for Caspian Studies 2003). Concerns over corporate reputation and technological risks associated with the BTC project led a major Italian investor to pull out of the consortium in 2004.

While the pipeline promises to bring much needed revenue to the region, concerns persist over the social and environmental price of the project. According to several studies, the societal burden of the BTC pipeline construction may outweigh its expected benefits. A study by Amnesty International found that the BTC commercial agreements could have been detrimental to the protection of human rights in the host countries and 'created disincentives for the three States to fulfil their current and future international human rights obligations' (Amnesty International UK 2003).

After publication of the report, the International Finance Corporation (the financial arm of the World Bank, which underwrote the BTC project) met Amnesty representatives. Amnesty International had also discussed its concerns with the European Bank for Reconstruction and Development and the UK Export Credits Guarantee Department. BP responded with a set of unilaterally adopted legal obligations, the so-called BTC Human Rights Undertaking. Here, the company, along with other consortium partners, pledged to abide by the prospective new laws introduced by the host governments for human rights or environmental protection and to refrain from advancing compensation claims that the earlier concluded agreements permitted for such instances (Baku–Tbilisi–Ceyhan Pipeline Company 2003).

Throughout 2003, BP held meetings with investors and NGOs to discuss issues of corporate social responsibility. This focused on transparency, security, safety and human rights protection. The same year, the consortium concluded environmental and social assessments for the BTC project and published a Joint Statement with NGOs and other stakeholders and a Citizen's Guide that outlined the purpose and scope of the agreement and explained its legal implications, security and human rights aspects. The Joint Statement reassured civil society actors by confirming the consortium and host governments' commitments to the norms of the International Labour Organization on such issues as forced labour, freedom of association, collective bargaining and equal opportunities. The company calls the Statement

> an unprecedented legal document in which the parties (1) reiterated their commitment to adhere to international best practices in environment, labour, human rights, security, social and corporate responsibility standards; (2) pledged to make the project 'a model in all respects'; and then (3) confirmed that these commitments are part of the prevailing legal regime governing the implementation of the project. (Citizen's Guide nd: 4)

By and large, TNCs reacted to public pressure and international lobbying with admirable energy. In both the BP Sustainability Report 2003 and the Caspian Location Report (2004), the issues of community and social investments, human rights, and protection of biodiversity have found their proper place. The company takes pride in its participation in the Global Compact, the UN-led initiative to promote corporate citizenship, human rights and labour standards, and pledges to abide by the Voluntary Principles for Security and Human Rights, now a key document regulating human rights aspects of the BTC project. The consortium runs social investment projects in Azerbaijan, Georgia and Turkey which are expected to total more than $30 million in 2003–6.

Good corporate citizenship is a quality that cannot be taken for granted. As the example of Transcaucasia shows, there is always room for improvement. In February 2004, the Georgian Trade Union Amalgamation had complained that the consortium was not following Georgian labour law and the international labour norms it had pledged to observe. Construction workers protested against 12–14-hour-long working days with no weekends, subsistence minimum wages, poor working conditions, discrimination against local employees and the capriciousness of the employer. Keti Kvinkadze, a lawyer representing the Georgian NGO Green Alternative, observed, 'The company is free to terminate an individual worker's contract at any time without compensation. When the IFC and the EBRD came to help finance this pipeline, it was claimed that their presence would guarantee the highest international project standards. Where are these banks now?' (CEE Bankwatch Network 2004).

In Azerbaijan, TNCs have invested millions to improve their image with local communities. An Enterprise Development Committee and its successor, Business Development Alliance (BDA), co-opt civil society groups and cajole them into approving business activities. An Oil Industry Forum promotes social investment initiatives in such areas as community investment, support for small and medium-size enterprises, good governance, administrative capacity-building and civil society development (Courier ACP-EU, January–February 2002: 55; Azerbaijan 2005). BP woos national and international NGOs by giving them contracts to implement various community investment programmes in the area.

At the same time, the government of Azerbaijan essentially flouted the so-called tripartite dialogue launched in London in 2000 to bring business, NGOs and government together. The Azeri authorities prevented marine scientists from conducting independent assessments of sea pollution around the oil-rich Apsheron peninsula. The state colluded with transnationals in pushing thorough the parliament a legislative amendment granting the American Frontera company drilling rights in a nature reserve (Golubchikov 2002: 94–5). Leaders of the Human Rights Centre of Azerbaijan and the Institute for Peace and Democracy (both critical of the BTC project) were publicly ostracized by the government, following which pro-regime thugs harassed them, broke into their offices and assaulted activists' relatives (Amnesty International 2004). The corporations themselves note that investments 'potentially encourage' corruption by government officials in what already is one of the most corrupt countries in the world (BP 2003).

In both Azerbaijan and Georgia, environmental regulations are trampled on by the consortium's bottom-line considerations. In July 2004, construction in the Borjomi national park of Georgia, which is internationally famous as a resort and mineral springs area, was started in the absence of construction permits from the government. As BP failed to apply for proper environmental certification, construction was temporarily suspended by the Georgian authorities (Baku-Ceyhan Campaign 2004). The so-called 'Letter of 50' addressed to President Saakashvili and signed by 50 Georgian scholars, NGO leaders and public figures criticized the pipeline construction in the environmentally unique region. The same year, environmental activists drew attention to the choice of safety coating for the BTC pipes, which, according to BP insiders, may not hold against potential oil leakages. By April 2005, BP faced legal action from its own contractors, who cited a scientific report critical of the pipeline's anti-corrosion coating (Timesonline, 17 April 2005).

The case of the BTC Co. adds extra weight to the argument of those who, together with Amnesty International's Irene Khan (2003), retain a healthy scepticism about TNCs' voluntary compliance with international labour, environmental and human rights standards. These activists of international civil society believe that 'while voluntary initiatives can be useful, they have very clear limits'. The role of civil society actors is to make sure that corporations make good on their pledges of corporate social responsibility. Because of the global scope and reach of corporate interests, civil society's work must be transnational in nature.

Conclusion

Globalization can be defined as technology-driven integration of the world capitalist markets. It brings deterritorialization of social space that erodes the regulating powers of the nation-state. As financial capital becomes delinked from a particular territory, individual states appear less capable of regulating it. In this environment, nation-centred forms of democratic participation prove vulnerable to pressures emanating from the transnational centres of corporate power. New forms of social and political participation are called into being. Transnational civic movements and solidarity campaigns engage societal forces that can no longer be fully articulated within the framework of a nation-state. The international civil society that these movements bring to life may well be crucial in promoting a truly global ethics of social responsibility.

Globalization transfers decision-making powers from states to multinational corporations, international institutions and non-governmental actors. At this historical juncture, marketization dominates all other aspects of the process. As Barber (2004: 17) notes, 'we have globalized our market institutions – markets in capital, markets in goods, markets in commodities, markets in labor, markets in currency – but we have hardly begun even to think about globalizing our politics: that civic and democratic envelope of free institutions in which, for the last four hundred years, capitalism has grown up and been founded, and in which markets and their contradictions have been tempered and moderated.'

The intensity of corporate globalization varies from region to region. The Caspian Sea area is attracting the active interest of transnational oil and gas companies. As emerging economies welcome foreign investments, they tend to put social and ecological concerns on the back burner. Yet the arrival of transnational corporations not only brings new life to the economy: it changes society and transforms the environment.

A growing body of evidence suggests that emerging economies are more vulnerable to social and economic disruptions and less protected from potential corporate abuse, which is routinely ignored by investment-happy governments. The forces of civil society are all too often not enough to prevent government–business collusion or counter its negative consequences. Because of that, civil activists in the Transcaucasian–Caspian region are establishing international connections and seeking assistance from their counterparts in the West. Persistent civic engagement on a transnational basis balances off corporate globalization and provides those anchors of moderation, responsibility and accountability that profit-motivated activities of transnational corporations rarely generate on their own. Thanks to these activities and internationally generated pressures, corporate behaviours are adapting and responding in a way that may bring the idea of sustainable development closer to reality.

References

Agenda 21 (1992) UN Department of Economic and Social Affairs, Division for Sustainable Development, http://www.un.org/esa/sustdev/documents/agenda21/english/agenda21chapter2.htm [Accessed 21 March 2005].

Amnesty International UK (2003) *Human Rights on the Line: The Baku–Tbilisi–Ceyhan Pipeline Project*, http://www.amnesty.org.uk/business/btc/ [Accessed 2 April 2005].

Amnesty International (2004) *Amnesty International Report 2004: Azerbaijan*, http://web.amnesty.org/report2004/aze-summary-eng. Accessed 2 April 2005.

Baku-Ceyhan Campaign (2004) *Baku–Ceyhan Pipeline stopped as BP Caught Violating Georgian Law*, http://www.bakuceyhan.org.uk/press_releases/georgia_halt.htm [Accessed 3 April 2005].

Baku–Tbilisi–Ceyhan Pipeline Company (2003) *BTC Human Rights Undertaking*, http://www.caspiandevelopmentandexport.com/Downloads/Human%20Rights%20Undertaking.pdf [Accessed 3 April 2005].

Barber, B. R. (2004), Can Democracy Survive Globalization in an Age of Terrorism? in T. M. Bateman and R. Epp (eds.) *Braving the New World*, 3rd edn. (Canada: Thomson Nelson), pp. 14–22.

BP (2003) *Ethical Performance*, The Caspian location report, http://www.bp.com/sectiongenericarticle.do?categoryId = 2010426&contentId = 2014940 [Accessed 3 April 2005].

BP (2005) *Azerbaijan*, http://www.bp.com/sectiongenericarticle.do?categoryId = 430&contentId = 2000578 [Accessed 3 May 2005].

BP Azerbaijan (2004) *Sustainability Report 2003*, http://www.caspiandevelopmentandexport.com/ASP/LatestNews.asp?ArticleID = 63&Lanuage = English [Accessed 30 April 2005].

Caspian Sea Region Country Analysis Brief (December 2004), Energy Information Administration, Official Energy Statistics from the US Government, http://www.eia.doe.gov/emeu/cabs/caspian.html≤caspconf [Accessed 21 March 2005].

CEE Bankwatch Network (2004) *BTC Workers Outraged by Oil Company's Violations*, Press release, http://www.bankwatch.org/press/2004/press07.html [Accessed 25 March 2005].

Citizen's Guide to the BTC Project Agreements: Environmental, Social, and Human Rights Standards (nd) http://www.caspiandevelopmentandexport.com/Downloads/citizens%20guide%20final.pdf [Accessed 3 April 2005].

de Santa Ana, J. (1994) The Concept of Civil Society, *Ecumenical Review*, 46(1): 3–11.

Diamond, L. (1994) Toward Democratic Consolidation, *Journal of Democracy*, 5: 4–17.

Eytchison, P. (2003) The Caspian Oil Myth, *Energy Bulletin*, 30 September, http://www.energybulletin.net/86.html [Accessed 25 March 2005].

Falcor.org (2003) We are Fighting for Our Future, Not for Oil, 25 March, http://www.falkor.org/news/newsarchive/btc%20developments.htm [Accessed 30 March 2004].

Golubchikov, S. (2002) NGOs Objections to Caspian Oil and Gas Projects, in *CIS Environment and Disarmament Yearbook 2002* (Jerusalem: Mayrock Centre), pp. 88–99.

Groups File Claim against BP and Pipeline Partners in 5 Countries, Press release (2003) http://www.foe.org/camps/intl/Appendices.htm [Accessed 30 March 2005].

Hill, F. and Spector, R. (2001) *The Caspian Basin and Asian Energy Markets*, The Brookings Institution, Global Economics, Conference Report 8, September, http://www.brook.edu/comm/conferencereport/cr08.htm [Accessed 4 October 2004].

International Centre for Caspian Studies (2003) *World Bank Backs Caspian Pipeline*, http://caspiancenter.org/news/01_12_2003_02.html [Accessed 2 April 2005].

Kaldor, M. (2003) Civil Society and Accountability, *Journal of Human Development*, 4(1): 5–27.

Karagiannis, E. (2002) *The Caspian Oil Market after Regime Change in Iraq*, European Rim Policy and Investment Council, Perihelion, November, http://www.erpic.org/perihelion/articles2002/november/caspianoil.htm [Accessed 2 October 2004].

Khan, I. (2003) *Taking Stock: Corporate Social Responsibility and Human Rights*, http://web.amnesty.org/library/Index/ENGIOR500032003?open&of = ENG-398 [Accessed 29 March 2005].

Klare, M. T. (2001) The New Geography of Conflict, *Foreign Affairs*, 80(3): 49–61.

Klein, N. (2001), Reclaiming the Commons, *New Left Review*, 9: 81–89.

Kretzmann, S. (2003), Oil, Security, War, *Multinational Monitor*, 24(1–2): 13.

Luft, G. (2004) *Fueling the Dragon: China's Race into the Oil Market*, Institute for the Analysis of Global Security, IAGS Spotlight, http://www.iags.org/china.htm [Accessed 2 October 2004].

Morgan, D. and Ottaway, D. B. (1998) Azerbaijan's Riches Alter the Chessboard, *Washington Post*, 4 October, A1.

O'Riordan, T. (1988) The Politics of Sustainability, in R. K. Turner (ed.) *Sustainable Environmental Management: Principles and Practice* (London: Belhaven Press), pp. 29–50.

Pezzy, J. (1992) *Sustainable Development Concepts: An Economic Analysis*, World Bank Environment Paper 2 (Washington, DC: World Bank).

Preamble, Agenda 21 (1992) UN Department of Economic and Social Affairs, Division for Sustainable Development, http://www.un.org/esa/sustdev/documents/agenda21/english/agenda21chapter1.htm [Accessed 20 March 2005].

Sen, A. (1983), Poor, Relatively Speaking, *Oxford Economic Papers*, 35: 153–169.

Sen, A. (2001) *Development as Freedom* (Oxford: Oxford University Press).

Sieff, M. (2004) Analysis: China Boosts Presence in Central Asia, United Press International, 24 September, http://washingtontimes.com/upi-breaking/20040924-120915-6882r.htm [Accessed 12 October 2004].

Solyanik, S. (2001) Opposition or Hesitant Collaboration? NGOs Seek Ways to Relate to TNCs, *Give & Take*, 3(4): 28–29, http://www.greensalvation.org/English/Facts/H_rights/opposition.htm [Accessed 15 March 2005].

Stiglitz, J. E. (2002) *Globalization and its Discontents*, New York: Norton.

UNCTAD (2003) *FDI in Brief: Azerbaijan*, http://r0.unctad.org/en/subsites/dite/fdistats_files/pdfs/Azerbaijan_brief.pdf [Accessed 5 December 2003].

UNCTAD (2005) *World Investment Report. Transnational Corporations and the Internationalization of R&D*. New York and Geneva: United Nations Conference on Trade and Development. Available at http://www.unctad.org/en/docs/wir2005_en.pdf [Accessed 5 May 2005].

WCED (World Commission on Environment and Development) (1987) *Our Common Future* ['The Brundtland Report'] (Oxford: Oxford University Press).

World Bank (1988) *Environment and Development: Implementing the World Bank's New Policies*, Development Committee Pamphlet 17 (Washington, DC: World Bank).

5

A Dance of Donors and Dependent States:[1] Dilemmas of Civil Society Actors in the Struggle for Accountability in India

Shalini Randeria

The new architecture of unaccountable global governance facilitates a game of 'passing the power', a game in which international institutions claim themselves to be powerless servants of their member states, and cunning states that delegate responsibility for unpopular policies to external actors by pointing to the demands of global capital, prescriptions from the International Monetary Fund (IMF) and World Bank or the legal framework of the World Trade Organization (WTO). Struggles for accountability at the local level against global players, be they multinational corporations or international organizations, have focused attention on the nexus between state and market but also on the interplay of international organizations, multinational corporations and the state in promoting neo-liberal globalization (Randeria 2003b). Civil society actors involved in a politics of contention around the issues of displacement, resource dispossession and the privatization as well as commercialization of common property resources have engaged in a variety of struggles at the local as well as the national level. Although they primarily address the state, they remain ambivalent about respecting its claims to sovereignty over its people or over natural resources in its territory. They question not only the definition of the common good as advanced by it, but also its monopoly over the definition of public interest.

Despite the spectacular successes of some transnational coalitions, for example that against the Narmada dam discussed here, or the one against the patenting of products of the Neem tree, which I have discussed elsewhere (Randeria 2006a), the national arena remains the main sphere of action for civil society actors in the South, for it is here that the majority of citizens mobilize, protest, seek judicial remedies and attempt to influence political decision-making. Social movements and NGOS have had to contend with the state as an adversary in these struggles for social justice but also rely on it as an ally to rein in the power of multinational corporations or negotiate at the WTO and make use of its dispute resolution mechanism. But civil society actors have also often used the leverage of the World Bank, and the opportunity afforded by the new quasi-judicial arena of its Inspection Panel, not only to challenge the policies and practices of the Bank but also to render states accountable to their own citizens.

Contrary to the rhetoric of many globalization theorists, the state is not being rolled back as a rule-making or rule-enforcing agency. Empirical material from India will be used here to argue instead that the state is not merely a victim of neo-liberal economic globalization as it remains an active agent in shaping these processes and their domestication. The three case studies presented analyse the interplay of international institutions and non-state actors engaged in shifting alliances with one another and with the state. In contradistinction to the widespread diagnosis of the decline of the state and a dismantling of its sovereignty, I argue that it would be a mistake to take this self-representation of states at its face value. We are faced not by weak, or weakening, states but by cunning states, which capitalize on their perceived weakness in order to render themselves unaccountable to both their own citizens and international institutions. If welfare states in the North were about the redistribution of risk and resources, cunning states in the South are about the redistribution of responsibility. Whereas weak states like Benin or Bangladesh are unable to protect their citizens from the consequences of the processes of globalization, cunning states like India, Russia or Mexico do not choose to do so.

Due to its salience in domesticating neo-liberal policies, the state remains an important interlocutor for civil society actors challenging these policies or seeking to mitigate their effects. However, grassroots NGOs and social movements in India are not only engaged in a struggle against the state and international institutions for the protection of the rights of indigenous peoples and other local communities, but are proactive in formulating new norms weaving together traditional collective rights, national laws and international standards. Their struggle for environmental justice is being waged through broad-based political mobilization and media campaigns but equally through the increasing use of national courts and international legal forums (Randeria 2003a). While recognizing the new constraints on the freedom of the state to design and implement their own laws and policies, it would thus be a mistake to accept the self-representation of the cunning state about its own weakness. The cunning state certainly has the capacity to decide which of the remedies prescribed in Washington for the ills of the national economy, or which of the rules of the WTO, should be administered selectively to different sections of its population.

The paradoxical consequences of the World Bank-supported biodiversity project for the protection of lions in Gujarat are considered in the first section. By unpacking both state and civil society, it explores cleavages within civil society just as it cautions against viewing the state as a monolithic or homogeneous unit. The second section deals with the ambivalent success of the anti-Narmada dam movement whose global victories were not matched at the local level. Though it brought about institutional reforms at the World Bank, the movement failed to meet the rehabilitation needs of those in the Narmada Valley in whose name it successfully mobilized transnational publics. I delineate some of the ambivalences of using the international arena and transnational political spaces to leapfrog subaltern states and render them accountable. An unintended consequence of such a strategy in the case discussed here was a strengthening of the power of the G7, and particularly of the US government, at the World Bank. Finally, I discuss the disappointing experience of civil society actors who filed claims on behalf of those adversely affected by World Bank projects before the Inspection Panel, an innovative transnational legal arena which has failed to realize its potential so far.

Biodiversity and the lions' share: the World Bank as an ambivalent ally against the state

Some of the cleavages within civil society as well as the ambivalences of civil society activists towards the state and the World Bank are evident, for example, in the controversy between environmentalist NGOs and the human rights groups, which have been at odds with one another over the protection of the rights of lions versus the rights of pastoral communities in the Gir forest in Gujarat. Whereas the environmentalists champion the cause of wild life protection, the human rights NGOs have been concerned with securing the livelihood and cultural survival of the pastoralists. The powerful transnationally connected NGO Worldwide

Fund for Nature–India (WWF–India) has used its financial resources and media links to make a case for the displacement of the pastoralists who, in its view, endanger the survival of the Asiatic lion. Against such a narrow environmentalist agenda, which pits people's rights to access common property resources against conservationist goals, human rights NGOs and the local people's movement have mobilized for the protection of traditional rights of access to, and use of, natural resources based on the customary rights of the pastoral communities. Both sides draw on different sets of international norms – environmentalist discourses of biodiversity preservation vs. the right to livelihood and cultural identity.

The fact that there is no transnational campaign or advocacy coalition in this case should not blind us to the transnational dimensions of this conflict. It illustrates the transnational dimensions of local politics of contention even though only local resources were used for purely local political mobilization and court cases, which only address regional and national audiences. The struggle between biodiversity conservation and the right to livelihood of local communities accompanied the eco-development project of the World Bank to improve the management of seven different Protected Areas of significant global biodiversity in India from its inception. The Gir sanctuary, the last intact habitat of 284 Asiatic lions estimated to be living within it, comprises a so-called Protected Area containing a smaller National Park. But unlike the model of protected areas consisting of pristine nature based on American notions of wilderness, the areas thus demarcated in India are all inhabited.[2] There are 54 traditional hamlets of pastoralists with an estimated population of 2,540 within the Protected Area of the Gir forest who raise livestock and sell milk products (World Bank 1996).

Whereas the pastoralists retained limited rights to graze their cattle and gather fodder, firewood and forest produce in the Protected Area, they had been forcibly evicted from the area of the forest demarcated as National Park long before the start of the World Bank project. Some families were permitted to resettle within the larger Protected Area demarcated as the sanctuary, whereas the majority were forced to leave the forest and resettle under an inadequate rehabilitation programme that gave them land in villages near the Gir sanctuary. This half-hearted attempt to turn pastoralists into farmers failed mainly due to the poor quality of land made available to the families and their lack of agricultural skills. Within a few years, many successful pastoralists were reduced to wage labour and rendered destitute (Ganguly 2000).

Those families which were resettled outside the Protected Area thus lost their livelihood as pastoralists and their customary access to

the commons. But the lions did not benefit from the eviction of the pastoralists along with their large herds of buffaloes from the National
Park either. No respecters of boundaries drawn for conservationist
purposes, the lions too were forced to move out into the rest of the sanctuary area and even outside in search of prey. Some of the lions had to
be shot as they began to predate cattle in the villages surrounding the
Gir forest and even turned to man-eating. As the pastoralists pointed
out to me, this could hardly be seen as a successful policy of wildlife
protection!

The rights of the pastoralists to live in the Gir forest, to move freely
within it, to collect forest produce, graze cattle, use forest land and water
resources are sought to be overridden by World Wide Fund for Nature–
India and the state government of Gujarat, which have made common
cause in the name of the greater common good of nature conservation.
They argue that the demand of the pastoralists for modern amenities
like roads and electricity as well as their traditional grazing practices
with large herds of buffaloes endanger both the fragile local ecological
system and the lions. Unable to protect the rights of the pastoralists
by recourse to the national legislation, which calls for the eviction of
local communities living within areas demarcated as national parks and
protected areas, local human rights NGOs and people's organizations
strategically invoked the norms against involuntary displacement contained in the World Bank's operational policy on resettlement. They
have so far been able to prevent involuntary displacement out of the
Protected Area and its conversion into a National Park by arguing
that this would violate the conditionalities of the World Bank for the
biodiversity project.

In terms of the overriding commitments accepted by the government
in its agreement with the World Bank (World Bank 1996), for the limited
duration of the project and within the six biodiversity project areas,
World Bank policies safeguarding the rights of indigenous peoples and
protecting those affected by a project from involuntary displacement
prevail over national laws which require the relocation of any person
living within an area demarcated as a National Park. However, it is far
from clear whether these World Bank conditionalities will have any
permanent or pervasive impact on national resettlement policies or
environmental laws beyond the duration of their operation. At the
national and local levels these norms and principles often compete
with, or may even override, national laws, as the Gir case illustrates.
However, when WWF–India took the central government to court for
the violation of the Wildlife Protection Act, the cunning state claimed

not to have the resources to implement its own laws, including the eviction of communities living within National Parks in the country.

The clash over biodiversity and human rights in Gir illustrates competing visions of cosmopolitanism within civil society between community-based human rights organizations drawing on a mix of customary rights and international norms and environmental NGOs advocating the implementation of global designs of biodiversity (Randeria 2003c). WWF–India has found an ally in the Gujarat government and the two have teamed up to protect the environment using national legislation. Human rights activists have found an ally in the central government which is forced to abide by its commitments to the World Bank standards laid down in its operational directives and policies. Ironically, the displacement envisaged by the Gujarat government and the WWF–India in consonance with national law has been temporarily averted by NGOs invoking World Bank norms. As forced displacement would have contravened credit conditionalities accepted by the national government as signatory to the agreement with the World Bank, the federal government prevailed on the regional government to stop all forced eviction. But this fine balance is likely to last only as long as the World Bank project.

However, there is a further twist to this tale, which links issues of displacement to the acute crisis of livelihood strategies of the poor in the face of rapid commercialization of the commons. Many of the large cement companies on the coast of Saurashtra depend for their supplies of limestone (a key ingredient for cement production) on the rich deposits in the Gir forest area nearby. Local contractors mine these deposits illegally as no such commercial mining activities are allowed in forests or areas classified as a Protected Area. Of the 14 large cement factories either operating or under construction on the Saurashtra coast, seven are close to the Gir forest. Several have been granted a licence to set up production in the area as they have promised to export cement, thus earning valuable foreign exchange for the state exchequer. The IMF and the World Bank are both advocating such an export-led model of economic growth but such an economic policy can be realized in this case only through violating the World Bank's own environmental norms and the aim of preserving biodiversity. The Gir case thus also bears testimony to the structural double-think of the World Bank which advocates contradictory policy goals simultaneously.

Legal plurality, i.e. the simultaneous operation of several, and even contradictory, legal orders within the territory of the state fractures its sovereignty but also makes available a set of alternative norms, which can be used to set aside national legislation (Günther and Randeria 2002; Randeria 2003b; 2006a). For example, different norms of involuntary displacement, resettlement and compensation apply to those under threat of forcible displacement from the Protected Areas of National Parks demarcated under a World Bank-financed project, or from the area of a dam financed by it, as compared to those affected by similar projects without World Bank assistance. The growing disjunction between law, state and territory as well as an increasingly heterogeneous legal landscape can have very different consequences for the rights of citizens in different countries and contexts. However, which set of norms will be applied depends not merely on the financial involvement of the World Bank but on the bargaining strength of civil society actors representing the interests of those affected by a project. Their bargaining power *vis-à-vis* the state and international institutions varies depending on the strength of local political mobilization and resistance but also on the transnational support and media attention which local struggles are able to generate.

The entire problem of the shrinking of the commons (i.e. of access to and use of common property resources) has acquired a new urgency due to the policies of liberalization and privatization introduced by the Indian state under the directive of the IMF and the World Bank. The central government itself admitted in the new draft National Policy for Rehabilitation of Persons Displaced as a Consequence of Acquisition of Land that economic liberalization and an increase in private investment will generate greater demand for land as well as for mineral resources and reserves located in regions inhabited primarily by indigenous communities. Yet instead of a just and humane rehabilitation policy (based on a process of consultation and respect for democratic rights of the displaced, which would take into account the complexities of land use and traditional rights to commons), the new policy seeks only to ensure efficient expropriation and legal security in the interest of investors. Here is where the 'enabling state', representing the sectional interests of industry in the name of 'national interest', comes increasingly into conflict with those of its vulnerable citizens who are dependent on access to common property resources for their survival. While the interest of private industry is redefined to be the 'public interest' in the provision of employment, a safeguarding of common property resources on which the livelihoods of the rural poor depends is defined out of the ambit of public interest and the common good. Paradoxically, the proliferation of national and supranational environmental and human rights law, and an expansion of its scope, goes hand in hand with the erosion of the collective rights of communities, their traditional access to the commons and their right to determine for themselves a vision of the good life.

Leapfrogging the state: some lessons from the transnational success of the anti-Narmada dam movement and its local failures

Given the fact that more and more citizens are now directly affected in their daily lives by the working of international institutions and their policies, it is not surprising that they choose to address these institutions directly with their protests, bypassing the national parliamentary arena in an attempt to transnationalize an issue. However, leapfrogging the national political arena through the use of campaign coalitions focusing on transnational arenas of action and jurisdiction comes at a price. Transnational linkages within a campaign, even if successful, may lead over time to a shift of agendas and priorities. As local mobilization and strategic action come to be focused increasingly on the activities of foreign donors with a view to ending their involvement in a project, local grievances are articulated increasingly in terms of discourses which have international legitimacy and legibility. The needs of local communities facing displacement and dispossession, in whose name transnational collective action is taken, may be sidelined or jeopardized.

The vocabulary of local activists as well as the timing of local protest action are often determined in such cases by the demands of the global arena and transnational constituency-building instead of seeking to work through regional and national political institutions, as Sen's (1999) excellent ethnography of the struggle against the Sardar Sarovar dam on the river Narmada in western India explores. Highly detrimental to the environment, the project was originally expected to displace 70,000 people (an estimate which subsequently had to be officially revised to 120,000) from a submergence area of approximately 370 km^2 (Morse and Berger 1992). The World Bank itself conceded that the eviction and resettlement of at least about another 120,000 people had been overlooked. It had neither been planned for in the project by the Indian bureaucracy nor taken into account at the time of its appraisal by the Bank (Shihata 2000).[3]

Due to intense pressure from a large transnational advocacy network comprising several Indian NGOs, environmental rights groups in the US, development aid groups in Europe (especially Germany), Japan and Australia, the World Bank belatedly sought to prevail on the Indian national government in the final stages of the project to meet the resettlement and compensation standards of the Bank. The government of India chose instead not to draw the last tranche of the World Bank loan, thus ending the involvement of the Bank in one of its most controversial infrastructure development projects ever. Subsequently, the government of Gujarat floated bonds abroad to attract capital from the Indian diaspora appealing to their nationalist sentiments. These funds enabled the construction of the dams, leading to a further submersion of villages with even more forced displacement. If the successes of the campaign against the dam can be attributed to its transnational character, support for the dam has a transnational dimension too, albeit a very different one. The emerging global civil society thus includes not only transnational politics of contention but also diaspora networks with an active involvement in the national politics of their states of origin.

Sen (1999) delineates some of the complexities and contradictions of the transnational advocacy coalition against the Narmada dam to show how the dynamics of resistance in the Narmada valley came to be shaped increasingly by the choice of the arenas of negotiation and the structures of the international institutions used as levers of power. He argues that, paradoxically, the campaign thus reduced democratic control over the structures of the World Bank by increasing the control of the US Congress and the concentration of power of the major shareholding states of the North (G7 members control about 60 per cent of the vote) over the staff of the World Bank. However, such a strategy whereby social movements and NGOs in the South linked up successfully with powerful Northern and especially North American NGOs to use US congressional hearings as a forum to reform multilateral development banks in general, and the World Bank in particular, has had some ironic if unintended consequences. It not only reinforces existing asymmetries in power between the North and the South, at the level of national legislatures, but also lends greater legitimacy to international institutions and the US Congress. Bypassing the national parliamentary arena in order to address the World Bank directly further undermines democratic decision-making in the domestic arena. Paradoxically, this is the arena in which the World Bank, the US government and the international community are trying to foster good governance, including transparency and accountability in borrower countries.

It may be easier to reform norms and policies at the World Bank than effect changes in domestic laws and policies, as the experience of the anti-Narmada dam movement shows. It succeeded in reforming the information disclosure policy of the Bank and in pressurising it into establishing an accountability mechanism in the form of the Inspection

Panel (Randeria 2003a). If the experience of Indian citizens at a transnational forum like the Inspection Panel (as argued below) have been disappointing, developments at the national scale after the withdrawal of the World Bank from the dam project have not been encouraging either. The anti-Narmada dam movement's failed attempt to seek judicial remedy in the Supreme Court exposed some of the limitations of the use of national courts as arena for social justice (Sathe 2000). It has been impossible in national forums or in the transnational arena to get judicial remedy against a state that has constantly flouted its own laws and policies.

The World Bank Inspection Panel: borrower sovereignty and dilution of standards

Should the World Bank be accountable to all its member states, or especially to the borrower governments among them? How compatible is this with demands for direct accountability to the poor in borrowing countries whom Bank projects are supposed to benefit and whose interests the borrower governments claim to further? International and local NGOs demanding transparency and public accountability from all multilateral development banks seriously questioned the benefits of the projects to the poor and claimed the right to represent their interests. Borrower governments fearing the infringement of their sovereignty were hostile to the setting up of an independent Inspection Panel at the World Bank and have not facilitated its functioning either (Udall 1998).

The Inspection Panel is by no means a full-fledged body for adjudication, but provides a forum for an appeal by any party adversely affected by a World Bank-funded project. Its primary purpose is to examine whether the Bank staff have complied with its own rules and procedures. Its influence on policy formation within the World Bank is probably limited (Kingsbury 1999). Barring a couple of exceptions, claims before the Panel so far have had only limited success as Bank staff have usually teamed up with the borrowing country in question to deny any violations. Together the donor and dependent states have subverted full-fledged field investigations by the Panel by hastily drawing up remedial action plans for the future. The larger and relatively more powerful borrowing countries, those I have termed cunning states (Randeria 2006a), have supported each other on the Executive Board of the World Bank in resisting Panel investigations, which they regard as interference in their country's internal affairs. So the Panel has been increasingly used by civil society actors, as much to publicize violations of international environmental and human rights norms by their own governments and to pressurize these into compliance as to seek remedy against the World Bank's non-implementation of its own operational policies.

Of the 39 requests filed before the Panel up to the end of 2005,[4] four were related to projects in India. I have analysed two of these in detail elsewhere (Randeria 2003a; 2006a).[5] In the earlier cases it was alleged that the Bank management had failed to comply with its own policies on environmental assessment, the displacement of indigenous people and involuntary resettlement. Although the Bank staff denied any breach of policies and procedures, the Panel felt that 'a significant potential for serious harm existed' (Shihata 2000: 135) as key premises in the design of the project appeared to be flawed. Despite these findings, and the potential of serious negative impact of the project on the indigenous communities in the area, the Bank's Board decided not to authorize any investigation in 1998. Instead, it merely asked the management, together with the government of Karnataka and the affected people, to address the issues raised in the Panel's report and intensify project implementation and micro-planning. Given the long history of non-compliance with Bank guidelines by its own staff (and by the government of Gujarat in the case of the Narmada dam project, as amply documented in the Morse Commission report on the Narmada dam commissioned by the World Bank), the Board's decision is cause for concern. Besides the power of the Bank staff, it reflects the success of executive directors from borrowing countries, including India, as a bloc in thwarting Panel investigations which they regard as an infringement of their country's national sovereignty. Under these circumstances, NGOs continue to be sceptical about the independence of the Panel, of its limited mandate and of the difficulties of access to it for people affected adversely by World Bank projects all over the world (Udall 1997).

In response to the request to the Panel to look into the NTPC power generation project in Singrauli, the World Bank management conceded, for the first time, its partial failure to implement some of the Bank's policies. It submitted to the Panel a detailed action plan of corrective measures agreed with the government of India. After a review of the records and a brief preliminary field visit, the Panel concluded that although the guidelines regarding indigenous people had not been breached, the possibility of serious violations by the Bank of policies and procedures relating to involuntary resettlement and environmental assessment needed investigation. The Panel's investigations confirmed these violations and it noted in its report that the failure 'appear[ed] more serious than previously assumed' (Shihata 2000: 132). The government of India, however, denied permission to the Panel for a full, field-based investigation into the complaints, leading the World Bank Board to allow only a desk review of the project. And the Panel watched helplessly as the World Bank remained inactive in the face of a backlash in Singrauli. Reprisals against the villagers, harassment and intimidation by local police and project authorities increased after the complaint was filed.

Even in the absence of its legal liability, what is striking is the World Bank's acceptance of 'a mythology of compliance' (Moore 2002: 339) and its infinite faith in the borrowing government's political will and capacity to implement environmental and human rights conditionalities contrary to all evidence. Despite the failure of the government of India to issue a national resettlement and rehabilitation policy, the World Bank continues to advance credits to it for infrastructure development projects involving forced displacement. Bank staff and bureaucracy in the borrowing country both know that full compliance with the Bank's policies are an impossibility given the resource constraints and lack of political will in India. In more recent infrastructure project loans, for example, for the construction of highways in Mumbai and in the state of Kerala, the Bank has, therefore, used a different strategy. It has sought to involve NGOs from the start to monitor the displacement and implement Bank guidelines on rehabilitation. Apart from the risk of cooptation run by the NGOs involved in organizing participatory (as opposed to forced) displacement, this has not prevented a complaint being registered before the Panel in the case of the Mumbai Urban Transportation Project, which is pending (Randeria 2006a).

It is not as if the Bank as an institution has not learnt from its past mistakes. Many of the norms enshrined in its operational policies reflect the experience of the Bank with the adverse effects of its earlier projects and are the result of sustained lobbying by, and consultations with, civil society actors and representatives of affected communities in many countries. So that World Bank standards often emerge from local sources and are then globally diffused to other international and bilateral development institutions and borrowing countries through their incorporation into Bank policies and practices. A good example of such a process is the norm of land-for-land compensation for those families displaced by a World Bank project instead of the earlier cash compensation for land acquired by the state. This standard was introduced after the experience of forced displacement and the struggle against the Narmada dam. But instead of ensuring compliance with it, it is being given up by the

World Bank under pressure from borrowing governments and private industries.

Although the World Bank continues to claim immunity from legal liability for the adverse impacts of its projects, parallel to the setting up of the Panel, Bank management began to convert operational directives and policies which were binding on the staff into 'non-mandatory recommendations' or 'Best Practices' in order to render them 'Panel-proof' by placing them beyond the jurisdiction of the Inspection Panel. The existence of the Panel has not led to greater compliance by the Bank staff with the institution's own rules and norms. Instead, ironically, the limited investigations by the Panel are already leading to a watering down of standards to make them conform to the Bank's and borrower's common practice of non-compliance with them.

Conclusion

This chapter has focused on some aspects of collective action in India against the World Bank and the state which has involved a (re)framing of local issues in a globally legible and translatable language. As my case studies show, World Bank norms and policies are not only a source of constraint but can also be deployed strategically by local actors to broaden their choices. The struggle in Gir forest against displacement and the dispossession of pastoralists reminds us of the pivotal, albeit contested, role of the state in transposing global designs to the local level. My analysis of the Narmada dam case alerts us to the fact that the involvement of the World Bank changes not only the context in which local processes of displacement occur but also the dynamics of collective action on the ground.

Paradoxically, however, a proliferation of supra-state governance and an increasing juridification of social life can go hand in hand with the erosion of customary rights of the poor to common property resources. If international norms and transnational processes shape and redefine local life-worlds, they can not only constrain choices but also empower activists at a national or local scale. Local communities and traditions are anything but bounded and static. Rather than a Russian doll model of the local, national, global as neatly demarcated spaces, each encapsulated within the next larger level as one moves up the scale, my case studies reveal the local and the national as fragmented spaces with plural, trans-local links. My empirical material illustrates some of the paradoxes and ambivalences of the processes of the transnationalization of these spaces and the dilemmas of civil society activists with multiple moorings who are forced into in shifting issue-based alliances with a variety of actors and institutions in a field of asymmetrical power relations.

Neo-liberal globalization has meant a shrinking of state responsibilities rather than a shrinking of the state apparatus. Similarly, it has not led to less state interventionism but rather to state intervention in favour of capital. Yet the capacity of the subaltern state seeking to domesticate neo-liberal governance to set its own agendas, and achieve them, is being limited from without and contested from within. It is forced to negotiate with both supranational organizations and with civil society actors with whom it enters into transient and issue-bound coalitions in order to implement various projects and policies. But if state responses are fragmented and context-specific, civil society alliances with and against the state are equally pragmatic. Cunning states are not weak states but states with enormous power and few duties towards their citizens. The dilemma that civil society actors in the South face is that of simultaneously working towards limiting the power of the state while broadening its social obligations.

The result is a fuzzy politics which defies easy classification in terms of ideologies or the binary opposition of national/transnational. Community-based grassroots NGOs and social movements, once harsh critics of the states, have rediscovered the merits of the state and its sovereignty in some contexts. Their anti-statism has given way to a recognition of the need to limited issue-based pragmatic partnerships with the state even as they continue to challenge its legitimacy to represent the public interest and the common good (Randeria 2006a). Faced by cunning states and non-accountable international institutions, civil society actors and coalitions in the twenty-first century will probably have neither permanent friends nor permanent enemies but only permanent interests.[6] For those in search of principled alliances, these may seem dangerous liaisons. But cunning states and unaccountable international institutions breed cunning civic alliances capable of mobilizing very different constituencies, attuning local priorities to a variety of global agendas, able to speak in different registers to different audiences, to redesign local issues for trans-local consumption while simultaneously addressing several publics in different locations.

Notes

1. The title is inspired by Sally F. Moore's felicitous phrase 'the international dance between funders and states' (2002: 351).
2. Randeria (2006b) traces the colonial legacies of contemporary national laws as well as global designs of conservation and environmental governance in India.

3. Estimates of the number of people displaced vary widely and were a highly contested issue between the state and the anti-dam movement. Large dams alone have displaced 16–38 million people in post-colonial India, 75 per cent of whom are still to be rehabilitated (World Commission on Large Dams Report 2000: 104, 108).
4. For a detailed analysis of the history of the Panel, its procedures and of the 17 cases which had come up before it up to 1999, see Randeria (2001).
5. These are the National Thermal Power Corporation (NTPC) power generation project in Singrauli (1997) and the eco-development project (of which the Gir project is a part) in the Nagarhole National Park in Karnataka (1998). On the results of the Panel investigations in these cases, see Umaña (1998). Randeria (2006a) analyses the latest complaints regarding the Mumbai Urban Transportation Project (2005).
6. See, for example, the International Annual Report of Greenpeace (1998) which states 'Greenpeace has no permanent allies or enemies'.

References

Ganguly, Varsha (2000) Impact of Displacement on Quality of life of Maldhari (Pastoral) Women of Gir Forest. PhD Thesis, South Gujarat University Surat.

Günther, Klaus and Shalini Randeria (2002) *Recht im Prozess der Globalisierung* (Frankfurt am Main: Suhrkamp Verlag).

Greenpeace (1998) International Annual Report of Greenpeace, http://archive.greenpeace.org/report98/index.html.

Krastev, Ivan (2002) The Balkans: Democracy without Choices, *Journal of Democracy* 13(3): 39–53.

Kingsbury, Benedict (1999) Operational Policies of International Institutions as Part of the Law-Making Process: The World Bank and Indigenous People, in G. S. Goodwin-Gill and S. Talmon (eds.) *The Reality of International Law: Essays in Honour of Ian Brownlie* (Oxford: Clarendon), pp. 323–343.

Moore, Sally F. (2002) An International Legal Regime and the Context of Conditionality', in M. Likosky (ed.) *Transnational Legal Processes. Globalisation and Power Disparities* (Wiltshire: Cromwell Press), pp. 333–352.

Morse, Bradford and Thomas Berger (1992) *Sardar Sarovar: Report of the Independent Review* (Ottawa: Resource Futures International).

Randeria, Shalini (2001) Local Refractions of Global Governance: Legal Plurality, International Institutions, NGOs and the Post-Colonial State in India. *Habilitation*, Faculty of Political and Social Sciences, Free University of Berlin.

Randeria, Shalini (2003a) Globalization of Law: Environmental Justice, World Bank; NGOs and the Cunning State in India, *Current Sociology*, 52(3/4): 305–328.

Randeria, Shalini (2003b) Domesticating Neoliberal Discipline: Transnationalization of Law, Fractured States and Legal Pluralism in the South, in Wolf Lepenies (ed.) *Entangled Histories and Negotiated Universals: Centres and Peripheries in a Changing World* (Frankfurt am Main: Campus Verlag), pp. 146–182.

Randeria, Shalini (2003c) 'Footloose Experts vs. Rooted Cosmopolitans: Biodiversity Conservation, Transnationalization of Law and Conflict among Civil Society Actors in India', *Tsantsa*, 8: 7–85.

Randeria, Shalini (2006a) The State of Globalization, *Theory, Culture and Society* (Summer).

Randeria, Shalini (2006b) Global Designs and Local Lifeworlds: Colonial Legacies of Conservation, Disenfranchisement and Environmental Governance in Postcolonial India, *Interventions: International Journal of Postcolonial Studies*, 8(1).

Sathe, S. P. (2000) Supreme Court and NBA, *Economic and Political Weekly*, 35(46): 3990–3994.

Sen, Jai (1999) A World to Win – But Whose World is it, Anyway? Civil Society and the World Bank, the View from the 'Front': Case Studies, in J. W. Foster and A. Anand (eds.) *Whose World is it Anyway? Civil Society, the United Nations and the Multilateral Future* (Ottawa: United Nations Association in Canada).

Shihata, Abraham F. I. (2000) *The World Bank Inspection Panel in Practice* (Washington, DC: Oxford University Press).

Udall, Lori (1997) *The World Bank Inspection Panel: A Three-Year Review* (Washington, DC: The World Bank Information Center).

Udall, Lori (1998) The World Bank and Public Accountability: Has Anything Changed? in J. Fox and L. D. Brown (eds.) *The Struggle for Accountability: The World Bank, NGOs and Grassroots Movements* (Cambridge, MA: MIT Press), pp. 323–436.

Umaña, Alvaro (ed.) (1998) *The World Bank Inspection Panel: The First Four Years (1994–1998)* (Washington, DC: The World Bank Information Center).

World Bank (1996) *Staff Appraisal Report: India. Eco-development Project.* Report No. 4914-IN, 3 August.

World Commission on Large Dams Report (2000) *Dams and Development: a New Framework for Decision-Making* (London: Earthscan).

Part II

New Social Movements within Transnational Civil Society

6
Critique of Capitalism in the Era of Globalization – Old Wine in New Bottles?[1]

Dieter Rucht

Social movements, especially working-class movements, have helped to restrain 'unbridled' capitalism by fostering state intervention, especially in the form of welfare state measures. Since the late 1970s, however, a neo-liberal offensive has gained momentum which aims to remove such restraints. With the accelerating pace of economic globalization, and encouraged by the end of the Cold War, neo-liberal forces and programmes have meanwhile come to play a powerful role within international political economies. Among the economic and political elites, an overwhelming majority praises not only the virtues of the market but, above all, the wholesale removal of barriers to free trade as an indispensable precondition for the development of general well being – including that of the poor countries in the southern hemisphere.

A heterogeneous alliance of groups and movements critical of globalization, most of which operate transnationally, vehemently challenges the assumption that neo-liberalism produces beneficial results. In their eyes, unfettered capitalism plays a decisive part in weakening nation-states and in widening the gap between rich and poor. Among other things, these groups are demanding transparency and democratic control over political and economic decisions of global magnitude, and greater solidarity with the poor and the underprivileged. Frequently casting themselves as representatives of civil society, critics of globalization – in opposition to the representatives of classical liberalism – are calling for measures to strengthen states and communities of states with the aim of containing market forces.

This raises two central questions which will be investigated in this chapter. The first concerns the way the critics of globalization view civil society, democracy and the state, and the role played by anti-capitalist positions and positions critical of capitalism in this context. The second asks whether there is any difference between current critiques of globalization and capitalism, and similar analyses undertaken in the past, and whether it is possible now, in contrast to the past, to identify a predominantly positive relationship to civil society.

The material for this reconstructive-hermeneutic analysis draws on declarations and manifestos issued by significant groups and on publications by individual experts and leading political thinkers that are referred to by groups critical of globalization inside and outside Germany. (The critique of globalization expressed in extreme right-wing circles will be ignored here.)

The rise of groups critical of globalization

With the emergence of the New Left in the 1960s, there was a renaissance of comprehensive social criticism which drew on the Marxist classics, psychoanalytic theories and the writings of the Frankfurt School. The 'hard core' of the New Left held firmly anti-capitalist positions. Anti-imperialist theories that glorified the various liberation movements in Third World countries also experienced an unprecedented renaissance. However, as the New Left declined as a political force, this form of social criticism waned, ceased to be of academic significance or exhausted itself in scholastic trench warfare between rival communist groups competing over 'correct theory'.

The 'new social movements' that have largely emerged from the New Left have shown nowhere near as much interest in theory as their predecessors. Although they too occasionally borrow from grand theories (e.g. dependency theories, world system theories, regulation theories and post-Fordism theories), theoretical debate generally plays a minor role. The new movements tend to focus instead on concrete problems and social injustices, whether in their own neighbourhoods or in countries of the Third World.

Partly rooted in the new social movements, a new generation of leftist groupings critical of globalization has finally emerged. Even though these groups have only really entered the public eye since the 'Battle of Seattle' (Thomas 2000; Smith 2001) which accompanied the World Trade Organization (WTO) summit at the end of 1999, their roots may be traced back much further (Rucht 2002). Although the term globalization was not commonly used at the time, groups had already started to appear in Germany by 1985 at the latest (e.g. at the G7 summit in

Cologne) which could be safely described as critics of globalization. Many of the patterns of criticism now in currency could be identified during the campaign against the World Bank and the IMF Conference in Berlin in 1988 (Gerhards and Rucht 1992; Gerhards 1993).[2] In the following sections, I shall clarify and discuss the extent to which critics of globalization have developed a distinctive critique of society and the state.

Nobody can seriously doubt that groups critical of globalization constitute a political force of no little significance. At one time largely ignored or greeted with pitying smiles, they can now no longer be overlooked (Canadian Security Intelligence Service 2000). They owe this change of fortune primarily to their appearance, which has had such a powerful impact through the media, at a number of international summit meetings (G7/G8, WTO, World Bank, International Monetary Fund, UN, EU Summit) (Fues and Hamm 2001; Pianta 2001). Although these protests have varied considerably in size, they have nevertheless continued to grow significantly over the recent years. Independently of the specific occasions for protest, these groups have developed and gradually consolidated a growing infrastructural base. They have also appeared before the world public at a number of World Social Forums (Gret and Sintomer 2002). In contrast to the first forum in 2001, which was a rather modest counterpart to the annual World Economic Forum in Davos, subsequent Social Forums have developed a momentum of their own. Their appeal has grown enormously. Approximately 50,000 people attended the second World Social Forum, which took place in the Brazilian city of Porto Alegre in January 2002. Just one year later, at the follow-up meeting at the same venue, the number attending had already more than doubled and – judging by the resonance in the media – outstripped the World Economic Forum (Wahl 2003). According to one optimistic account: 'Where there was once only impotent moral protest, a movement of movements has now developed' (Brand and Brie 2003). Indeed, more than 40,000 turned up for the first European Social Forum in Florence in November 2002 (Wahl 2002). It was absolutely crowded and culminated in a demonstration attended by about half a million people.

Initial analyses show that globalization critics can certainly count on the support of a broad section of the population, not to mention the left and the politically – but not the economically – liberal press (Rucht 2003a). New groups such as Attac have spread across a large part of the globe and are growing fast in a number of countries, including Germany (Eskola and Kolb 2002; Kolb 2005). Furthermore, despite their disapproval, established politicians are beginning to take these emerging currents seriously. The pensive comments made by a few high-ranking politicians at the 2002 World Economic Forum, which was held in New York (instead of Davos), is indicative of this. Also revealing is the fact that the Belgian Prime Minister, Guy Verhofstadt, for example, who had previously made his mark with an 'Open letter to the anti-globalization movement' (Lettre ouverte aux anti-mondialistes,[3]) foundered in his attempt to gain permission to speak at the Social Forum 2002 in Porto Alegre.

The critics of globalization and their critique of society and the state

Although the term 'anti-globalization movement', which probably originated in the media, was initially adopted by those thus designated, many people have meanwhile come to view this term as inappropriate for a variety of reasons (George 2001; Graeber 2001; Smith 2001). Some, arguing tactically, object to being associated with a 'No' only and want to escape Niklas Luhmann's polemical verdict that brands the new social movements the 'Niet Set'. The arguments dealing with their content are far more serious, however. On the one hand, with the aid of global communications technologies, groups critical of globalization are creating networks that are increasingly transnational and ultimately global in character. On the other, these groups constitute a force that is in a way demanding and fostering globalization. For with the exception of the right-wing opponents of globalization (see Leggewie 2003: 54ff), these groups are seeking to gain acknowledgement for the principles of transnational and trans-class solidarity and for the worldwide democratization of politics. It is therefore only logical that self-designations such as the global solidarity movement, global justice movement and global civil society should be gaining currency, particularly in the United States, whilst in France, the term altermondialistes is catching on (instead of antimondialistes).

If, therefore, neither anti- nor pro-globalization movement can be considered an appropriate designation, the question remains regarding the smallest common denominator of the groups involved. The simplest response, which is probably accepted by most, is that they are united in their struggle against neo-liberal globalization (Rucht 2003). Whilst many of the more moderate groups in particular can identify with this definition of their position, sections of the radical left only seem to accept this denominator in order to remain suitable partners for alliances, as grumbling voices in these circles confirm: 'Instead of grasping globalised capitalism theoretically, people often refer to a vaguely defined concept of neo-liberalism which then has to serve as an explanation for all kinds of social injustices' (Wissen nd: 15).

Although the term neo-liberalism is a somewhat vague common denominator, people nevertheless associate with it a range of concrete strategies and measures: a high regard for competition and the competitive principle, the removal of all barriers to free trade (for capital, goods, services and labour), the extensive privatization of state-owned services, far-reaching de-bureaucratization and deregulation, more flexible employment conditions and the demand that individuals assume direct responsibility for risks to their lives. The critical feature of these liberal principles, which are by no means new, lies in their radicalization and universalization within the framework of an aggressive globalization strategy. Advocates of this strategy argue that it contains a promise: that neo-liberal principles and strategies are, in the long term at least, the best guarantee for promoting the welfare of all human beings and nations. And these are precisely the assumptions that the critics of globalization challenge. For in their eyes, globalizing neo-liberalism (or the Washington Consensus[4]) is not the solution but the problem. The central criticisms of globalization are that it widens the gap between the rich and poor both in and between the different countries across the globe (especially between North and South), disempowers nation-states with their functions of providing social security and redistributing wealth, removes momentous economic processes from democratic control and, finally, buttresses – in the name of freedom – existing imbalances of power and influence (for one example among many, see Chomsky 2000).

Globalization critics of all shades are likely to agree with this assessment. Opinions are, admittedly, divided when it comes to identifying the driving forces behind globalizing neo-liberalism, determining how radically criticism of this development should be formulated, and ascertaining which forms of resistance are necessary. The comparison between moderate reformists and anti-system radicals, which recalls the debate on reformism conducted within the Social Democratic parties in the early part of the twentieth century, merely provides a starting point for answering these questions: but it cannot do justice to the complexity of the overlapping positions.

Three variations on the critique of capitalism

In his survey of the political ideas of the critics of globalization, Markus Wissen, a member of the *Bundeskoordination Internationalismus* (BUKO,

Federal Co-ordination Group Internationalism[5]), identified three main currents (Wissen nd, 13ff.):

1   The first current is treated under the sub-heading: 'International civil society: Protest in diplomatic circles'. The central actors here are NGOs working in the fields of environmental and development policy. By internationalizing their protest, they have been able to grow in importance, especially since the Rio conference of 1992. Many of these groups have 'emerged from the bankrupt's estate of the new social movements' (ibid.: 12) and lent expression to the illusory hope, shared by many at the end of the Cold War, that they 'could use what appeared to be greater political freedom to create more social, ecological and democratic conditions throughout the world' (ibid.). However, the limits of the practical involvement of many of these NGOS have become very apparent. For although they have undoubtedly influenced UN negotiations and thus gained recognition as 'players', they generally romp around the playground of symbolic politics and 'by concentrating on UN conferences, put their money on the wrong horses or tried to ride them with questionable means' (ibid.: 14).

2   More than anything else, it was the Seattle protests that rehabilitated radical criticism by shifting attention away from the 'political side-show of UN conferences' and onto the institutional centres of neo-liberal globalization and the WTO as the embodiments of global power relations. As a result, the protest assumed 'the form of a symbolic attack', and a 'second, anti-state current ... [gained in] ... importance' (ibid.) alongside the by no means outdated professionalized policies of the NGOs. Representatives of this current include groups such as Tute Bianche from Italy, the international network Peoples' Global Action (PGA) and those who share the Zapatista conception of politics. In contrast to the professional NGOs and traditional left-wing parties, these groups reject state-centred political strategies, aim to combine diverse emancipatory approaches, advocate non-hierarchical forms of organization and cultivate a confrontational style of politics. In Tute Bianche's case, this strategy is aimed at exposing the violence immanent to the system.[6]

3   Under the heading 'Keynes international', Markus Wissen notes a third current, which, more than any other, characterizes the present international protest movement. This current considers itself explicitly anti-neo-liberal and (in contrast to NGOs, which place their faith in dialogue) advocates 'mobilization from below' in order to put pressure

on the state. This strategy seeks to impose restraints on an uncontrolled economy by pursuing left-wing Keynesian policies and implementing appropriate reforms. Wissen sees Attac and the group Raison d'Agir, which was inspired by Pierre Bourdieu, as representative of this current, who sometimes seem to have 'an idealised view of Fordism' (ibid.: 16). Raison d'Agir's prime goal is to get Europe's social movements to merge. These groups apparently do not see capitalism *per se* as a problem. Furthermore, they have taken up hardly any other issue – such as racism, patriarchal relationships and the destruction of nature – apart from that of capitalist power relations.

With the exception of Wissen's judgements, which stem from his support for the second position,[7] his typification of these three currents provides a valuable starting point for categorizing this bewildering spectrum of positions.[8] In the following, when I refer to these three currents, I shall speak for simplicity's sake of the moderate reformism of the NGOs, the anti-systemic critique of the left-wing radicals and the radical reformism of the broad coalition movements. Yet one should remember that each current has a highly differentiated composition entailing complex mixing ratios and alliances, thus making it impossible to proceed from the existence of a clearly structured, static field. It is difficult to classify these groups precisely, because they often propose vague ideological compromises or conceal differences in political positions both to allow tactical coalitions and to avoid scaring off large sections of the middle class. Applying the typology presented above, we shall now take a closer look at these positions (albeit in a different order) in the light of their divergent critiques of capitalism.

Moderate NGO reformism

The broadly defined term 'non-governmental organizations' which – from a purely formal standpoint – includes commercial enterprises, parties, economic associations, cultural and leisure associations, etc., came to be defined more narrowly in the domain of international politics during the 1990s. It now primarily refers to non-commercial associations that care for or campaign for 'weak interests' (Willems and von Winter 2000). Consequently, these NGOs tend to give priority to human and civil rights, peace, environmental protection and poverty, social issues and health. These groups have mushroomed over the past few decades. From the local to the international level they have sought to influence the formulation of political objectives and decisions. Second, and this is more of an implicit semantic shift, the term NGO is increasingly being used for organizations that do not (primarily) see themselves as representing grass-roots movements, but principally operate as specialized groups of experts and lobbyists. Even though these different areas overlap[9] and NGOs (in the narrower sense of the term) occasionally participate in unconventional protests, their work typically centres on negotiating with governments and local authorities. NGOs' interaction with governments sometimes necessitates their becoming involved in advisory committees and delegations or in implementing specific projects. This, in turn, encourages and calls for considerable professionalization, which means that NGOs have to tailor their activities towards 'what is feasible'. Consequently, they tend to avoid fundamental questions of ideological significance and devote themselves instead to finding pragmatic solutions.

NGOs' decidedly 'unideological' attitude is also linked to their ambiguous attitude towards, or a reluctance to involve themselves in, debates on the socio-political order. They rarely raise questions about the 'character of the state' or the 'logic of capitalism' or the 'role of civil society', at least not in such general terms. Although NGOs press for structural changes in many problematic areas and remind people of the necessity of making them, they believe such changes must be made gradually, one step at a time. NGOs of this type tend to display – both implicitly and in their actual actions – faith in the willingness and capacity of national and international governments to institute reforms. That the gulf between these NGOs and governmental institutions is not so wide is ultimately illustrated by the fact that time and again professionally experienced representatives of NGOs leave their jobs for positions in governments and administrations. This is regarded with mixed feelings,[10] to say the least, by the NGOs, and seen as betrayal by radical groups.

The radical reformism of transnational mass movements

In addition to the above-mentioned NGOs, which occasionally have an elitist and meritocratic bias, there are now many broadly based groups which often operate at the transnational level. Some observers interpret their emergence as a reaction to the fact that 'the tendency of most NGOs to focus on lobbying has prevented them from transcending their own narrow boundaries' (Hierlmeier 2002: 159).

Mass movements critical of globalization reveal two main characteristics: first, they see themselves as open, participatory social movements with a decidedly grass-roots organizational form and a predilection for public and peaceful (mass) protest.[11] As such, they may well include, or ally themselves with, NGOs specializing in a certain field without being overly influenced by them. Second, although members on the fringes may see things quite differently, these movements basically stand for radical reformism, so that they adopt positions on key questions about the social order. Among these groups one frequently encounters attitudes that are not only critical of capitalism, but also go as far as to oppose 'the new colonial rule of companies' (Goldsmith 2002: 54). It must be said, however, that this opposition seldom includes an attempt theoretically or systematically to analyse the dynamics of capitalism. Rather, their critique of capitalism is generally a response to specific social injustices, which are ascribed to an unrestrained – or insufficiently restrained – striving for power or profit. These critics propose moderate reforms. Furthermore, they are willing to become involved in specific political issues, but stubbornly avoid committing themselves exclusively to individual projects. On the whole, these movements comprise a broad political spectrum that ranges from Christians to Social Democrats, Green politicians and democratic socialists (or former reform communists) to anti-institutional grass-roots movements within the moderate left-wing camp.

When it comes to long-term strategies and questions of social order, they tend to hold rather vague political positions – if only to allow them to enter a broad range of alliances. The international spokesperson for Attac France expressed some self-critical comments on these issues:

> Nobody discusses the question of power. That is a grave limitation. There is no real strategy. And avoiding these questions enables us to reach a broad consensus within the movement and hold meetings such as the ESF (European Social Forum, D.R.). But it is also a weakness. The movement does not have an answer, because it wants to change the system at an international, European or even national level. (Aguiton 2003: 11)

This critique is mainly directed at the concrete behaviour of individual governments, groups of companies and at certain institutional regulations, whilst questions concerning the system are either not addressed at all, or only very indirectly. Thus, for instance, while neo-liberalism is declared to be the enemy,[12] the capitalist principle inherent to it is rarely discussed, and if it is, then only in terms of its excesses or absolute forms. Implicitly, then, not capitalism and the market as such are the subject of debate: rather, the aim is merely to restrict their field of operation. Consequently, free trade is not rejected *per se*. Even so, many demand that individual countries or sectors be exposed only gradually and cautiously to the pressures of international competition and that some spheres of the economy be permanently excluded from the market. They want to retain or reintroduce Keynesian[13] policies and closely related mechanisms of economic control. Their basic goal is to implement on a global scale the idea of the social market economy, which was originally created for national economies. This strategy would also involve taking measures to introduce protective and compensatory mechanisms for the economically weak, to reduce speculative transfers and tax evasion, and to strengthen state institutions *vis-à-vis* corporate interests, namely, the big companies with international operations. Thus, it is not difficult to understand that broad sections of the trade union movement see themselves as being the natural allies if not the original basis of mass movements that are committed to these positions. It is here, however, that the contradictory demands of reformers critical of globalization become apparent. Whereas some of the trade unions in the North advocate (albeit to different degrees) protectionist measures, the unions in many Southern countries demand that the core capitalist countries take free trade seriously and abolish their import controls, such as those on agricultural produce.

Like the reformist NGOs, the radical reformers also place their hope in the flexibility of international political institutions. They formulate their appeals accordingly, submit constructive proposals to solve problems (including the much-cited Tobin tax) and advocate applying political pressure, which means, above all, 'the pressure of the street'. On the left-wing margin of this spectrum, there are more or less broad transitional zones, which vary in accordance with the vehemence of the groups' critique of capitalism and even include decidedly anti-capitalist positions, which deserve especial attention within the framework of this essay.

Anti-systemic critiques by the left-wing radicals

Left-wing radicals, who draw very sharp dividing lines between one another at times, call attention to the principle of exploitation and destruction, which is inherent to capitalism and is being to pushed to its limits by the 'definitive internationalisation of capitalist relations – euphemistically referred to as globalization' (Grigat 2001). Many regard the globalization strategies now being forced through under the banner of neo-liberalism as imperialism in new clothes, which no longer has recourse to thundering gunboat politics but assumes an apolitical face, approaching quietly, in the service of supposedly purely economic interests. According to this critique, class rule has always functioned in this way in practice. Hence, the starting point for any solution is seen as a radical break. The very idea that this system can be reformed from within and improved is regarded as mere wishful thinking. Instead of trying to push for reforms, which can at best bring about no more than superficial changes, they believe it is necessary to reject 'the system' altogether and, ultimately, overthrow it. Hence, their globalization policy slogan is 'Smash the WTO', and when it comes to the system as a whole: 'Smash Capitalism'. Groups such as Attac, which are politically more moderate and less ideological, appear quite naïve from this perspective. Where the criticism voiced by the more moderate left-wing radical spectrum tends to be more restrained and is designed to attract support,[14] representatives of an uncompromising anti-capitalist stance are inclined to resort to ridicule and distance themselves from such tendencies: 'There is not much left of the insights gained from the critique of capitalism. The revolutionary demand: "Abolish capitalism" has been transformed for the foreseeable future into: "Be nice to one another"' (Fahrenheit No. 6 'Gegen verlängerten Kapitalismus und verkürzte Kritik' [Against the Prolongation of Capitalism and Superficial Criticism]).

Hard-core leftists also accuse mainstream groups critical of globalization of playing down the problems, of being fixated on the state, and of idealizing it as the guardian of the common weal. Such groups, they allege, romanticize capitalism's past, and portray capitalism as if it had once been 'tamed'. Mainstream groups are also accused of succumbing to the illusion that one need only apply sufficient social pressure plus a few good arguments for things to get better (see, e.g., Heinrich nd). This critique is inconsistent, however, when it attacks the way the majority of globalization critics see a democratic process which the latter judge positively. On the one hand, there are those who claim that all these processes are by no means the result of 'a cunningly thought-out diversion on the part of the rulers, who have a tight grip on the situation and know, from the very start, exactly what they want' (ibid.: 23). Maria Mies, on the other hand, an anti-capitalist feminist, writes that, 'nowadays, it is the "economy", in other words the big banks and groups of companies, that makes the political decisions and not vice versa, i.e. the (sovereign) people who determine economic policy through their elected representatives' (Mies 2001: 185). The Trotskyist camp has a very similar assessment of the situation: 'The democratic representatives, the parliaments and gossip shops are not the real power in capitalist society. Behind them are the administrative and repressive apparatuses, which are designed to defend private property' (global red 2001: 86).

Those who hold this perspective condemn local endeavours to carry out reforms – such as the participatory decisions on Porto Alegre's public sector budget – as 'democratic puppet shows' designed to 'satisfy the middle classes' and see the World Social Forum of globalization opponents as a 'trick on the part of those who are trying to push the anti-capitalist movement towards a policy of class collaboration and participation in bourgeois elections'.[15]

Even though left-wing reformism is under attack from the far left, an attempt must still be made to take up the thread of the discussion and the politicization processes underlying it. 'In any case, the left', so the argument runs, 'should become involved in this process with everything it has to offer in the way of a critique of capitalism and the state' (ibid.: 23).

The significance of civil society for global justice groups

The three positions described above determine the way the various currents relate to civil society. Both the reformist NGOs and the mass movements that tend to advocate radical reforms generally fall back unreservedly on the idea of civil society. Perceptible differences in positions seem to be of secondary importance here. NGOs are more likely than other groupings to emphasize their role as representatives or organs of society *vis-à-vis* the state. And in so doing, they accommodate the state's need to legitimate its policies, since the state wants to present itself as democratic and sympathetic to its citizens' needs. NGOs generally regard civil society as a positive concept and lay claim to it for their own purposes. As a result, international governments and institutions tend to accept rather than reject them. For even though governments find NGOs uncomfortable at times, they generally find them easy to deal with. This state of affairs enables governments to declare that political decisions have been reached through 'consultation' and 'dialogue' and in co-operation with members of 'civil society', thus strengthening, in turn, NGOs' claim that they embody civil society. It is no accident that both sides view approvingly the concept of governance.

However, the very vagueness of the term NGO and of the NGOs' conception of civil society also provides for points of overlapping interest with avowed opponents of globalization critics: i.e. with economic interest groups that try to portray themselves as legitimate representatives of civil society *vis-à-vis* the organs of the state. The current debates on corporate citizenship and corporate social responsibility must also be seen in this context.

In contrast to the NGOs, the mass movements, which claim to speak for civil society, emphasize their broad support among the population. They see themselves as the authentic embodiment of civil society, and not simply as its representatives or champions.[16] They make inflationary use of stylized images presenting them as participants in a 'global civil society'. Also significant in this context is the fact that the connotations attached to the role of the 'citizen' and not least of the world citizen are far more positive now than they were in the 1960s. Emphatic commitment to a global civil society is on the agenda (for a sceptical assessment, see Roth 2001). Susan George, Vice-President of Attac France and one of the figureheads of pro-reformist globalization critics, has a vision of a 'planetary social contract'. And even Walden Bello, the Director of Focus on the Global South, who is generally considered an advocate of a radical approach, appeals to an 'international civil society'. The vague and positive connotations of the term civil society have proved to be very valuable here, since they push political dividing lines into the background.

Not all globalization critics, however, subscribe to an emphatic concept of civil society. To 'revolutionary' anti-capitalists, for example, the concept of civil society has negative connotations. Similar to the way some viewed the citizens' initiatives of the 1960s and 1970s, they now consider all the talk about civil society as a means of euphemistically veiling the real relations of power, exclusion and oppression. Hence, any commitment to civil society is seen as reflecting a wilful or naive acceptance of a delusion or an empty promise of peacefulness and tolerance, which is totally absurd given the real conditions. Characteristic of this attitude is the position held by Thomas Ebermann, a left-wing radical critic of the old school,[17] who wants to save less staunch leftists from their illusions. Thus, in response to the hope expressed by discussion participants that the Middle East would undergo democratization, he replied: 'Democracy is an effective but expensive form of class rule. It doesn't work in places where scarcity prevails.' He added that the people on the left had always viewed this as a self-evident truth 'until they became friends of civil society, in other words: until they became imbeciles'.[18]

According to Werner Pirker, a member of the Antiimperialistische Koordination Wien, critique of the 'myth of civil society' is also linked to the 'tendency of anti-globalization elites to develop a kind of parallel movement (instead of a counter movement) to global penetration. The concept of civil society – in contrast to Gramsci's position, which viewed civil society as an instance mediating between the bourgeoisie's ruling interests and the base of society – suggests a neutral space within class society, a discourse among equals. It is impossible to imagine a more radical departure from Marxist thought. The consciousness of one's own moral superiority – a consciousness that views itself as the world's conscience – combined with opinionated and self-righteous goody-goodyism and singing songs of compassion are, in fact, almost intolerable features of the new left. They say much about the origins and history of the movement: a history that did not begin in Seattle, but – intellectually at least – had its roots in the left-wing middle-class revolt of the '68 generation' (Pirker 2001).

In line with their ideological radicalism, when it comes to specific conflicts the advocates of such positions claim a 'right to resist' and uphold the legitimacy of militant (including violent) forms of protest (which are not to be confused with civil disobedience). Unlike the activists in the 'Black Block', for whom the issue is simply taken for granted, other groups start shilly-shallying when it comes to the question of violence. Trotsykist revolutionaries, for instance, try to negotiate a path between the wing that promulgates 'non-violent direct action' and the 'anarchist-influenced Black Bloc'. As both paths ostensibly lead to self-destruction, people are expected to take matters into their own hands. 'Peaceful and legal mass demonstrations' are seen as 'our goal', but only with the following proviso: 'To achieve this we need democratically controlled self-defence units that are able to offer resistance against police attacks and, at the same time, prevent a few idiots from giving the police a pretext for attacking the demo' (ibid.: 38f). These tactical suggestions notwithstanding, the overall strategy is clear: 'Fighting against the power of the capitalists with your bare hands when they are armed to the teeth is a suicidal strategy. We need to mobilise and arm a mass movement, and demobilise and disarm the enemy' (ibid.: 86).

This not only suggests a potential break with the NGOs, 'most of whom ... must be seen as parts of an extended neo-liberalised state', in any case (Hierlmeier 2002: 123). It also indicates a gulf between them and the reformist movements, which advocate offensive yet non-violent forms of protest and have shown that they can be very imaginative in the process (Graeber 2001), or they try to escape the trap of violence by explicitly demanding or passively accepting the spatial and temporal separation of various forms of protest and demonstration (as, for example, in the protests in Prague in September 2000).

Just as the militant groups sometimes offers the peaceful groups a not unwelcome 'radical flank effect',[19] the latter can in turn give the numerically weaker radicals the welcome aura of a broad-based, grass-roots movement. Consequently, both sides have an interest in avoiding sharp divisions. There are, admittedly, groups in both camps that insist on making their positions clear: on the one hand, the militants who sneer at the harmlessness of what they refer to as Latschdemos (a pejorative German word for demos where people simply go along with it with little sign of energy or enthusiasm) and, on the other hand, those who firmly advocate solving conflicts civilly and denounce what they see as senseless ritualised violence, without becoming advocates of lobbying strategies themselves.

The above shows that the debate on the content and attraction of civil society, which at first sight may be perceived as a kind of empty talk, can have very real consequences in practice. Those who approvingly appeal to civil society commit themselves explicitly or implicitly to its normative content, i.e. to 'civility', which ultimately means solving conflicts peacefully and respecting one's political opponent. On the other hand, anyone who grasps civil society as a political sedative, analogous to the role Marx assigned to religion, will be less inclined to submit to the principle (inherent in civil society) of acknowledging others and of solving conflicts by moderate means.

For all its vague non-committal character, the term civil society none the less marks a political dividing line that cannot be reduced to a simple distinction between peacefulness and violence (Reichardt 2003). First, these concepts are themselves open to interpretation and subject to semantic and normative changes. Second, one can neither ignore the fact that the state monopoly of violence has stabilized civil societies, nor that dictatorial misuse of this monopoly of violence legitimates the use of violence by civil societies as sanctioned by the Christian doctrine of tyrannicide.

Appraisal

When the Cold War ended, positions critical of capitalism found themselves on the defensive. However, due to the geostrategic absence of competition from a different system they gradually revived. It is no longer automatically assumed that anyone criticizing capitalism openly or secretly sympathized with 'real existing socialism'. Furthermore, the revival in criticism of capitalism is mainly due to the emergence of global justice groups which have presented on a global scale extensive if not undisputed evidence of the urgent need for political intervention against neo-liberalism. In this, they have found influential allies among the trade unions, the churches and progressive (and not only intellectual) elites, as well as in some governments in the North and South (Leggewie 2003).

There is a growing mood for a change in direction. Trotskyists see in the 'anti-capitalism of hundreds of thousands of youths and working-class people ... a refreshing sign after all the counterrevolutionary developments of the early 1990s' (global red nd: 6). According to the Antifaschistische Aktion Berlin: 'Placed on the agenda by rioting, discussion on the consequences of contemporary capitalist development is now experiencing a revival in many places, and not only among the left. As a consequence, the anti-globalization movement has been the first left-wing current since the collapse of the Soviet Union to succeed in challenging humanity's fateful subjection to capitalism.' None the less, the group adds the following critical comment: 'For all its heroism and impact on the media, the anti-globalization movement has come up with few new ideas since it first appeared on the scene. Its pluralism is generally celebrated as its strength; on closer inspection, however, it turns out to be a mixture of fragments of various left-wing currents that have failed' (Antifaschistische Aktion Berlin nd: 84).

The idea that the global justice movements are simply a collection of failures seems a slight exaggeration. This view ignores the influx of new and remarkably undogmatic currents in the North and the involvement of some very democratic grass-roots movements in the countries of the Southern Hemisphere. What is true, however, is that many global justice groups apparently attach little importance to theoretical analysis and, above all, to analysis of society as a whole. Nor does one see the conspicuous insignia of the radical student left of the 1960s: Marx's collected works and Mao's little red books, *Capital* courses, discussion clubs, theoretical journals and their respective circles of readers. There is also a dearth of theories of society that go beyond mere sloganeering. In any case, most contemporary left-wing theoreticians,[20] even those writing on globalization, are unknown to the majority of activists inside the mass movements critical of globalization, let alone in the NGOs. The ranks now tend to be closing on the other side. Quite a number of (old) left-wing theoreticians and political economists sense their opportunity and want to take part in the new movement. And they are doing so partly by citing familiar phrases and offering familiar solutions like those proposed by the left-Keynesian economist Jörg Huffschmid. At times, however, one is overwhelmed by a flood of new concepts (for instance, Hardt and Negri 2002), only to discover that there is little that is genuinely original behind all the murmuring and incessant name-dropping. Others offer a version of vulgar Marxism that contains a mixture of falsified history, phraseology and platitudes. A prime example of this is the book *Globalisierung, Antikapitalismus und Krieg* (global red 2001),[21] which comes from the Trotsykist camp. Despite the assurance given the reader at the end of the book that it does not have all the answers, the text is peppered with statements oozing with absolute self-certainty and promises of salvation. For example:

> The capitalist state cannot be taken over and used to introduce socialism. It must be destroyed, smashed by a revolution. There is only one way this can be done: by building an alternative power, a power based on the democratic councils of the masses chosen from delegates elected by the working class and subject to recall at all times.
>
> If the councils are to assume power, the mass of the people must be ready to fight and revolutionaries have to organise an uprising in order to disarm the exploiters and drive them from power. (ibid.: 86)

Measured against this yardstick, it would appear that everyone else on the left, with its 'professional writers from the middle classes' (ibid.: 61), were on the wrong track: reformist representatives of global justice movements such as Susan George, David C. Korten, George Montbiot, Pierre Bourdieu and Elmar Altvater, as well as figures such as Walden Bello. He is generally viewed as belonging to the radical camp of globalization critics; he has vehemently fought for the poor in the South and at least demands that the institutions of Bretton Woods should not be reformed, but dissolved or neutralized, or that their powers should be drastically curtailed (Bello 2002). Yet the ultra-leftist verdict is that 'Bello is no more anti-capitalist than Susan George', and adds: 'his petit-bourgeois alternatives divide the working classes along North–South lines and leave the real power and property in both parts of the world in the hands of big capital and its politicians' (ibid.: 74).

Even if one ignores the cruder forms of fetishizing revolution, the overall impression remains that global justice movements show no signs of having developed an elaborate, up-to-date theory or of engaging in anti-capitalist political practice. A search through countless brochures and websites would by and large unearth oft-repeated clichés. Theories are verified not by systematic empirical data but – if at all – by carefully chosen examples.

On the one hand, there is the radical fringe of the left-wing spectrum whose politics are dominated by a woolly and rather crude form of anti-capitalism. Simple slogans ('One Solution – Revolution'), the trading in political devotional objects on the fringes of demonstrations (e.g. T-shirts and flags with portraits of Che Guevara) and the idealization of resistance movements (especially the Zapatista movement MLFN, and MST, the movement of landless peasants in Brazil) reflect the powerful desire among many to stylize their own organizations into revolutionary forces. Some proud revolutionaries come to mind here, such as the British Socialist Workers Party, whose protagonist Chris Harman (2001) simply repeats well-known positions. The only new additions are concepts such as globalization and the use of gender-neutral terms, for instance. Large sections of the radical left now tend to ignore stale-sounding terms such as revolution, class consciousness and false consciousness, yet they too refuse to make an effort to develop a more forward-looking theory. The mere reference to capitalism is often seen as evidence of critical thinking, as when Fausto Bertinotti, for example, admonishes the Italian party Rifundazione Comunista: 'One cannot speak of neo-liberalism and remain silent about capitalism' (http://www.istendency.net/docs.php). There are also, however, more aggressive contributions to the debate, in which the participants accuse one another with conspicuous frequency of making a 'superficial critique of capitalism'. However, the critics' own positions, which are meant to be the embodiment of a profound theory, generally turn out to be rather superficial. Exchanges are often limited to picking out a few sentences from the work under criticism and countering them with the occasional quote from Marx to illustrate the correctness of the writer or speaker's critique (see Hanloser 2001).

Among NGOs that are not theoretically minded, one finds a wealth of literature focusing on concrete injustices, and a professionalized approach to critical writing that examines specific details in certain fields such as genetic engineering, agriculture, water, tropical wood, fair trade, and so on. The state is increasingly coming to recognize and reward this kind of specialized knowledge on specific fields, as well as organizations' readiness to co-operate and to enter into solution-centred negotiations.[22]

Caught and torn between the two sides are the groups that are pushing for radical reform. They are open and (left-wing) pluralist, and present themselves as forums, platforms and as 'an educational movement that emphasises expertise and learning through doing'.[23] They seek a path outside the Scylla of monopolization by others and the Charybdis of (self-) exclusion. Their mass basis, coupled with their ideological openness and their (in some cases) political naivety makes them attractive to small and tactically shrewd groups such as Linksruck, a German group which is close to the British Socialist Workers Party.[24] Such tendencies try to infiltrate ideologically flexible global justice organizations and networks such as Attac; once in these environments, however, they are compelled to change their discussion style. Consequently, some traditional left-wing groups (such as the Italian Rifundazione Comunista) have developed a new sensibility towards their potential allies, who adamantly reject their all too well-known avant-gardism and respond allergically to revolutionary clichés. It remains to be seen who will have the greater influence on whom. To the best of my knowledge, however, such attempts at political infiltration have not been very fruitful, at least not in Germany. Although there is no denying that there could be a split into reformers and revolutionaries in future, the strength of the critics of globalization lies in the existence of a large middle camp with broad overlaps on both sides.

What distinguishes most 'centre-left' globalization critics from the new left of the 1960s is their pragmatic attitude and endeavour to attract attention and to win over broad sections of the population. A characteristic sign of this is their fine feeling for 'political education'. The concept of civil society, whose value lies precisely in its vagueness, plays an important role here, and its use by many globalization critics reflects their desire to represent wide-ranging interests, which include those of the greater part of the (world's) population. Whereas the New Left, in best Marxist tradition, would contemptuously look down on 'bourgeois society', many globalization critics refer positively to an all-inclusive civil society, which is expected to exert pressure on 'external' actors, particularly on the state and the economy. Others, in the form of moderate NGOs, place their hopes in the state and civil society working with them to find co-operative solutions. The radical critics of globalization are alone in expressly distancing themselves from the idea of a civil society, which, in their eyes, is nothing other than a means of disguising the real, existing divisions within society.

Another point distinguishing strategically thinking minds among the reformist globalization critics from a large part of the New Left is their cautious treatment of grand theories. A large part of the radical left has abandoned the self-confident pose of the lecturer and the ambition to pronounce political truths in favour of working with others to find solutions.[25] Ulrich Brand, a member of the Bundeskoordination Internationalismus (BUKO), for example, approvingly cites the motto of the Zapatista EZLN: 'preguntando caminamos' (we advance with questions in our minds) (Brand 2003). In many cases, the departure from grand theories is also a conscious result of the decision to accept ideological pluralism, which is one of the distinguishing features of Attac, for instance.[26]

Even if there are no rigorous debates on social theory, or those that do take place involve small circles only, there are still signs that a learning process is gradually gaining ground within sections of the radical left. The left now seems to show greater tolerance towards those who think differently and less of a tendency to exclude others. Agitation undertaken with missionary zeal, fervent attempts to lecture and convert others may not have disappeared completely, but they have lost much of their former importance. Many now realize that there is little to be gained by proclaiming the 'pure doctrine' within a small circle of kindred spirits. 'If the critique of globalization is to go beyond the level of a critique and bring about some real changes, the classical left alone will not be powerful enough to achieve this, despite the clear signs of an influx of (mainly young) people into left-wing organisations and a greater interest in a fundamental critique of society' (Wahl 2003).

There is certainly an opening for 'fundamental critique of society' at present, especially given the widespread indignation and moral finger pointing at glaring real social injustices. The causes of such injustices are primarily blamed on the global economic system and the international finance regime. At present, however, there is no sign of a new theory in new (or old) bottles that could serve as a guide to broad-based political activity. Whether practice will really suffer as a result remains to be seen.

Notes

1. I wish to thank Dieter Gosewinkel and Felix Kolb for their stimulating suggestions for this chapter.
2. In this campaign, an updated critique of imperialism created a kind of masterframe to which groups active in specific areas (feminists, ecologists, human and civil rights' campaigners, etc.) are able to relate.
3. *Le Soir*, 26 September 2001, 17.
4. The term Washington Consensus stems from the US economist John Williamson who, in 1989, set out ten points (ranging from fiscal discipline to property rights) as part of a strategy for consolidating the economies of Latin America. The concept has meanwhile taken on a life of its own, independently of its creator: it is often considered synonymous with neo-liberalism and is frequently used pejoratively to brand aggressive and ruthless free-trade policies and all they imply. In their zeal, people occasionally ascribe to Williamson positions that he has never advanced in this form. Maria Mies

(2001a), for instance, claims that the first of Williamson's ten 'dogmas' states: 'The most important goal for the economy is growth. Growth creates jobs, wealth, development, equality and democracy.'

5. Until 2002, co-ordination at an all-German level was carried out under the name Bundeskonferenz entwicklungspolitischer Aktionsgruppen (BUKO). BUKO has existed since 1977 as a loose network of groups (approximately 150 in the meantime) with a decidedly left-wing orientation. It describes itself as follows: 'Whilst many groups working internationally have devoted themselves to lobbying over the past few years, BUKO continues to see its political point of reference in social movements. Grass-roots democracy is an essential part of its self conception. BUKO's activities centre on questions concerning practical perspectives in the fight against global capitalism, racism and patriarchal society' (http://www.buko.info/bulo/bulo.html). It is from this position that BUKO representatives criticise the rather vague ideological position of Attac.

6. Tute Bianche, so-called because its activists choose to dress in white overalls, formed at the beginning of the year 2000 during the course of activities directed at a deportation prison in Milan. Their appearances at various subsequent globalization protests have been quite spectacular. The activists, who turn up equipped with gasmasks, foam-rubber padding, life-jackets and tyre tubes, among other things, use their bodies antagonistically in confrontations, without, however, resorting to the standard means of brute force: such as batons, stones or even weapons (see Tute Bianche 2001).

7. This goes hand in hand with his endeavour to win over the third current, which he considers politically suspect yet nevertheless capable of learning and of entering into alliances.

8. Desai and Said (2001) provide a very different and puzzling classification; they speak of a cross-party 'movement against global capitalism' and identify four variations: 1) *isolationists* ('the only global civil society response which openly claims to be anti-globalization', e.g. Friends of the Earth, Focus on Global South, 50 Years is Enough, Walden Bello, Noam Chomsky 'and media outlets such as *Le Monde Diplomatique*'), 2) *supporters* (of global capitalism, sic), 3) *reformists* (among these they include Oxfam, Attac and Jubilee 2000) and 4) *alternatives* (Zapatistas, Adbusters, Reclaim the Streets, Naomi Klein). They confuse a number of issues here. The authors' classifications and divisions of categories are not only problematic in individual cases (e.g. they fail to see the close relationship between Attac and *Le Monde Diplomatique* and the overlap of people involved in both); they even go so far as to mention *the supporters* as a variant of the 'movement against global capitalism'. They specifically name 'the Chamber of British Industry in the UK, the American Enterprise Institute in the US, *The Economist*, *The Wall Street Journal*, the Meltzer Commission, and Thomas Friedman' (ibid.: 66).

9. Social movement researchers in particular make a distinction between genuine movement organizations (Social Movement Organizations – SMOs; Transnational Social Movement Organizations – TSMOs) and NGOs, although NGO researchers and many NGOs themselves have difficulties relating to this distinction.

10. Reactions are mixed for the simple reason that, on the one hand, the co-opting of NGO representatives signifies a certain degree of recognition of the NGOs

concerned and gives them easier access to contact partners in governments and the authorities. On the other hand, it drains the NGOs, since their partners woo experts and strategically experienced NGO representatives away from them.

11. The question of violence is still being vehemently discussed among these organizations; even so, the overwhelming majority of organisations are committed to peaceful forms of protest. Although Attac – in Germany at least – professes to be in favour of non-violent protest, some Attac members insist on subtle distinctions between 'non-violent' and 'peaceful' actions. Then there are members of Attac who do not want to distance themselves from violent groups, even though these members see themselves as non-violent. That said, the organizers of the World Social Forum in Porto Alegre in 2003, which representatives of armed groups from Latin America had hoped to attend, refused to allow these groups to participate.

12. A declaration of social movements issued at the gathering of more than 50,000 critics of globalization in Porto Alegre in February 2002, stated: 'We are a global solidarity movement united in our determination to fight against the concentration of wealth, the proliferation of poverty and inequalities and the destruction of our earth. We are constructing alternative systems and using alternative ways to promote them.' The World Social Forum itself sees itself, however, as a platform and in this capacity will not, or rather cannot, draw up any resolutions.

13. 'One can view ATTAC's analyses and proposals as a form of modernised left-wing Keynesianism' (Hierlmeier 2002: 160).

14. Conspicuous here is the carefully formulated argument, designed to attract support, expressed by members of the Bundeskoordination Internationalismus and addressed to Attac. The argument avoids any hint of a 'know-all' attitude and places its trust in collective learning processes, although it does call for greater consistency: 'On the one hand, there is the question of a confrontational attitude toward the dominant state institutions, especially the international ones. This means formulating demands that intensify certain contradictions' (Brand and Wissen 2003).

15. Resolution of the anti-capitalist youth in Porto Alegre (Eine andere Welt ist nur durch die Zerstörung des Kapitalismus möglich! [A Different World Can be Created only by Destroying Capitalism]), reproduced in global red (2001: 32–34).

16. The declaration issued during the Seattle protests in 1999 is quite revealing: 'We salute those who came to Seattle to be counted in the call for the involvement of Civil Society in assessing the impact of the WTO on people, governments and the environment.'

17. Ebermann was originally a member of the Kommunistischer Bund (Communist Alliance) and later of the Grün-Alternative Liste (coalition of Greens and Alternative List, GAL) in Hamburg. After they turned to *realpolitik* he left the GAL and has been working as a publicist and lecturer ever since.

18. Cited by *Tageszeitung* of 15 February 2003, 34 ('Nicht nur linker Mainstream' [Not only the Mainstream Left]).

19. 'Radical groups may bring about a greater level of responsiveness to the claims of the moderates, either by making the latter appear more "reasonable"

or by creating a crisis which can be solved by the lesser concessions required by the moderates' (Haines 1988: 269).

20. For a brief survey of some of the relevant authors, see Hierlmeier (2002a).
21. By and large this is a translation of the English brochure *The Anti-capitalist Movement: A Guide to Action.*
22. Co-operation has come about in particular with 'progressive' national governments (e.g. in Scandinavia and the small island states) and a few international committees (e.g. CEPAL, the UN Economic Commission for Latin America and the Caribbean as well as parts of the World Bank). Many critics of globalization also place great hopes, which are the subject of internal controversy, in the EU as one of the 'civilizing forces' in world politics.
23. Cf. Attac Deutschland's self-description in the supplement to *Tageszeitung*, 19 July 2002.
24. Linksruck, which arose from an eponymous Jusos (SPD young socialist organization) network, is – like the Socialist Workers Party – a member of the umbrella organization, the International Socialist Tendency (IST), which sees itself in the tradition of the Trotskyist Fourth International.
25. A detailed analysis of the political conception and framing of the EZLN ends in a general summary: 'The current phase of trans-nationalization of the Left is much more heterogeneous than previous phases. This also implies a clear movement away from any notions of vanguardism' (Olesen 2002: 227).
26. 'Convinced Christians see in Attac an organisation of both environmentalists and anti-capitalists ... Preserving this ideological pluralism is a key to Attac's success. For only in this way is it possible work together with so many different people and organisations' (Eskola and Kolb 2002: 207f.)

References

Aguiton, Christophe (2003) Die Sozialforen sind ein Markt der Ideen. Interview mit Christophe Aguiton, *INKONTA-Brief*, Jg. 23, H. 123: 11.

Andretta, Massimiliano, Donatella della Porta, Lorenzo Mosca and Herbert Reiter (2003) *No Global – New Global. Identität und Strategien der Antiglobalisierungsbewegung* (Frankfurt am Main: Campus).

Antifaschistische Aktion Berlin (ed.) (nd) *Global Resistance* (Berlin: Eigenverlag Antifaschistische Aktion Berlin).

Bello, Walden (2002) 'Saurierfonds', in Jerry Mander and Edward Goldsmith (eds.) *Schwarzbuch Globalisierung* (Munich: Riemann), pp. 202–208.

Brand, Ulrich (2003) Fragend geht's voran. Wie die Bewegung auf den Begriff kommt, in Wo steht die Bewegung? Eine Zwischenbilanz der Globalisisierungskritik. Sonderheft der *blätter des informationszentrums 3. welt*, Ausgabe 265: 54–55.

Brand, Ulrich and Michael Brie (2003) 'Was ist uns Porto Alegre?' Sonderheft des *FREITAG*, 7 February.

Brand, Ulrich and Markus Wissen (2003) Zwischen Staatsreformismus und Herrschaftskritik. Ambivalenzen im Politikverständnis von Attac, *INKONTA-Brief*, 23(123): 18–19.

Canadian Security Intelligence Service (2000) Anti-Globalization – A Spreading Phenomenon. Report, 2000/08, http://www.csis-scrs.gc.ca./eng./miscdocs/200008e.html.

Chomsky, Noam (2000) *Profit over People. Neoliberalismus und globale Weltordnung* (Hamburg and Vienna: Europa Verlag).

Desai, Meghnad and Yahia Said (2001) The New Anti-Capitalist Movement: Money and Global Civil Society, in Helmut Anheier, Marlies Glasius and Mary Kaldor (eds.) *Global Civil Society 2001* (Oxford: Oxford University Press), pp. 51–78.

Eskola, Kaisa and Felix Kolb (2002) Attac – Globalisierung ist kein Schicksal, in Christiane Frantz and Annette Zimmer (eds.) *Zivilgesellschaft international. Alte und neue NGOs* (Opladen: Leske & Budrich), pp. 199–212.

Fues, Thomas and Hamm, Brigitte I. (eds.) (2001) *Die Weltkonferenzen der 90er Jahre: Baustellen für Global Governance* (Bonn: J. H. W. Dietz).

George, Susan (1999) *A Short History of Neo-liberalism: Twenty Years of Elite Economics and Emerging Opportunities for Structural Change*, http://www.millenium-round.org/.

George, Susan (2001) Another World is Possible, in *Dissent*, http://www.Dissentmagazine.org/archive/wi01/george/shtml.

Gerhards, Jürgen (1993) *Neue Konfliktlinien in der öffentlichen Mobilisierung. Eine Fallstudie* (Opladen: Westdeutscher Verlag).

Gerhards, Jürgen and Dieter Rucht (1992) Mesomobilization: Organizing and Framing in Two Protest Campaigns in West Germany, *American Journal of Sociology*, 98(3): 555–595.

Global Red (2001) *Globalisierung, Antikapitalismus und Krieg. Ursprünge und Perspektiven einer Bewegung* (Berlin: Verlag Martin Mitterhauser).

Goldsmith, Edward (2002) Entwicklung des Kolonialismus', in Jerry Mander and Edward Goldsmith (eds.) *Schwarzbuch Globalisierung* (Munich: Riemann), pp. 33–57.

Graeber, David (2001) The Globalization Movement: Some Points of Clarification, in *Items & Issues* (published by the Social Research Council), 2(3–4), pp. 12–14.

Gret, Marion and Yves Sintomer (2002) *Porto Alegre. L'espoir d'une autre démocratie* (Paris: La Découverte).

Grigat, Stephan (2001) Idealistische Weltmarktkritik und globale Hexenmeister, in *Jungle World* 27/2001, http://www.cafecritiuqw.priv/at.pdf.

Haines, Herbert H. (1988) *Black Radicals and the Civil Rights Mainstream, 1954–1970* (Knoxville: University of Tennessee Press).

Hanloser, Gerhard (2001) Geist gegen Bewegung, in *Jungle World*, 28, http:www.nadir.org/nadir/periodika/jungle world/_2001/28/05a.htm.

Hardt, Michael and Tonio Negri (2002) *Empire. Die neue Weltordnung* (Frankfurt am Main: Campus).

Harman, Chris (2002) *Antikapitalismus – Theorie und Praxis* (Eng. orig. 2000) (Frankfurt am Main: edition aurora).

Heinrich, Michael (nd) Entfesselter Kapitalismus? Zur Kritik der Globalisierungskritik, in Antifaschistische Aktion Berlin (ed.) *Global Resistance* (Berlin: Eigenverlag Antifaschistische Aktion Berlin), pp. 18–23.

Hierlmeier, Josef (Moe) (2002) *Internationalismus. Eine Einführung in die Ideengeschichte des Internationalismus – von Vietnam bis Genua* (Stuttgart: Schmetterling Verlag).

Hierlmeier, Moe (2002a) Die Konjunktur der Krise. Ein Crashkurs über neuere Kapitalismustheorien, in Wo steht die Bewegung? Eine Zwischenbilanz der

Globalisiserungskritik. Sonderheft der *blätter des informationszentrums 3. welt*, Ausagbe 265: 30–33.

Kolb, Felix (2005) *The Impact of Transnational Protest on Social Movement Organizations: Mass Media and the Making of ATTAC Germany*, in Donatella della Porta and Sidney Tarrow (eds.) *Transnational Protest and Global Activism* (Lanham, Boulder and New York: Rowman & Littlefield), pp. 95–120.

Leggewie, Claus (2003) *Die Globalisierung und ihre Gegner* (Munich: C. H. Beck).

Mies, Maria (2001) *Globalisierung von unten: Der Kampf gegen die Herrschaft der Konzerne* (Berlin: Rotbuch).

Mies, Maria (2001a) *Globalisierung von unten, Widerstand und neue Perspektiven*. Rede auf dem 29. Evangelischen Kirchentag in Frankfurt am Main, htttp://www.ikvu.de/kirchentag/mies.html.

Olesen, Thomas (2002) Long Distance Zapatismo. Globalization and the Construction of Solidarity. Unpublished PhD dissertation, Department of Political Science, University of Aarhus, Denmark.

Pianta, Mario (2001) Parallel Summits of Global Civil Society, in Helmut Anheier, Marlies Glasius and Mary Kaldor (eds.) *Global Civil Society 2001* (Oxford: Oxford University Press), pp. 169–194.

Pirker, Werner (2001) Die Bewegung gegen die Globalisierung und das Elend ihrer liberalen Interpretation, *Junge Welt*, 9 August; see also: http://www.kommunisten-online.de/aktuelles.htm.

Reichardt, Sven (2003) Zivilgesellschaft und Gewalt. Einige konzeptionelle Über-legungen aus historischer Sicht, in Dieter Gosewinkel et al. (eds.) *Zivilgesellschaft – National und Transnational* (Berlin: edition sigma), pp. 61–81.

Roth, Roland (2001) NGO und transnationale soziale Bewegungen: Akteure einer 'Weltzivilgesellschaft'? in Ulrich Brand, Alex Demirovic, Christoph Görg and Joachim Hirsch (eds.) *Nichtregierungsorganisationen in der Transformation des Staates* (Münster: Westfälisches Dampfboot), pp. 43–63.

Rucht, Dieter (2001) Transnationaler politischer Protest im historischen Längsschnitt, in Ansgar Klein et al. (eds.) *Politische Partizipation im Zeitalter der Globalisierung* (Opladen: Leske & Budrich), pp. 77–96.

Rucht, Dieter (2002) Rückblicke und Ausblicke auf die globalisierungskritischen Bewegungen, in Heike Walk and Nele Boehme (eds.) *Globaler Widerstand. Internationale Netzwerke auf der Suche nach Alternativen im globalen Kapitalismus* (Münster: Westfälisches Dampfboot), pp. 57–82.

Rucht, Dieter (2003) Social Movements Challenging Neo-liberal Globalization, in Pedro Ibarra (ed.) *Social Movements and Democracy* (New York: Palgrave Macmillan), pp. 211–228.

Rucht, Dieter (2003a) Media Strategies and Media Resonance in Transnational Protest Campaigns. Paper presented at the Conference 'Transnational Processes and Social Movements', Villa Serbelloni, Bellagio, 22–26 July.

Rucht, Dieter (2004) The Quadruple 'A': Media Strategies of Protest Movements since the 1960s, in Wim van de Donk et al. (eds.) *Cyber Protest: New Media, Citizens and Social Movements* (London: Routledge), pp. 29–56.

Schulz, Martin (1998) Collective Action across Border: Opportunity Structures, Network Capacities, and Communicative Praxis in the Age of Advanced Globalization, in *Sociological Perspectives*, 41(3): 587–616.

Smith, Jackie (2001) Made in (Corporate) America: Looking Behind the Anti-Globalization Label. Unpublished manuscript.

Smith, Jackie (2001) Globalizing Resistance: The Battle of Seattle and the Future of Social Movements, *Mobilization*, 6(1): 1–19.

Thomas, Janet (2000) *The Battle in Seattle: The Story Behind and Beyond the WTO Demonstrations* (Golden, CO: Fulcrum).

Tute Bianche (2001) Die 'Tute Bianche'. Interview mit Chiara Cassurino (Genua) und Federico Martelloni (Bologna), in *Arranca!* 22 (Summer), http://aranca.nadir.org/artikel.

Wahl, Peter (2002) Seattle, Genua ... und jetzt Florenz. Eine Bilanz des Europäischen Sozialforums in Florenz. Unpublished manuscript.

Wahl, Peter (2003) In den Zwickmühlen des Erfolgs. Eine Bilanz des Dritten Weltsozialforums in Porto Alegre. Unpublished manuscript.

Willems, Ulrich and Thomas von Winter (eds.) (2000) *Politische Repräsentation schwacher Interessen* (Opladen: Leske & Budrich).

Wissen, Markus (nd) Zwischen Dialog und Staatskritik. Akteure und Politikansätze in der internationalen Protestbewegung, in Antifaschistische Aktion Berlin (ed.) *Global Resistance* (Berlin: Antifaschistische Aktion Berlin), pp. 12–17.

7
Global Democratic Protest: The Chiapas Connection[1]

Thomas Olesen

Since their uprising in 1994, the Zapatistas in Chiapas, Mexico have been an important and globally recognized source of inspiration in the formulation of a democratic critique of neo-liberalism. This chapter illuminates the radical democratic character of the Zapatistas' social and political struggle on the local and national levels of Chiapas and Mexico and it discusses how the Zapatista democratic vision is applied and visible in the work of political activists outside Mexico.

Since the so-called Battle in Seattle in late 1999, scholars, activists and journalists have 'invented' a new phenomenon: the global justice and solidarity movement.[2] I say 'invented' because this movement cannot be fixed in time or place. It has no recognized leaders, no manifesto and no common strategies. Is it not almost contradictory, then, to insist that something like a movement exists? Not quite. Joseph R. Gusfield (1981: 326) once remarked that 'a social movement occurs when people are conscious that a movement is occurring'. From this perspective social movements become fluid phenomena, a social current rather than concrete organizations.[3] This is not simply an exercise in conceptual definition. A fluid conception of movements requires us to ask an extremely important question: what holds the movement together, despite the lack of common leaders and strategies? The question is important for two reasons: first, it promises to take us to the core of the phenomenon we are studying; and second, it gives us a chance to diagnose some broader social developments that point beyond the movement itself. The potential of a fluid view, as Gusfield (1981: 323) sees it, is precisely that it is much more 'alive to the larger contexts of change'.

If we look at this larger context today we find a fundamental struggle over the meaning of democracy (Olesen 2004). This struggle is evident in the global justice and solidarity movement. In other words, the 'something' that holds it together, however loosely, is a quest for more and better democracy to confront neo-liberal globalization. I am not alone in this observation. In fact, it is a key point in most accounts of the movement (e.g. Klein 2001; Smith 2001; Ross 2003; Hardt and Negri 2004; Rucht in this volume). Many of these authors also mention how Mexico's Zapatistas have been an important source of inspiration in the formulation of a democratic critique of neo-liberal globalization. Still, none of them pays more than passing attention to the Zapatista vision of democracy and how it overlaps with the global justice and solidarity movement. The aim of this chapter is to provide a more systematic analysis of these issues. I hope to accomplish two things. First, I shall try to illuminate the radical democratic character of the Zapatistas' social and political struggle in Chiapas and Mexico. This discussion takes place in the first section. Second, since the Zapatistas both reflect and inspire democratic concerns in the global justice and solidarity movement, a closer examination of their democratic vision can improve our under-standing of what democratic protest today actually means and what its sources are. This is the topic of the second section. I conclude with some critical remarks about the potential and future of democratic protest after 9/11, as well as about the internal democratic problems that exist in the global justice and solidarity movement.

The Zapatistas and social change: from revolutionary rhetoric to democracy

The Zapatistas have undergone an enormous transformation since the early days of its armed uprising in Chiapas in 1994.[4] In their first public communiqués (e.g. EZLN 1994) they threatened to march on the capital to bring down the government. This seemed to confirm what the weapons and revolutionary attire evident in the first images of the upris-ing suggested; that the Zapatistas were only the last incarnation in Latin America's long history of armed uprisings. But there was something different about them; or at least they became different. For within a few months of the uprising the Zapatistas changed tack, now speaking of democracy and civil society as the engine of social and political change. Since then the armed aspect has played a more symbolic role and today the Zapatistas are best seen as a political movement struggling on the level of words and ideas rather than on the level of armed confrontation (Castañeda 1995; Kampwirth 1996). The combination of armed struggle and democracy may appear to be an oxymoron. This enticing paradox has led Jorge G. Castañeda (1995) to label the Zapatistas armed reformists and Alain Touraine (1996) to refer to Subcomandante Marcos, spokesman and leader of the Zapatistas, as an armed democrat. These characterizations all make implicit references to the strategies adopted by traditional armed movements in Latin America and elsewhere, a tradition from which the Zapatistas consider themselves to be significantly different. The Zapatistas' transformation since the 1994 uprising has, as I have already more than suggested, been evident in their adoption of a democratic discourse. But in what way does their democratic discourse differ from official interpretations of democracy? I propose that we speak of the Zapatista democratic vision as a vision of radical democracy and that we contrast this with the liberal vision of democracy espoused by most of the world's governments, including the Mexican. Before I go on to the analysis of Zapatista democracy I pause to clarify what is meant by radical democracy.

Radical democracy: three lines of thinking

It is possible to synthesize at least three broad lines of thinking on radical democracy: the broadening, delegation and deepening of democracy. The broadening of democracy refers to the extension of democratic principles to more and more societal areas. This perspective has two dimensions: it denotes a situation in which the economy is under some degree of democratic control (Wood 1995; Fotopoulos 1997); as well as a situation with an element of democratic control in all areas of decision-making (Mouffe 1992, 1993). The delegation of democracy refers to the creation of autonomous spaces with a level of authority to govern independently from the state. This view mainly entails the aspirations of minorities who feel excluded or repressed by the state (Esteva 1999, 2001). The deepening of democracy refers to the empowerment of civil society through social action. There are two aspects here. First, it points to a normative ideal where an active, organized and politicized civil society is seen as a vital part of democracy (Lummis 1996).[5] Second, it rests on a notion of civil society as a sphere penetrated by power relations (Gramsci 1971) or by the colonization of system rationalities (Habermas 1987); a situation which can only be changed through social action at the level of civil society.

Democracy in the radical perspective is generally seen as an unfinished project and as something obtainable only through social action and struggle. Notions of radical democracy are therefore highly political as they denote a critique (but not rejection) of existing liberal democratic arrangements and their focus on elections and institutions. As such, the idea of radical democracy clashes with any proclamation of liberal democracy as the end of history and places itself within a leftist political framework. This will become clear in the following analysis of the Zapatistas, which is structured by the three-component framework of radical democracy laid out above.

'To rule by obeying': the Zapatistas and the broadening of democracy

The Zapatistas have a dual relationship with democracy – they distinguish between two democratic levels, one based in civil society the other in the political institutions. Shortly before the presidential elections in July 2000, the Zapatistas (EZLN 2000) issued a communiqué outlining this view:

> For the Zapatistas, democracy is much more than the electoral competition or the alternation of power. ... Therefore we say that electoral democracy does not exhaust democracy, but it is an important part of it. ... We want to find a politics that goes from the bottom to the top, one in which 'to rule by obeying' is more than a slogan. ... In the Zapatista idea, democracy is something that is constructed from below and with everyone ... [6]

As demonstrated by the quote, the Zapatistas have not renounced electoral democracy. Their definition revolves around the concept 'to rule by obeying'. This vision is influenced by the traditions of decision-making within indigenous communities (Harvey 1998: 208). The type of democracy enacted in the Zapatista indigenous communities is different from that offered by liberal democracy. This is especially marked in the way democracy is based on continuous consultation and debate aimed at the establishment of consensus. Subcomandante Marcos (Le Bot 1997: 281), however, acknowledges that this vision has its limitations: 'I think that this form of democracy is only possible in community life. It works in an indigenous community ... but I do not think that it is transferable or generalizable to other contexts, for example the urban, or to larger levels, state or national.'[7] However, he also notes how some of the basic ideas of this vision should find their way to the national level. In an interview with Marta Durán de Huerta (1999: 271–2), Marcos describes the idea of 'to rule by obeying' and its implications for democracy beyond the community level. This would involve a system allowing for a permanent evaluation of a government's work and entail the possibility of reversing political decisions if they are not made in accordance with the mandates given by the electorate.

The notion of 'to rule by obeying' is mainly tied to the relationship between citizens and government. But the idea of broadening democracy also moves the question of democracy beyond the purely political and into the realm of the economy. This is most clearly seen in the Zapatista interpretation of neo-liberalism as a development model at odds with democracy:

> The Zapatista uprising contributed to an expansion of democracy in the domain of political society but also beyond it, into civil society and the cultural sphere. In addition, it has sought to expand democratization to the economic realm in order to address the social costs of neoliberal market reforms. ... The exacerbation of socio-economic disparities following free-market reforms provoked the EZLN to question the relationship between economic marginalization and political exclusion and the extent to which this hampers democracy. (Gilbreth and Otero 2001: 24–5)

The Zapatistas, then, do not make a watertight distinction between political and civil rights and social and economical rights, as is the case in most versions of liberal democracy. Social and economical marginalization is dehumanizing and limits the opportunities to make meaningful use of civil and political rights.

Indigenous autonomy: the Zapatistas and the delegation of democracy

Lynn Stephen (2002) has summed up the main pillars of democracy in Zapatista communities in the following way:

- 'to rule by obeying', that is, to govern through listening, obeying the ideas of the community;
- consultation with base communities through community assemblies in which everyone is supposed to have an opportunity to speak, including women and children;
- the use of local and regional councils to communicate opinions formed at the community level;
- respect for difference, that is, the ability to reach solutions that allow for individual variation and difference of views;
- governance as service.

To be a member of a community, one provides service through serving the community. The major efforts of the Zapatistas have gone in the direction of securing a degree of autonomy for the indigenous people in order to establish a legal recognition of these practices of government and decision-making. It is important to advance at least two qualifications in regard to the Zapatistas' quest for autonomy for the indigenous people. First, although the Zapatistas' demands echo the wishes of a large part of the indigenous population, they do not represent the aspirations of all Mexico's 56 ethnic groups. Second, the search for autonomy should not be equated with a search for secession from the Mexican state (Esteva 2001). The Zapatistas have an eminently national character and constantly engage in debates concerning the appropriation of national Mexican symbols and Mexican history (Olesen 2005a: ch. 6).

The Zapatista aspiration to autonomy has revolved round a proposal prepared in late 1996 by COCOPA (Commission of Concordance and Pacification), a forum made up by Mexican legislators. The COCOPA proposal was an attempt to revive the peace process that had stalled since the signing of the so-called San Andrés Accords between the Zapatistas and the Mexican government in February 1996. The negotiations began in March 1995, and were encoded in the Law of Dialogue, Conciliation and Dignified Peace in Chiapas, which established the Zapatistas as a legitimate social actor with legitimate demands. The COCOPA proposal built on the San Andrés Accords, and was accepted by the Zapatistas in 1996, but rejected by President Ernesto Zedillo (1994–2000). The COCOPA issue reappeared in the new political climate following the PAN (National Action Party) and Vicente Fox's accession to presidential power in December 2000. Fox put the question of indigenous rights high on his agenda and sent the COCOPA proposal to congress. The Zapatistas followed up on this by trying to generate a public debate on the issue of indigenous rights and the COCOPA proposal. This resulted in the March for Indigenous Dignity in early 2001, which ended in Mexico City and with Zapatista commanders delivering speeches in the Congress. However, the expectations and awareness raised by the march and the new political signals from the Fox government were disappointed when Congress approved a proposal that differed significantly from the COCOPA proposal. The proposal led the Zapatistas (EZLN 2001) to break off any contacts with the government until the original COCOPA proposal is constitutionally recognized.[8] Despite the fact that indigenous autonomy has not yet been enshrined *de jure* in the Constitution in the form desired by the Zapatistas, the formation of autonomous municipalities in Chiapas means that *de facto* autonomy is currently being practised in a number of areas with Zapatista influence, albeit in a climate of constant military and paramilitary conflict and violence.

The empowerment of civil society: the Zapatistas and the deepening of democracy

The concept of civil society is vital to understanding the Zapatistas' radical democratic vision. The focus on civil society in radical democracy differs significantly from the role accorded to civil society in liberal democracy. In order to bring out these differences, I suggest (with Jean L. Cohen and Andrew Arato 1992), that we apply a distinction between civil society as respectively the terrain and the target of social movements. The main difference between liberal and radical democracy lies in the fact that the latter views civil society not only as a terrain, but also as a target of social action. This entails an emphasis on the politicization of civil society. The Zapatistas have engaged in a number of activities aimed at civil society.[9] Although these initiatives have had different objectives, they have one in common; to activate and politicize civil society by creating public space. In the these activities, the Zapatistas have either served as a facilitator for a meeting between Mexican and non-Mexican civil society actors, invited civil society actors to vote on different issues or invited civil society actors to participate in events sponsored by the Zapatistas. On the one hand, these initiatives have aimed at giving voice to social forces excluded by the political system in Mexico. Their demands, however, do not stop there, but strive to forge a more fundamental change in the relationship between those who govern and those who are governed:

> Rather than making war to take power and impose its vision from above, the EZLN sought to open political spaces in which new actors in civil society could press for democracy and social justice from below. ... In Gramsci's terms, the EZLN changed its strategy from a 'war of movements' challenging state power through the force of arms to a 'war of positions' contesting the moral and intellectual leadership of Mexico's ruling class. (Gilbreth and Otero 2001: 8, 19)

Whereas a war of movement, according to Gramsci (1971), may be fought by a small number of rebels, a war of positions involves a larger portion of society. The Zapatistas' strategy would not, in other words, have been conceivable without the participation of a wide range of civil society actors. We cannot, however, apply Gramsci's framework without some qualifications. Gramsci was basically a Marxist revolutionary who saw the working class as the leader of a new counter-hegemony (Laclau and Mouffe 1985: 69). In the context of the Zapatistas, Gramsci's thinking may be more usefully applied along the lines of Cohen and Arato's (1992) concept of self-limiting radicalism. Social movements that display a self-limiting radical character have abandoned the revolutionary aspirations inherent in Gramsci's thinking and do not consider the working class (or other classes) the natural leaders in social struggle. The Zapatista strategy of self-limiting radicalism renounces any role of leadership or vanguard. Instead, the Zapatistas engage in a formulation of the relationship between particularity and universality. This relationship is central to the notion of radical democracy as advanced by Laclau (1990, 1996) and Mouffe (1992, 1993), whose emphasis on plurality and particularity does not entail a rejection of universalism. Difference is acknowledged and accepted on the grounds that respect for difference rests on a notion of universality that grants everyone the right to be different (Laclau 1996: 49). This universal right to be different should, according to Laclau and Mouffe, be continuously contested and constructed through a democratic matrix. The empowerment of particularities and identities through a democratic matrix is at the heart of the Zapatista radical democratic vision.

The global justice and solidarity movement: exploring the Chiapas connection

So far, the discussion has focused on the national Mexican context. In this section, I turn to the implications and traces of the Zapatista radical democratic vision outside of Mexico. The centrality of democracy in the Zapatista struggle and in the global justice and solidarity movement must be understood in its historical context. The end of the Cold War did two things for radical activism: on the one hand, it created an identity crisis, a vacuum in which radical politics had to be redefined, a redefinition which, I argue, has taken place around the concept of democracy; on the other, it provided social movements with new political opportunities.[10] The Zapatistas have not been the main authors of the redefinition processes on the left following the Cold War, but they have, as most observers agree, played a significant role, not least because they appeared at an early point when the world (and the left) was still trying to find their feet after the momentous changes in the late 1980s and early 1990s. In particular, the Intercontinental Encounter for Humanity and against Neo-liberalism convened by the Zapatistas in 1996 and held in Zapatista territory became an important point of reference and inspiration for many of the activists who later became involved in the global justice and solidarity movement. Before I discuss how and where this inspiration can be seen, I will comment on the Cold War as a new political opportunity for democratic protest.

The end of the Cold War: a new opportunity

The new opportunities arising from the end of the Cold War resulted from the cessation of the bipolar conflict. The Cold War had had a highly restrictive effect as authorities interpreted the nature of contentious social action through a bipolar logic. This, in turn, provided authorities with legitimacy and a wide room for manoeuvre in dealing with instances of contention. Especially, the margins for where social ideas and actions were considered to be Soviet and socialist-inspired were rather narrow. This also significantly limited the reach of the concept of democracy. During the Cold War, the West tolerated authoritarian and non-democratic governments as long as they were seen as a bulwark against the spread of socialist ideas (Shaw 2000: 135). Evidently, the end of the Cold War to a large extent eliminated the legitimacy of this rationale (Donnelly 1993: 133) (although there are signs, which I discuss in the conclusion, that the recent War against Terror has led to its resurrection). This argument suggests that it is now possible for contentious social movements to engage in struggles over the definition of democracy without being categorized as Soviet sympathizers and legitimate targets of repression. In other words, authoritarian regimes are having an increasingly hard time, as they can no longer refer to the imperative of the Cold War as a source of legitimacy. In contrast, contentious social movements have access to a large number of global and regional institutions that serve as guarantors of democracy and human rights and may be used as allies by social movements that criticize, for example, the conditions of democracy in their home countries (Shaw 2000: 167).

Direct democracy and decentralization: the Zapatista influence

The influence of Zapatista ideas is primarily visible in the global solidarity network that coalesced around the Zapatistas in the mid- to late 1990s. In this section I focus on this solidarity network but, as will be evident in this section and the next, the Zapatista solidarity network is strongly entwined with the global justice and solidarity movement. I have already referred to the importance of the intercontinental encounter in 1996 in spurring the diffusion of Zapatista ideas to settings outside of Mexico. At the closing ceremony of the intercontinental encounter in Chiapas in 1996, the Zapatistas presented their vision of global struggle against neo-liberalism as a network without hierarchies or leaders (EZLN 1996). This approach is seen by the majority of activists as an important value in itself, something which is also reflected in the way they view the global Zapatista solidarity network. In the words of an anonymous interviewee and activist, diversity within the global network supporting the Zapatistas is viewed as a quality, not a problem:

> There are groups with differing politics and projects, but I don't see any serious divisions that hamper anyone's work. For example, some organizations are more Zapatista-centred and others are more church-centred (they support the diocese in San Cristóbal and indigenous communities, not the armed struggle). I think this is due to the loose nature of the network and the diverse nature of solidarity groups' responses to the situation in Chiapas. This bottom-up type of organization is actually encouraged by the Zapatistas and allows for diverse types of work with less conflict.

Put differently, the relationships between groups, organizations and individuals participating in global struggles against neo-liberalism and in the Zapatista solidarity network are relationships between independent and autonomous actors who share concerns but are not subsumed under the leadership of one or more specific actor. The vision of organization as a loose network of autonomous groups is a common normative trait in much contemporary protest activities. This approach has visible similarities with the Zapatistas' radical democratic vision discussed earlier. David Martin (2000), a Denver-based Zapatista solidarity activist, suggests that one of the inspirations coming from the Zapatistas to activists outside Mexico lies exactly in their emphasis on direct democracy and grass-roots organization:

> with the example of the Zapatistas you can talk about grassroots democracy and local control and local democratic practices … and I think that is what we are trying to do here in terms of organizing coalitions for economic justice, we are saying, we need to get the power into the hands of grassroots organizations and have more democratic forms of government … what we are trying to do is create … grassroots democratic structures so that we can start building

momentum to have more influence politically, but also practice democracy amongst our own groups before we try to exercise power.

Kerry Appel (2000) of the Human Bean Company in Denver echoes Martin by pointing out how it is the democratic organizing efforts of the Zapatistas rather than the armed aspect that lies at the core of the organization:

[A] lot of people come to the Zapatista struggle because they are enamored with this idea of armed indigenous resistance, they want to go down and volunteer, they want to go down and join, they want to pick up a gun, but the guns have almost nothing to do with the Zapatista struggle, they haven't fired a shot since January 12th 1994 ... but the main activity of the Zapatistas is just organizing, organizing, organizing, locally, nationally, and internationally, talking, having *consultas*, having *encuentros* ... the hard boring stuff, so a lot of the people go to the Zapatistas because of this glamour, and they will say, is there any way I can join the Zapatistas, I want to run around the mountains with a mask on and a gun, and the Zapatistas will say no, if you want to help the Zapatistas, go home and fight for justice in your own lands, because if there is justice in your own lands, there will be justice here as well because it is all the same struggle.

The last part of the quote directs our attention to the widespread belief that solidarity with the Zapatistas involves radical democratic organizing for social change in the local and national settings of solidarity activists. The Texas-based organization Acción Zapatista has drawn strongly on the Zapatista radical democratic vision in an attempt to apply the Zapatista idea of *encuentro* (encounter) to the local setting of Austin. Manuel Callahan (2000) of Acción Zapatista explains the inspiration from the Zapatistas as follows:

[W]e wanted to introduce this whole strategy of *coyuntura* ... it is a strategy of analysis that allows for everybody in the room to make a contribution ... they use it in Chiapas all over the place ... and the other thing we want to introduce is the notion of councils, which we weren't very clear of, we had this vague notion of how councils were operating in Chiapas ... we were still having trouble getting some really good material on how the Zapatistas actually organized themselves and used education as a vehicle to organize all the levels of

the Zapatistas ... so we are kind of testing it on ourselves, experiment-
ing what we vaguely have an sense of is happening in Chiapas ... .

As this quote shows, the Zapatista radical democratic vision is considered
to originate in the decision-making structures of the indigenous communities of Chiapas. In other words, the perception of democracy in the
indigenous communities seems to fit well with the anarchist and new
social movement currents already present in activist circles, especially in
the US and Europe (I discuss these currents further in the next section).
It is worth recalling here my reservation that democratic processes in the
indigenous communities influenced by the Zapatistas do not necessarily
reflect decision-making practices in other indigenous communities. At
the same time, and as suggested by the quote, the understanding of democratic practices in indigenous communities is not always substantial,
and information on how democracy actually works in the Zapatista communities is scant. What is of interest here, however, is not whether the
Zapatista and indigenous inspiration for radical democratic activities is
rooted in perfect knowledge of the way democracy works in Chiapas. The
important issue is the fact that the Zapatista and indigenous form of
democracy has become a symbol of radical democracy beyond Mexico's
borders.

Democracy in the global justice and solidarity movement: reformists and anarchists

The discussion has demonstrated areas in which the influence of the
Zapatistas radical democratic vision is directly visible in the actions and
ideas of social actors outside Mexico, but especially those involved in
solidarity activities related to the Zapatistas. In the following I broaden
the view to the global justice and solidarity movement. The aim is not
to so much show direct application of Zapatista ideas, but rather to establish an argument pointing to similarities between the Zapatista radical
democratic vision and those that guide political action within the global
justice and solidarity movement.

Considering the variety of actors and purposes in the global justice
and solidarity movement it may seem imprudent to propose any similarities. Nevertheless, and in line with what was said in the introduction,
I contend that the struggle over definitions of democracy constitutes
such a unifying factor. This view is echoed by Smith (2001: 16):

If one had to identify a common thread among the demands of
activists in this movement, it would be a demand for democracy.

As governments seek to coordinate policies at the global level, they have systematically excluded ever greater numbers of people from decision-making. Against this exclusion, activists call for greater access to information about the free trade agreements that governments are negotiating. Many were surprised to learn that even their elected legislators could not obtain a copy of the negotiating text for the Free Trade Area of the Americas (only a heavily censored version of the text was released, months after the Québec summit). These agreements have an enormous impact on everyday life in local communities, and so the members of these communities are beginning to demand a say in their negotiation.

This interpretation is largely shared by Lori Wallach, one of the key figures in the protests in Seattle in 1999. In an interview with Moisés Naím (2000) of *Foreign Policy*, Wallach suggests the following diagnosis and cure for the democratic deficit in the institutions that embody neo-liberal policies, for example the WTO and the IMF:

> There would be a global regime of rules that more than anything create the political space for the kinds of value decisions that mechanisms like the WTO now make, at a level where people living with the results can hold the decision makers accountable. Right now, there are decisions, value-subjective decisions, being shifted into totally unaccountable, international realms where, if the decision is wrong, there's no way to fix it.

This emphasis on the extension of democracy as a social change strategy is also reflected in the ideas that have inspired the World Social Forum held since 2001. The forums are open to everyone who is critical of neo-liberalism, and in many ways they continue the ideas and spirit of the intercontinental encounter held in Chiapas in 1996. The relationship is evident in the guiding principles of the World Social Forum (2001):

> The World Social Forum is a plural, diversified, non-confessional, non-governmental and non-party space that, in a decentralized, networked fashion, interrelates organizations and movements engaged in concrete action at levels from the local to the international to build another world. ... The World Social Forum asserts democracy as the avenue to resolving society's problems politically. As a meeting place, it is open to the pluralism and to the diversity of activities and ways of engaging of the organizations and movements that decide to participate in it, as well as the diversity of gender, race, ethnicity, and culture.

These three quotes partly echo the Zapatistas' demands for a democracy built on the principle of 'to rule by obeying'; that is, a democracy with less distance between those who govern and those who are governed and affected by political decisions, and with a more effective democratic control over the market. This comparison must be qualified in a number of ways. First, we should remember that the Zapatistas have mainly used the concept of 'to rule by obeying' in the national context of Mexico. Second, the Zapatistas' fundamental critique of neo-liberalism and its demands for the protection of the Mexican state and nation may seem to entail a rejection of the international institutions of neo-liberalism rather than a demand for further democratization of these institutions as suggested in some of the above quotes. The point here, however, is not to discuss whether or not the Zapatista democratic vision of 'to rule by obeying' is directly applicable on a global level, but to register how it overlaps with some of the radical democratic aspirations within the global justice and solidarity movement.

It is, of course, too simple to take the comments advanced in the above quotes as common denominators for the democratic aspirations of all participants in the global justice and solidarity movement. The quotes from Smith and Wallach reflect a specific position where international institutions such as the WTO and the IMF are not fundamentally questioned. Rather, demands go in the direction of subjecting these institutions to closer democratic scrutiny and opening them to the influence of civil society actors. In relation to the Zapatista radical democratic vision, this critique of democracy is located primarily in the dimensions of the deepening and broadening of democracy and its proponents may be described as global transformers (Held and McGrew 2002: ch. 8). Another important current in the global justice and solidarity movement consists of activists working from an anarchist point of view. But as noted by Epstein (2001: 1), the anarchist inspiration in the movement is not necessarily built on strict adherence to the theoretical roots of anarchism:

> For contemporary young radical activists, anarchism means a decentralized organizational structure, based on affinity groups that work together on an ad hoc basis, and decision-making by consensus... . Many envision a stateless society based on small, egalitarian communities. For some, however, the society of the future remains an open question. For them, anarchism is important mainly as an organizational structure and as a commitment to egalitarianism.

Compared to the quotes from Smith (2001) and Wallach (Naím 2000), anarchist tendencies seem to put more emphasis on democracy within and between groups and organizations, and less on the democratization of what is largely considered to be illegitimate international institutions. Polletta (2001: 26) describes the consensus-oriented decision-making procedures in the New York branch of the anarchist-inspired Direct Action Network, which plays an important role in the global justice and solidarity movement:

> I had seen the group's decision-making style in action at one of its Sunday meetings. Participants sat in a circle and were called on by two facilitators who also kept track of the agenda. A time-keeper alerted the group to the fact that it had used up the time allotted for an issue; in this meeting, participants 'consensed' that they would devote ten more minutes to discussion. A difficult question about whether to fund a project – a hundred or so dollars – required two extensions in this meeting. Tempers flared during the discussion, and people signaled their intention to block what seemed to be an emerging consensus. The solution slowly hammered out was that DAN would not fund the project and people instead would contribute voluntarily. There was consensus and a hat was passed around and quickly filled. The next issue was taken up. Again, discussion seemed to go round and round; again, consensus was eventually reached.

Apart from its ideological and theoretical roots in anarchism, similarities may be identified in what has generally been referred to as the new social movements of the 1970s and 1980s. The debate on new social movements is extensive and will not be taken up here. It is, however, useful to dwell briefly on the new social movements' visions of direct or grass-roots democracy as these display important areas of similarity with the radical democratic vision of the Zapatistas and many of the organizations and networks involved in the current global justice and solidarity movement. Scott (1990: 27) sums up the anti-authoritarian characteristics of the new social movements:

> Anti-authoritarianism shifts the emphasis towards direct or grass-roots democracy, and away from formal representative democracy... . Representative democracy is distrusted because it weighs power in favour of the representatives who enjoy extensive autonomy, and away

from those who they represent, who must, by and large, rely on the integrity of those who act in their name and call on their, largely passive support. This critique of formal democracy is turned not merely upon existing social institutions, but also upon the social movements who have allowed themselves to be drawn into institutionalized politics and have developed large bureaucratic and oligarchic organizational forms in the process.

This approach to the question of democracy is different from the one presented in the quotes from Smith (2001) and Wallach (Naím 2000). What is interesting in the context of the discussions in this chapter are not the differences and the tensions they may cause, but the fact that this anarchist and grass-roots-oriented approach to democracy is echoed in the Zapatista radical democratic vision. The similarities are not so much in the concept of 'to rule by obeying', but rather in the question of autonomy defended by the Zapatistas. In other words, the anarchist current primarily resembles the delegation dimension in Zapatista radical democracy.

Conclusion

This chapter has revolved around the notion of radical democracy. Radical democracy differs significantly from liberal democracy, which is expressed mainly in electoral and institutional approaches to democracy. Radical democracy is considered to imply a broadening, delegation and deepening of democracy as understood in the liberal interpretation. The broadening of democracy denotes an aspiration to make democratic decision-making procedures penetrate institutions and markets. In regard to the Zapatistas, this is evident in the notion of 'to rule by obeying', which demands a closer relationship between those who govern and those who are governed. The issue of the broadening of democracy is also visible in their interpretation of neo-liberalism and its socio-economic consequences as fundamentally at odds with democracy. The delegation of democracy denotes an aspiration to form more or less autonomous areas within the context of nation states in which alternative democratic practices may be exercised. In the Zapatista case, this aspect is especially evident in regard to demands for indigenous autonomy. The deepening of democracy denotes an increasing empowerment of civil society actors and an increasing politicization of civil society. This aspiration rests on two assumptions: that an active civil society is the basis of a more substantive democracy; and that civil society is a sphere penetrated by power relations that can only be countered through changes on the level of civil society. In regard to the Zapatistas, this aspect is evident in its many initiatives to activate civil society and create a space for civil society politics.

The changes leading up to and following the end of the Cold War gave democratic ideas a dominant position in the new world order. This development may be seen as a political opportunity for social movements, as it has relaxed the ideological straitjacket imposed by the Cold War logic. The Zapatistas have been at the forefront of the formulation of radical democratic ideas in the post-Cold War period and have been an important source of inspiration for the global justice and solidarity movement, which made its first important mark at the WTO protests in Seattle in 1999. Zapatista radical democratic ideas are directly visible in the activities of global Zapatista solidarity activists in at least two ways: in Zapatista solidarity activists' emphasis on the value of decentralized and autonomous action and interaction; and in the adoption of what is considered to be Zapatista democratic practices in settings outside of Mexico. The Zapatista radical democratic vision is more indirectly visible in the global justice and solidarity movement in at least two ways: in the demands for more democratic accountability in international institutions such as the WTO and the IMF; and in anarchist and new social movements inspired rejections of centralized authority.

I will close this chapter with a couple of problematizing notes: one regarding the present state and future of radical democratic protest and the other regarding what we could call internal democratic problems in the global justice and solidarity movement.[11]

The events of 9/11 and its aftermath have significantly changed the conditions for the global justice and solidarity movement and its radical democratic visions. The terrorists and those committed to destroying them respectively place themselves outside and on the borders of what is democratically permissible. This situation is laden with great insecurity and may jeopardize the democratic potentials set in motion by the end of the Cold War. The War against Terror may, in other words, install imperatives similar to those that dominated world politics during the Cold War. For many social activists, this situation is already narrowing the space for contentious action (e.g. Ayres and Tarrow 2002; Glasius and Kaldor 2002; Kaldor et al. 2003).

Radical democratic activists also face a number of democratic challenges that are more internal. Three issues are particularly pertinent. First, global activists are a self-constituted and often numerically small force that has not been democratically elected. This raises important questions as to whom the activists represent and what sources of legitimacy they draw on. Second, the global justice and solidarity movement cannot deny a Western bias and a persistence of inequality between Western and Southern activists (Smith and Bandy 2005). This bias does not lie in a focus on issues and problems in the West, but rather in the fact that most activists are based in Europe and the US. While global activists often deal with issues related to the South, the overweight of Western activists may in some cases lead to analyses and solution proposals that are out of tune with local and national desires. When this is the case, activists commit some of the very same democratic errors for which they fault current policies. Third, the function and form of democracy in the relationships between activists is a contested issue. In general, activists agree that flat and networked structures of organization are preferable to centralized and hierarchical forms, but serious disagreements have surfaced – for example, around the staging of the World Social Forum (Waterman 2003). Controversy has arisen over the organizing process and the running of the forum that, according to critics, has been undemocratic and in the hands of a small circle of people. Such controversies reflect fundamental differences in the perception of democracy between anarchists and more reformist and hierarchically inclined activists (Ross 2002). Conflicts like these are a major challenge for the future of the global justice and solidarity movement and perhaps even suggest that it is problematic, as I have done in this chapter, to speak of it as a 'movement'.

Notes

1. This chapter builds on chapter 7 of a book-length study of the Zapatistas and the solidarity network surrounding them (Olesen 2005a).
2. I prefer to speak about the global justice and solidarity movement rather than the anti-globalization movement. As has been noted by several observers (e.g. Smith 2001), activists are *against* the globalization of a neo-liberal development model, but *for* global co-operation and exchange and universal human rights values.
3. Gusfield contrasts the fluid conception with a linear conception that focuses on social movements as organizations. The fluid conception of social movements is what allows activists and researchers to speak of the women's movement, the peace movement, the environmental movement, and so on.
4. The official name of the Zapatistas is the EZLN (Zapatista Army of National Liberation). Here I will use EZLN only when referring to Zapatista documents.
5. At first sight, this view may not appear to differ significantly from liberal democracy, which also presupposes an active civil society as the foundation for democracy. In the perspective of liberal democracy, however, civil society is made up by interest groups that do not question social, economic and cultural values in fundamental ways. In contrast, radical democratic visions

of civil society focus on civil society as an arena of conflict and politics and the development of contentious alternatives.

6. My translation from the Spanish.
7. My translation from the Spanish.
8. At the time of writing (June 2005) there are still no official contacts between the government and the Zapatistas and the issue of indigenous autonomy remains unresolved. In the last four years the Zapatistas have concentrated on a restructuring of the political organization of the Zapatista communities in Chiapas and have also been less active in regard to global activism.
9. The most important activities have been 1) the National Democratic Convention (CND) in Chiapas in 1994; 2) the National Consultation for Peace and Democracy in 1995; 3) the First Intercontinental Encounter for Humanity and against Neoliberalism in Chiapas in 1996; 4) the visit of 1,111 civilian Zapatistas to Mexico City to celebrate the formation of the FZLN in 1997; 5) the National Consultation Concerning the Legal Initiative on Indigenous Rights of the Commission of Concordance and Pacification and for an End to the War of Extermination in 1999; and 6) the March for Indigenous Dignity in 2001 aimed at the approval of the COCOPA proposal on indigenous rights.
10. This argument builds on the so-called political opportunities approach within social movement theory. This theory argues that social movement form and mobilization is strongly affected by structural changes in their political environment (see, for example, Tarrow 1998).
11. These arguments build on Olesen (2004, 2005b).

References

Appel, Kerry (2000). The Human Bean Company, Denver, CO. Interview Denver, 24 October.

Callahan, Manuel (2000) Acción Zapatista, Austin, TX. Interview Austin, TX, 5 October.

Ayres, Jeffrey and Sidney Tarrow (2002) The Shifting Grounds for Transnational Civic Activity, www. ssrc.org/sept11/essays/ayres.htm.

Castañeda, Jorge G. (1995) *Sorpresas te da la vida: México, fin de siglo* (México D.F.: Aguilar).

Cohen, Jean L. and Andrew Arato (1992) *Civil Society and Political Theory* (Cambridge, MA: MIT Press).

Donnelly, Jack (1993) *International Human Rights* (Boulder, CO: Westview Press).

Durán de Huerta, Marta (1999) An Interview with Subcomandante Insurgente Marcos, spokesman and military commander of the Zapatista National Liberation Army (EZLN), *International Affairs*, 75(2): 269–279.

Epstein, Barbara (2001). 'Anarchism and the Anti-Globalization Movement', Monthly Review (September): 1–14.

Esteva, Gustavo (1999) The Zapatistas and People's Power, *Capital & Class* (Summer): 153–182.

Esteva, Gustavo (2001) The Meaning and the Scope of the Struggle for Autonomy, *Latin American Perspectives*, 28(2): 120–148.

EZLN (1994) *Declaración de la Selva Lacandona*, www.ezln.org/documentos/1994/199312xx.es.htm.

EZLN (1996) *Segunda Declaración de la Realidad*, www.ezln.org/documentos/1996/19960803.es.htm.

EZLN (2000) *Communiqué* (June 19), www.ezln.org/documentos/2000/20000619.es.htm.

EZLN (2001) *Communiqué* (April 2001), www.ezln.org/documentos/2001/ezln010429b.es.htm.

Fotopoulos, Takis (1997) *Towards an Inclusive Democracy* (London and New York: Cassell).

Gilbreth, Chris and Gerardo Otero (2001) Democratization in Mexico: The Zapatista Uprising and Civil Society, *Latin American Perspectives*, 28(4): 7–29.

Glasius, Marlies and Mary Kaldor (2002) The State of Global Civil Society: Before and after September 11, in Helmut Anheier, Marlies Glasius, and Mary Kaldor (eds.) *Global Civil Society* (Oxford: Oxford University Press), pp. 3–33.

Gramsci, Antonio (1971) *Selections from the Prison Notebooks*, ed. and transl. Quintin Hoare and Geoffrey Nowell Smith (New York: International Publishers).

Gusfield, Joseph R. (1981) Social Movements and Social Change: Perspectives of Linearity and Fluidity, *Research in Social Movements, Conflict and Change*, 4: 317–339.

Habermas, Jürgen (1987) *The Theory of Communicative Action*, vol. 2 (Cambridge: Polity Press).

Hardt, Michael and Antonio Negri (2004) *Multitude: War and Democracy in the Age of Empire* (New York: Penguin Press).

Harvey, Neil (1998) *The Chiapas Rebellion: The Struggle for Land and Democracy* (Durham, NC: Duke University Press).

Held, David and Anthony McGrew (2002) *Globalization/Anti-Globalization* (Cambridge: Polity).

Kaldor, Mary, Helmut Anheier and Marlies Glasius (2003) Global Civil Society in an Era of Regressive Globalization, in Mary Kaldor, Helmut Anheier and Marlies Glasius (eds.) *Global Civil Society Yearbook 2003* (Oxford: Oxford University Press), pp. 3–33.

Kampwirth, Karen (1996) Creating Space in Chiapas: An Analysis of the Strategies of the Zapatista Army and the Rebel Government in Transition, *Bulletin of Latin American Research*, 15(2): 261–267.

Klein, Naomi (2001) Reclaiming the Commons, *New Left Review*, 9 (May/June): 81–89.

Laclau, Ernesto (1990) *New Reflections on the Revolution of Our Time* (London: Verso).

Laclau, Ernesto (1996) *Emancipation(s)* (London: Verso).

Laclau, Ernesto and Chantal Mouffe (1985) *Hegemony and Socialist Strategy* (London: Verso).

Le Bot, Yvon (1997) *El sueño zapatista* (Barcelona: Plaza y Janés).

Lummis, Douglas (1996) *Radical Democracy* (Ithaca, NY: Cornell University Press).

Martin, David (2000) Denver Peace and Justice Committee, Denver. CO. Interview in Denver, 24 October.

Mouffe, Chantal (1992) Preface: Democratic Politics Today, in Chantal Mouffe (ed.) *Dimensions of Radical Democracy: Pluralism, Citizenship, Community* (London: Verso), pp. 1–14.

Mouffe, Chantal (1993) *The Return of the Political* (London: Verso).

Naím, Moisés (2000) The FP Interview: Lori's War, *Foreign Policy* (Spring): 29–55.

Olesen, Thomas (2004) The Struggle inside Democracy: Modernity, Social Movements, and Global Solidarity, *Distinktion*, 8: 19–35.

Olesen, Thomas (2005a) *International Zapatismo: The Construction of Solidarity in the Age of Globalization* (London: Zed Books).

Olesen, Thomas (2005b) World Politics and Social Movements: The Janus Face of the Global Democratic Structure, *Global Society*, 19(2): 109–129.

Polletta, Francesca (2001) 'This is What Democracy Looks Like': A Conversation with Direct Action Network Activists David Graeber, Brooke Lehman, Jose Lugo and Jeremy Varon. *Social Policy*, Summer.

Ross, Stephanie (2002) Is This What 'Democracy' Looks Like? The Politics of the Anti-Globalization Movement in North America, *Socialist Register 2003*: 281–304.

Scott, Alan (1990) *Ideology and the New Social Movements* (London: Unwin Hyman).

Shaw Martin (2000) *Theory of the Global State: Globality as an Unfinished Revolution* (Cambridge: Cambridge University Press).

Smith, Jackie (2001) Behind the Anti-Globalization Label, *Dissent* (Fall): 14–18.

Smith, Jackie and Joe Bandy (2005) Introduction: Cooperation and Conflict in Transnational Protest, in Joe Bandy and Jackie Smith (eds.) *Coalitions across Borders: Transnational Protest and the Neoliberal Order* (Lanham: Rowman and Littlefield), pp. 1–17.

Stephen, Lynn (2001) University of Oregon. Interview: e-mail received 16 January.

Tarrow, Sidney (1998) *Power in Movement: Social Movements and Contentious Politics*, 2nd edition (Cambridge: Cambridge University Press).

Touraine, Alain (1996) Marcos, el demócrata armado, *La Jornada Semanal*, 22 December.

Waterman, Peter (2003) Second Thoughts on the Third World Social Forum: Place, Space and the Reinvention of Social Emancipation on a Global Scale, received from the author.

Wood, Ellen Meiskins (1995) *Democracy against Capitalism: Renewing Historical Materialism* (Cambridge: Cambridge University Press).

World Social Forum (2001) www.forumsocialmundial.org.br/esp/2cartas.asp [Accessed 26 January 2002].

8
'Flirting with the Enemy': Green Alliances in Global Environmental Governance

Harry Bauer

Introduction

The notion that a transnational or global civil society is emerging has become a commonplace in recent cosmopolitan and globalist literature.[1] In spite of its 'contagious appeal' the concept of civil society itself remains, however – like all central conceptualizations in political thought – contested and polarizing: whereas sceptics find its use and definition as awkward as 'nailing a pudding to a wall' (M. Brumlik) or even demur that 'the formation of such society has hardly started anywhere except in philosophers' study rooms' (Z. Bauman), others promote global civil society's function as a crucial, third force for progress in world politics. In International Relations (IR),[2] therefore, a fierce debate about the concept's normative implications and analytical value has recently been sparked. Notably, its widespread simplifications have come under attack, e.g. the common modelling of state, market and civil society as autonomous spheres determined by their own logics and the frequent equation of non-governmental organizations (NGOs) and their activities with (global) civil society as a whole (for an introduction into the debate see Laxer and Halperin 2003; Amoore and Langley 2004).

This chapter stands in line with a growing number of studies that propose a more nuanced understanding of transnational civil society and its workings. It is especially meant to contribute to our knowledge of the nexus between actors from the apparently adversarial spheres of state, market and civil society. Before this backdrop, the chapter argues that one significant (and for some, surprising) feature of global environmental governance after the Rio Earth Summit 1992 has been the increasing emergence of 'green alliances', formal and informal collaborations of environmental NGOs (ENGOs) and private corporations. The overall rationale for paying attention to such collaborations is twofold. First, and as indicated, their existence casts doubt on common conceptions of inter- and transnational politics. Being private, voluntary environmental policy arrangements green alliances call into question state-centric concepts of governance and politics; as coalitions between market forces and (global) civil society they question all too simplistic, antagonistic understandings of the relationship between the two. Second, a close analysis of green alliances can broaden IR's research beyond the widely established consensus that 'private actors matter' in international relations by asking why, when and how they do.

In the following, I propose that green alliances reflect significantly broadened room for manoeuvre for ENGOs. Faced with the enormously slow, resource- and time-consuming as well as ineffective workings of international environmental politics and fostered by the new *idée directrice* in environmental discourse, 'sustainable development', such private voluntary arrangements, has been heralded as one alternative, 'new policy instrument' in environmental governance (see Jordan, Wurzel and Zito 2003). According to the terminology of some analysts, new windows of opportunity have opened for NGO–business collaborations (Lober 1997). Therefore, this chapter starts with an analysis of the new conditions for the possibility of green alliances. This more contextual overview is followed by a taxonomy of green alliances themselves, covering their diversity of inter-actions, both formal and informal, market-oriented as well as policy-oriented. As green alliances are relatively new, still limited in quantity and quality, and involve parties that were quite often former antagonists, their robustness and effectiveness may be questioned. Hence, the next section suggests that a variety of factors, such as coalition form, power relations, political discourse and 'rules of the game', impinge on the stability – and therefore possible efficacy – of such collaborations. The final section speculates about the perspectives of such partnerships and their implications, and proposes possible directions for further research in this area.

The remodelling of environmental governance

During the last decade of the twentieth century relations between ENGOs and business – and thus the relationship between (global) civil society and market forces – have become increasingly complex. Whereas relations in the 1970s and 1980s had been restricted to corporate phi-lanthropy on the one hand and determined environmentalist criticism of almost all industrial activity on the other, current interactions range from 'the strongly antagonistic to the "strangely" collaborative' (Bendell 1998: i). From the first emergence of green alliances in the early 1990s they have come a long way indeed. In 1990 the cooperation of the Environmental Defence Fund with McDonald's in order to improve the restaurants' waste management was still seen as an 'odd coupling' (Livesey 1999), today green alliances and their activities are widespread: just think of the growing number of schemes monitoring and verrifying sustainable corporate performance and production.[3] Undeniably, the range of environmental issues being addressed, as well as the variety of participants involved, have significantly increased in recent years as have the complexity and frequency of such collaborations (for an overview, see Stafford and Hartman 1996; Crane 1998; Bendell 2000b; Wymer and Samu 2003).

Asking about the reasons for the emergence of green alliances, one has to refer to fundamental, interlinked transformations in both global environmental politics and the political domain of society, encompassing modified views on governance as well as on the relationship between state, market and civil society. The literature on globalization and governance with its intensified interest in the privatization of regulation and authority has reflected these trajectories and offers a major vantage point for the study of green alliances. Broadly speaking, the question of business–ENGO collaboration fits into the *problematique* of new governance beyond the state, domestically as well as internationally.

A narrow definition of governance, as in Czempiel and Rosenau's seminal *Governance without Government*, suggests that governance connotes 'a mode of governing that is distinct from the hierarchical control model characterizing the interventionist state. Governance is the type of regulation ... where state and non-state actors participate in mixed public/private policy networks' (Mayntz 2002: 21). Governance is therefore seen as the counterpart to traditional top-down, command-and-control approaches to the provision of social order and common goods. It includes private actors, multiple spatial and functional levels of politics and the emergence of new spheres of authority beyond the state. In this sense green alliances are a form of environmental governance but a distinct form, as they encompass private actors from civil society and market only. Their institutional arrangements 'structure and direct actors' behavior in an issue-specific area. These structuring effects resemble the "public" governing functions of states and intergovernmental institutions, and for this reason the notion of governance, and indeed authority, has been applied to private actors' (Falkner 2003: 73). As

Jennifer Clapp (1998) has pointed out, this 'privatization of global environmental governance' includes a growing number of voluntary codes of conduct and private or hybrid standard-setting bodies recognized by organizations such as the WTO.

But why have these forms of private governance and authority emerged in the first place? IR's literature on globalization provides us with three paradigmatic answers briefly sketched here (see for the following Falkner 2003: 74–83). First, there is the widespread assertion that an ever more globalized, unregulated economy is coupled with the shift of power and authority from the public to the private domain. This inevitably leads to a decline and *Retreat of the State* (Strange 1996) with a turn away from state-centric models of governance to new forms of authority mainly to be found within the global economy. Second, the emergence of private governance is linked to transnationalism and the expansion of global civil society, which figures as

> a transnational domain in which people form relationships and develop elements of identity outside their role as a citizen of a particular state ... that transcends the self-regarding character of the state system and can work in the service of a genuinely transnational, public interest ... overcoming the many impediments associated with statist politics. (Wapner 2000: 261)

In this perspective private governance is the product of pressure exerted by ENGOs and activist groups directly on corporations. In this line of reasoning, as an instrument for the promotion of environmental sustainability, it has become a vital element in the political repertoire of civil society actors.

A third concept of private governance can be found in critical political economy (cf., for instance, Cox 1983, 1987; Gill 1993). Based on a Gramscian or historical materialist perspective, the privileged capitalist class engages in building cooperation with a variety of state and civil society actors so as to restructure the dominant capitalist economic order better to serve its own interests. The current rise of private governance signifies a new phase in the process of restructuring global hegemony, in which transnational and multinational corporations seek to establish environmental standards with the clear intent of shifting the ideological focus in global environmental politics towards market-oriented, deregulatory systems. The instigation and sponsoring of such environmental regimes is therefore a reaction to the ecological crisis meant to cement the control by the domineering class and to silence anti-capitalist forces.

These three claims raise central questions about the importance of private environmental governance for the conditions under which green alliances can become feasible. They point to 1) a change in the relationship between and weight of private actors as well as states; 2) an increased opportunity for ENGOs and environmental movements to shape global environmental politics and accompany a shift in authority; 3) a shift in the ideological underpinning of environmental governance.

Overall, the debates about these assertions caution against hasty, simplistic conclusions. Therefore, the observation that private actors play an increasing role in global environmental governance and that private regimes and authority have emerged, for example in international trade, the global insurance industry among accountancy firms and credit rating agencies (Cutler, Haufler and Porter 1999; Hall and Biersteker 2002), should not be equated with the general demise of the state. States remain the central – though not the only – actors in world politics and if we wish to claim that the relationship between states and private actors has changed, this has to be qualified. Indeed, many private governance arrangements do not undermine the governance functions of states and the state system; on the contrary, they appear to be beneficial to states, easing their burden of implementing standards by leaving it to the private sector. Various government initiatives as well as international organizations such as the World Bank and the United Nations with their Global Compact have therefore tried to endorse and facilitate such regulation (Tesner 2000; Oliviero and Simmons 2002: 88–9). Furthermore, examples of private governance regimes such as the ISO 14000 standards and the Forestry Stewardship Council (FSC) indicate that their particular strength derives from the support and recognition states and international organizations have lent them. Yet, states are utterly dissimilar entities; corporations might find themselves equipped with far more constraining power on the autonomy of developing countries than on countries in the industrialized world.

Doubtless, the rise of private governance has strengthened the position of ENGOs and activist groups in global environmental politics. A key argument of current transnationalist research has been the central role ENGOs play in

> creating global environmental awareness, spreading ecological values across borders, and targeting private actors in their campaigning efforts. In the era of globalization, which provides the 'infrastructure' in the form of global communication systems, for new forms of 'world civil politics' private governance thus emerges not in a political

vacuum but in an increasingly politicized space of transnational interaction. (Falkner 2003: 79)

From such a perspective, corporate self-regulation is less motivated by a desire for autonomy than by a necessity to be responsive to public pressure. On the other hand, private governance provides civil society actors with political capital and leverage beyond the state system. In sum, 'as either business provocateurs or partners, NGOs are playing catalytic roles in changing corporate policy and practice' (Bendell 2000b: 246).

Public campaigns consequently become an indispensable factor in the expansion of private environmental governance. As studies show, two major ways remain open to ENGOs for fostering this development. First, ENGOs focus on individual corporations, holding them accountable for environmentally damaging conduct with the intention of altering their behaviour and of reminding other businesses of the need to comply with higher standards. Here Greenpeace's Brent Spar campaign comes to mind. Second, entire business sectors become the target of environmental campaigns that establish sector-wide environmental standards. Prominent examples for global private regimes outside the domain of established state-centric environmental regulation are the Worldwide Fund for Nature (WWF) and the Unilever-led Maritime Stewardship Council (MSC: since 1995), the FSC (since 1993) and the Tea Sourcing Partnership (TSP: since 1997). All work towards sustainable practices in their field by certifying corporations' compliance with established criteria, standards and procedures (see Bendell 2000a).

Faced with the ability to target and become involved with the corporate sector, some analysts have argued that environmental activism has opened up a new space for activity beyond the realm of traditional state-system regulation. Even more, private environmental governance may provide a potentially more effective and quicker way of achieving international environmental regulation than the conventional lobbying of states. As one NGO leader said, when stressing the need for green alliances: 'You cannot just sit back and wait for governments to agree, because this could take forever' (in Bendell and Murphy 2000: 69).

However, there have also been cautioning voices, which express scepticism concerning the role of civil society actors in private environmental governance. There is concern that close cooperation might tame environmental activism. New relationships might jeopardize the independence of civil society actors since collaboration might entail corporate funding, the need to compromise and the legitimization of corporate activities. Further warnings may well be in order. First, corporate partners will sooner or later face great difficulties in accommodating the increasingly demanding sustainability agenda of their civil society partners, which in turn will threaten the corporate short-term financial horizon. Second, ENGOs could risk alienating their memberships and their own fundraising base. And third, resourceful ENGOs 'may not exist so ubiquitously' (Usui 2004: 236) as one would wish. Elkington and Fennel even warn that the army of well-resourced independent activist groups is likely to run short soon of the rising demand from corporate players. So much so that 'the corporations leading off in forging strategic alliances with key civil society organizations may be doing so just to enjoy a "first-mover" benefit' (Elkington and Fennell 2000: 152–3).

A third, and related, view of private environmental governance is that it indicates a shift not only in authority but also in its ideological underpinnings. In this view the growing preference for business-friendly, market-oriented approaches in environmental management increasingly sidelines more holistic understandings of environmental issues. Privatization is seen as undermining established, state-centric, relatively open models of global governance by promoting a neo-liberal agenda that also impedes the progressive power of global environmental activism. The impact corporate actors have sought to apply to the global environmental agenda has become especially visible in the preparation phase of the Rio Earth Summit 1992. In particular, the Business Council on Sustainable Development (BCSD) and the International Chamber of Commerce lobbied for the notion of joint ventures between the corporate sector, environmentalists and states in pursuit of environmental solutions. This idea of a reconciliation between ecological and economic interests markedly brought forward by Stephan Schmidheiny (1992), founder of the BCSD, and incorporated in the notion of 'sustainable development' became a kind of blueprint for a market-oriented and self-regulatory approach to global environmental governance.

This conception has received numerous criticisms, not least for framing environmental concerns as issues of management and resources avoiding a fundamental critique of capitalism as the source for ecological degradation (see, for instance, Kütting 2004). However, such a perception is, as Robert Falkner argues, in 'danger of overstating the influence of business in setting the global agenda and understating the continuity of a fundamentally liberal consensus enshrined in the global environmental agenda' (Falkner 2003: 83). What has happened in recent years is therefore not a shift towards a neo-liberal, market-oriented ideology, but a strengthening of those liberal political and economic ideas, which have already been present in the practices of global environmental governance.

In a similar vein, Steven Bernstein (2001) has suggested that this *Compromise of Liberal Environmentalism* has less to do with the impact of the corporate sector than with a consensus among the leading personnel of policy networks and international organizations such as the OECD. If there is an ideological shift to discover, then it is one within liberal environmentalism itself and concerns a move away from the ideal of free markets towards their domination by an oligopoly of potent corporations.

I have stressed that the remodelling of global governance can be understood along three axes: the role of states and private actors, of civil society activism and its ideological underpinnings. However, besides these debates firmly grounded in IR, renewed discussions about domestic and regional public policymaking have also had an impact on the trajectories of environmental governance from the early 1980s onwards. Here the involvement of a broad range of private actors was experimented with, for instance in the fields of urban regeneration and local economic development. In general, it is the unprecedented success of the welfare state itself, incorporating an ever-increasing section of society within its range that exceeds governments' capacities to provide and maintain social order and public goods. It is for this reason that governments seek to delimit their activities by new instruments of policy steering, new actor constellations and by privatizing, outsourcing and sharing the provision of public goods.[4]

ENGOs' activities: what room for manoeuvre?

Now what do these considerations mean for the activities of ENGOs and especially for their efforts at modifying corporate behaviour towards a more sustainable performance? The overview in Figure 8.1 indicates that ENGOs' room for manoeuvre has indeed significantly broadened with the changing notions and praxis of governance in recent years (see areas in grey). Both style and orientation of ENGOs' actions have widened. The previously confrontational approach to corporate actors has been complemented by collaborative efforts. Whereas in the past all activity was concentrated outside the marketplace, activities inside the market now make it possible both to collaborate with and to target corporate actors. Jem Bendell has captured this in the quartet 'forcing', 'facilitating', 'producing' and 'promoting' change (see for this and the following Bendell 2000b: 242–5).

The traditional approach to alter the behaviour of corporate actors is certainly the enforcement of change (cell 1). This comprises the traditional instruments of environmental activism where ENGOs employ voluntary

Orientation	Approach	
	Confrontational	**Collaborative**
Market external	**(1) Forcing change** Boycott, direct action, critical research, court action, lobbying for legislation	**(2) Promoting change** Agreements, advice on and endorsement of best practice, research, product and technique development
Market internal	**(3) Producing change** Providing alternative products and creating markets	**(4) Facilitating change** Consultancy services, product endorsement, certification and accreditation schemes

Figure 8.1   NGO activities to alter corporate behaviour

donations of time, money and other resources. The mobilization of consumers to boycott particular goods or companies, as in the case of Shell, has been an efficient tool to impose change in a variety of industries, as has direct action against the field trials of genetically modified crops or the publication of critical research putting into doubt claims made by corporate actors. Finally, court action and lobbying for legislation continue to remain powerful strategies by drawing on states and state authority.

Another group of activities that can be located outside the market and which therefore rely on voluntary donations of time, money and other resources can be characterized as promoting change (cell 2). Such collaborative activities encompass negotiating agreements with corporate management, giving advice on and endorsing best practice, carrying out and publishing research or engaging in the joint development of new products or techniques. Greenpeace International's solutions campaign in the 1990s with the development of an eco-friendly freezer or a fuel-efficient car has utilized almost all of these instruments (see Rose 1997).

In contrast, the last two categories of activity rely on the generation of revenues from market-oriented activities. Various NGOs have in recent years offered consultancy services to corporations in order to facilitate change (cell 4). Such advice can include the change of internal working procedures as with the introduction of ISO 14000 standards, the endorsement of products or the running of certification schemes. Others have specialized in the monitoring of labour and environmental standards, for instance in connection with the FSC and MSC.

The last group of ENGO activity concerns the production of change in the market via the provision of alternative, sustainable product lines and the creation of alternative markets. NGO-owned trading companies like Havelaar or Fairtrade Foundation are well-known examples. Of course, such activities make the success of ENGOs dependent on their economic achievements. These activities are competitive in the sense that ENGOs compete with other corporations in the marketplace and try to use the ethical and ecological qualities of their products as selling point. Therefore the mobilizing of consumer politics plays a significant role in the success of ENGOs both in their confrontation with corporations outside the market via strike and boycott as well as within the market via product preferences.

This overview has highlighted the variety of activities ENGOs can engage in if they wish to alter corporate behaviour. The categories suggested are not meant to distinguish between different groups of NGOs. The reality of environmental activism suggests that an activist group might use a broad range of activity depending on circumstances and policy. However, most NGOs might start with one kind of activity, primarily forcing change, before they develop a wider set of instruments. For the analysis of green alliances (cells 2 and 4) it is most important that the trend towards collaboration with corporate actors inside and outside the marketplace has tremendously increased in recent years.

The depth and breadth of green alliances

The previous line of reasoning has shed light on the deep-rooted changes in the notion and praxis of global environmental governance. In particular, I have argued that these transformations have enhanced ENGOs' range of instruments and activities tremendously, including collaborative approaches to corporate actors and activities in the marketplace. What organizational forms can these collaborations now take? Building on the earlier considerations and integrating previous attempts to categorize green alliances (see Hartman and Stafford 1997; Glasbergen and Groenenberg 2001), I suggest categorizing them according to their degree of institutionalization and orientation. It should, however, be noted that these categories are only meant as heuristic tools. Hybrid forms of green alliances such as informal roundtables dealing with research projects are common.

A green alliance can therefore be placed along a continuum from informal, low institutionalized cooperation to formal, highly institutionalized cooperation. In view of the incremental development of such collaborations, most observers have proposed a simple, multi-stage model of private collaboration-building and assume an almost 'organic' growth from simpler to more formal forms of green alliances. They can

	Level of Institutionalization	
Orientation	Low, informal	High, formal
Policy-oriented	(1) Regular consultation and information, round-tables	(2) Green public policy alliance, joint research
Market-oriented	(3) Product endorsement, advice on and endorsement of best practice, corporate sponsorship	(4) Agreements, certification and accreditation schemes, product and technique development

Figure 8.2   A taxonomy of collaborations of ENGOs and corporate actors

also been classified as either policy-oriented or as market-oriented, as strategies directed towards the alteration of public policy or as aiming at alterations within the marketplace. This is summarized in Figure 8.2 in order to cover the diversity of green alliances within four different categories.

From the standpoint of complexity, cell 1 contains the simpler forms of collaboration, because *ad hoc* roundtables and regular exchange of information keep the level of commitment on both sides relatively low. This seems to alter steadily when progressing to cells 2, 3 and 4. Where the level of institutionalization increases, the level of mutual commitment increases as well. Green alliances such as these differ in their advantages and disadvantages. Less formal and extensive collaboration has the benefit of being open and flexible on the one hand, but will hardly generate much environmental impact on the other. The opposite is true for certification and accreditation schemes, for example. If successful, they can be efficient in environmental terms, but the nature of a joint venture forces ENGOs to operate as businesses, which may have some negative consequences as well (see the discussion on 'inside market approaches').

Stable 'private environmental policy arrangements'?

Whereas an examination of the debates about global governance has helped to clarify the political and institutional context conditions for the emergence of green alliances, I now turn to Bas Arts' concept of 'green alliances' as 'private environmental policy arrangements' to identify those factors that impinge on the stability and therefore potential efficacy of such collaborations. The term 'policy arrangement' 'refers to the temporary stabilization of the content and organization of a policy domain' (Arts 2002: 30), including policy programmes and discourses as content, and actors, their coalitions and power relations as organizational features. Arts' conception of policy arrangements is heavily influenced by the notion that modern society is undergoing a process of reflexive modernization covering developments already touched on in the governance debate: key elements of industrial modernity such as the nation-state as 'container' of politics (A. Giddens), the regulatory state and the manageable society have become weakened in function and legitimacy in the face of emerging difficulties in steering and governing under increasing complexity. This affects policy domains and their actors by forcing them to adapt to radically altered states of affairs. One major result of such macro-societal processes is a turn away from static, state-centric forms of governance; new directions as well as new coalitions such as those between the corporate sector and civil society are formed. Policy arrangements are shifting gradually under the influence of new relationships between state, market and civil society, and under the weight of new views on modes of governance.

Equipped with such a conceptual apparatus, Arts includes green alliances in his conception of 'private environmental policy arrangements' (2002: 28), as both NGOs and companies are private actors, at least in form (for these distinctions, see Reinalda 2001). They differ, however, in aim, NGOs having a public aim (e.g. promoting a common good), companies having a private one (profit-making). Yet, this distinction is to some extent blurred, as many ENGOs, such as Greenpeace, have become businesses themselves, while ever more companies have acknowledged their societal responsibilities (see Held 2002). As far as ENGOs and corporations participate in green alliances, they both strive for a public aim, namely to improve environmental conditions by setting up and implementing environmental policies. As a result, we can characterize green alliances as 'private environmental policy arrangements'. There are four important dimensions for their workings as entirely private governance institutions suggested by Arts (2002: 30–3): the specific form the interaction of the involved parties takes, the internal power relations, the 'rules of the game' and the dominant discourses.

Actors and coalitions

The two parties engaged in a green alliance are ENGOs on the one hand, and corporations on the other. Both form specific coalitions ranging, as we have seen, from less formal to highly institutionalized coalitions with market or policy orientation.

An excellent example might be the issue of sustainable forestry (see Lipschutz and Fogel 2002: 127, 131; Bartley 2003). With the failure of the United Nations to broker an international forest regime between developed and developing countries from the 1980s onwards, WWF, frustrated at the breakdown of international negotiations, launched a dialogue with industry, leading to the establishment of the FSC in 1993. The council has developed a product label, the FSC certificate, which binds the labelled timber wood to standards of sustainability. Mainly under the pressure of activist groups, retailers have made FSC-certified wood available to their customers. Overall, the FSC can be seen as a modest success. It has managed to introduce sustainable forestry and furthermore has realized a market share of about 5 per cent in developed countries such as the United Kingdom and the Netherlands.

Yet, this accomplishment stands on shaky grounds regarding coalition-building. 'It has become clear that (1) most consumers are not acquainted with FSC-wood; (2) the supply of FSC-wood has remained limited; (3) the prices of FSC-products are generally twice as high as those of non-labeled products; (4) the market share has ... [stagnated]; and (5) last but not the least, FSC timber has not developed into "the core business" of most companies' (Arts 2002: 32). The major issue, however, is that the market share of FSC products cannot be increased. Here, market-oriented strategies seem to reach their limits. Therefore, one may pose the question of whether state intervention in the form of incentives for both producers and consumers could overcome an otherwise saturated market.

This touches on the issue of whether green alliances might reach a point where cooperation with governments becomes crucial. Put differently, it might be difficult for a green alliance alone to turn a market into a green one. In the light of failing voluntary environmental agreements one OECD study has suggested that 'mixed policy packages' with the involvement of state, market and civil society might be a more effective alternative (OECD 2003).

Power relations

Green alliances are made up of very disparate parties. Conventional knowledge takes corporations as more powerful than ENGOs, even more than states. For a green alliance a power imbalance between the parties could lead to the domination of the corporate actor involved. This will render such collaboration highly volatile, as marginalized ENGOs will lose the incentive to be part of a relationship it can no longer influence. However, for the assessment of the power relations within a green alliance a refined concept of power is needed. Of course, corporations have an advantage when it comes to material resources, ENGOs, however, might counterbalance this lack with political, social and cultural capital or expertise. ENGOs are therefore not necessarily weaker than corporations. On the contrary, when it comes to policymaking, the ability to engage with the public or to make an impact in public debates ENGOs might even have an advantage. Hence, the distribution of power may be less uneven than it seems at first sight. Yet, as far as both opportunities and constraints are concerned, resources are far from equal.

The appeal of a strong alliance might therefore lie in the combination of unequal but complementary parties. A mutual exchange of resources – material, social, political, normative and ideational – to the benefit of the parties in the end establishes the foundation of a successful collaboration as long as unanimity can be maintained. Internal rifts, however, might lead to a confrontational climate, giving the imbalance of power new importance. Here we touch on a potential weakness of green alliances: 'in-built tensions as a result of unequal power relations' (Arts 2002: 32). Both NGOs and corporations should realize this, and look for strategies, at least if they wish to be successful, to soften imbalances. One such strategy is, of course, building mutual respect; another is setting up green alliances only with partners who can exchange considerable amounts of resources. This implies that alliances of big companies and small NGOs – or, less common, small companies and big NGOs – will probably not work well. Again reflecting on the different types of green alliances, it is plausible to assume that the closer and formalized a collaboration gets, the more sensitive the parties become *vis-à-vis* perceived imbalances in their power structure.

The rules of the game

As collaborations move along a continuum from informal to formal institutions, actors cannot avoid developing routines and perceptions about appropriate behaviour and determining legitimate norms and procedures leading to the intended policy outcomes. Again in this regard, both parties differ widely. Corporations prefer formal, contract-based cooperation, reflecting their relationship with long-standing external business partners, whereas civil society actors prefer softer, less binding, open forms of collaboration, involving flexible networks and *ad hoc* coalitions. It seems that both types of interaction practice characterize green alliances. As far as collaboration is dialogue-oriented, the *ad hoc* and open character of these 'rules of the game' will probably prevail. But as soon as it turns into a project, formalization will take over. This might put the ENGO under such constraint that it may wish to end the cooperation altogether.

Policy discourse

Understanding policy discourse as a 'specific ensemble of ideas, concepts, and categorizations that are produced, reproduced and transformed in a particular policy domain through which meaning is given to the physical and social realities of that domain' (Hajer 1995), especially the sustainability discourse, has become paramount for environmental governance. Green alliances are therefore one expression of the immense success liberal environmentalism, and the gradual convergence of norms of environmental protection with liberal economic norms, have had in recent decades. In particular, the discourse about sustainable development, shaped by the Brundtland Commission, in its report *Our Common Future*, UNCED's Agenda 21 and other UN-related initiatives has made the (partial) integration of opposite views on ecological and economic issues possible (WCED 1987): 'combining the view of economists, industrialists and governments (who interpret the ecological issues only in terms of economics) with the views of environmentalists and ecological scientists (who tend to interpret economic issues only in terms of ecology)' (Arts 2002: 33). Sustainable development, however, aims at integrating economics and ecology. Both mainstream economists and environmental activists have embraced the concept of sustainability. This has paved the way for remarkable 'discourse coalitions' such as those between NGOs and business in green alliances.

Yet the concept is, according to the critics, vague, imprecise and too broad (see Redclift 1987). 'Although these characteristics have made the construction of unexpected discourse coalitions possible, they also have the disadvantage that parties continue to disagree at the more fundamental level of core values and worldviews. In fact, the discourse of sustainable development can be deconstructed into a number of 'sub-discourses' that are to some extent incompatible [... (Bernstein)]. As a result, potential conflict is part of any broad sustainability coalition' (Arts 2002: 34).

Conclusion

Overall, green alliances stem from two interrelated developments: first, from the changes in the idea and praxis of global environmental governance; and second, from the rise of the *idée directrice* of environmental discourse, sustainable development. Additionally, the professionalization of environmental activism, on the one hand, and the development of a more pro-active environmental approach by (some) corporations, on the other, have fostered the establishment of green alliances.

Green alliances have definite potential but, as indicated in this chapter, the hitherto beneficial circumstances might change for the worse. However, they are flexible, non-bureaucratic coalitions blending different resources for private environmental policy-making. In doing so, they are examples of putting the concept of liberal environmentalism into operation. But green alliances 'remain weak if they are not – or hardly – embedded in the "core business" of companies' (Arts 2002: 34) and in formal environmental public policymaking. And, of course, such collaborations are rife with contradictions, antagonism and problems caused by the conflicting 'nature' of the parties in terms of their resources, worldviews and orientations. This gives green alliances a potentially volatile character apart from 'serious questions regarding representation and democratization' (Lipschutz and Fogel 2000: 136), which have not been addressed here. In sum, green alliances have under certain circumstances the ability to solve environmental issues; but whether they are the panacea they are widely heralded to be has to be treated with caution.

Although green alliances are popular in practice as well as in academic literature, our knowledge about their impact and theoretical implications remains limited. In stark contrast to management and organizational studies, the relationship between ENGOs and corporations remains under-researched. Empirical evidence largely continues to be unsystematic and anecdotal, hampering a well-founded conclusion about the effectiveness of green alliances. Here again scepticism has to prevail, as voluntary environmental policy has not lived up to its expectations.

On a more conceptual level, the above analysis has shown research into private actors to have almost exclusively focused so far on the conditions for the possibility of such actors' success. While policy windows, political opportunity and governance structures have been paramount research objects, NGOs have indeed been 'black boxed' to date. Future research agendas should therefore take into account that internal organizational dynamics and habits have an effect on ENGOs' actions and therefore on their impact, their success and failure. An interrelated focal point of future inquiry could lie with the conduct of green alliances. Thus far research has mainly looked at the conditions for the emergence of green alliances but has neglected how they can be maintained. Another aspect of such a research agenda has to be the question of how legitimate private policy arrangements actually are. As these arrangements have a political impact but exclude direct public participation *per se*, their success will probably be measured not only in terms of effectiveness but also in terms of public approval – a rather tall order.

To conclude: do green alliances really represent a frivolous flirtation with the enemy, as the title of this chapter suggests? Time will tell whether conditions remain favourable and whether green alliances might be able to work under adverse circumstances. The key to the success of green alliances lies in their ability to keep internal rifts at bay, to avoid the danger of cooptation and to connect their activities to core business and public policy. As part of mixed policy packages, they may provide a much needed push for global environmental governance.

Notes

1. For the purpose of the argument, I treat transnational and global civil society synonymously. Although the difference between the two remains blurred on the whole, they seem to imply different perspectives: the former alludes to the emergence of trans-border communities with a shared sense of solidarity, purpose and common interest, the latter to the materialization of a progressive global order.
2. Following convention, I will use capital letters to denote the academic field of International Relations (IR) and lower case when referring to what is construed as its empirical subject matter.
3. Similar systems have, for instance, developed in the fields of human and social rights, labour standards and so forth; for a comprehensive overview, see Oliviero and Simmons (2002).
4. Multiple narratives and concepts capture this trajectory. One of the most prominent has been Beck's (1996) contrast between 'simple' and 'reflexive modernity'.

References

Amoore, L. and P. Langley (2004) Ambiguities of Global Civil Society, *Review of International Studies*, 30(1): 89–110.

Arts, B. (2002) 'Green Alliances' of Business and NGOs: New Styles of Self-regulation or 'Dead-end Roads'? *Corporate Social Responsibility and Environmental Management*, 9(1): 26–36.

Bartley, T. (2003) Certifying Forests and Factories: States, Social Movements, and the Rise of Private Regulation in the Apparel and Forest Products Fields, *Politics and Society*, 31(3): 433–464.

Beck, U. (1996) World Risk Society as Cosmopolitan Society? Ecological Questions in a Framework of Manufactured Uncertainties, *Theory, Culture & Society*, 13(4): 1–32.

Bendell, J. (1998) Editorial – Special Issue: Business-NGO Relations and Sustainable Development, *Greener Management International*, (24): i–iv.

Bendell, J. (ed.) (2000a) *Terms of Endearment: Business, NGOs and Sustainable Development* (Sheffield: Greenleaf Publishing).

Bendell, J. (2000b) Civil Regulation: A New Form of Democratic Governance for the Global Economy? in J. Bendell (ed.) *Terms of Endearment* (Sheffield: Greenleaf Publishing), pp. 239–255.

Bendell, J. and D. Murphy (2000) Planting the Seeds of Change: Business – NGO Relations on Tropical Deforestation, in Bendell, *Terms of Endearment*, pp. 65–78.

Bernstein, S. (2001) *The Compromise of Liberal Environmentalism* (New York: Columbia University Press).

Clapp, J. (1998) The Privatization of Global Environmental Governance: ISO 14000 and the Developing World, *Global Governance*, 4(3): 295–316.

Cox, R. W. (1983) Gramsci, Hegemony and International Relations: An Essay in Method, *Millennium: Journal of International Studies*, 12(2): 162–175.

Cox, R. W. (1987) *Production, Power, and World Order: Social Forces in the Making of History* (New York: Columbia University Press)

Crane, A. (1998) Exploring Green Alliances, *Journal of Marketing Management*, 14(6): 559–579.

Cutler, C. A. V. Haufler and T. Porter (eds.) (1999) *Private Authority and International Affairs* (Albany, NY: State University of New York Press).

Elkington, J. and S. Fennell (2000) Partners for Sustainability, in Bendell, *Terms of Endearment*, pp. 152–153.

Falkner, R. (2003) Private Environmental Governance and International Relations: Exploring the Links, *Global Environmental Politics*, 3(2): 72–87.

Gill, S. (ed.) (1993) *Gramsci, Historical Materialism and International Relations* (Cambridge: Cambridge University Press).

Glasbergen, P. and R. Groenenberg (2001) Environmental Partnerships in Sustainable Energy, *European Environment*, 11(1): 1–13.

Hajer, M. A. (1995) *The Politics of Environmental Discourse: Ecological Modernization and the Policy Process* (Oxford: Clarendon Press).

Hall, R. B. and T. J. Biersteker (eds.) (2002) *The Emergence of Private Authority in Global Governance* (Cambridge: Cambridge University Press).

Hartman, C. L. and E. R. Stafford (1997) Green Alliances: Building New Business with Environmental Groups, *Long Range Planning*, 30(2): 184–196.

Held, D. (2002) Globalization, Corporate Practice and Cosmopolitan Social Standards, *Contemporary Political Theory*, 1(1): 59–78.

Jordan, A., R. K. W. Wurzel and A. R. Zito (2003) 'New' Environmental Policy Instruments: An Evolution or a Revolution in Environmental Policy? *Environmental Politics*, 12(SI): 201–224.

Kütting, G. (2004) *Globalization and the Environment: Greening Global Political Economy* (New York: State University of New York Press).

Laxer, G. and S. Halperin (eds.) (2003) *Global Civil Society and its Limits* (Basingstoke: Palgrave).

Lipschutz, R. D. and C. Fogel (2002) 'Regulation for the Rest of Us?' Global Civil Society and the Privatization of Transnational Regulation', in R. B. Hall and T. J. Biersteker (eds.) *The Emergence of Private Authority in Global Governance* (Cambridge: Cambridge University Press), pp. 115–140.

Livesey, S. M. (1999) McDonald's and the Environmental Defense Fund: A Case Study of a Green Alliance, *The Journal of Business Communication*, 36(1): 5–39.

Lober, D. J. (1997) Explaining the Formation of Business – Environmentalist Collaborations: Collaborative Windows and the Paper Task Force, *Policy Sciences*, 30(1): 1–24.

Mayntz, R. (2002) Common Goods and Governance, in A. Heritier (ed.) *Common Goods: Reinventing European and International Governance* (Lanham, MD: Rowman & Littlefield), pp. 15–27.

OECD (2003) *Voluntary Approaches for Environmental Policy: Effectiveness, Efficiency and Usage in Policy Mixes* (Paris: OECD).

Oliviero, M. B. and A. Simmons (2002) Who's Minding the Store? Global Civil Society and Corporate Responsibility, in M. Glasius, M. Kaldor and H. K. Anheier (eds.) *Global Civil Society* (Oxford: Oxford University Press), pp. 77–107.

Redclift, M. (1987) *Sustainable Development: Exploring the Contradictions* (London: Methuen).

Reinalda, B. (2001) Private in Form, Public in Purpose: NGOs in International Relations Theory, in B. Arts, M. Noortmann, and B. Reinalda (eds.) *Non-State Actors in International Relations* (Aldershot: Ashgate), pp. 11–40.

Rose, C. (1997) Greenpeace – Implementing Solutions, *Marine Environmental Management*, 4: 81–84.

Schmidheiny, S. (ed.) (1992) *Changing Course: A Global Business Perspective on Development and the Environment* (Cambridge, MA: MIT Press).

Stafford, E. and C. Hartman (1996) Green Alliances: Strategic Relations between Businesses and Environmental Groups, *Business Horizons*, 39(2): 50–59.

Strange, S. (1996) *The Retreat of the State: The Diffusion of Power in the World Economy* (Cambridge: Cambridge University Press).

Tesner, S. (2000) *The United Nations and Business: A Partnership Recovered* (Basingstoke: Macmillan).

Usui, M. (2004) The Private Business Sector in Global Environmental Diplomacy, in N. Kanie and P. M. Haas (eds.) *Emerging Forces in Environmental Governance* (Tokyo: United Nations University Press), pp. 216–259.

Wapner, P. (2000) The Normative Promise of Nonstate Actors: A Theoretical Account of Global Civil Society, in P. Wapner and L. E. J. Ruiz (eds.) *Principled World Politics: The Challenge of Normative International Relations* (Lanham, MD: Rowman & Littlefield), pp. 261–274.

WCED (1987) *Our Common Future* (Oxford: Oxford University Press).

Wymer, W. W. J. and S. Samu (2003) Dimensions of Business and Nonprofit Collaborative Relationships, *Journal of Nonprofit and Public Sector Marketing*, 11(1): 3–22.

Part III

Humanitarianism within a New World Order

9
Transnational Risks and Humanitarian Crises: The Blind Alley of UN Interventionism

David Rieff

'Even solidarity is sick,' wrote Adorno in *Minima Moralia*. That was in 1951. Despite all assertions to the contrary about the growth of solidarity in what the American political theorist Richard Falk has called 'an emerging global village', and the rise of a new global order based on the clichés any reader of a decent broadsheet newspaper can recite – rule of law, human rights, democracy, cosmopolitan citizenship (you are just as capable of elaborating the rest of the inventory as I am) – there is little reason to believe that the patient has grown healthier over the course of the past 56 years. What is true, certainly, is that while states remain the fundamental building blocks of the international system, various pressures on this system, ranging from the unforeseen consequences of capitalist development (the environmental crisis), to the globalization of mass culture, above all the media (what, following Guy Debord, one might call the 'spectacular' crisis), the demographic explosion in the poor world and the demographic collapse of the rich world (the migration crisis), and the (further) denationalization of capital (the crisis of social democracy), together impose an international dimension on spheres that hitherto were national or sub-national.

Laying both hopes and fears aside, what has been the result? The obvious pathologies have manifested themselves and are not difficult to enumerate: utopianism on the left in the form of fantasies of cosmopolitan citizenship and world government, and utopianism on the right in the form of the permanence of capitalism (Fukuyama's end of history) and the ideology of redemptive materialism that goes with it (the work of the American journalist Thomas Friedman is a good example of this); xenophobia on the 'old right'; nihilism, whether in its deep green or neo-fascist versions among the disenchanted youth of the rich world; religious fundamentalism – above all, in the Islamic world but not inconsequentially in the United States and India. But among people who do not want to join one of these cults, what has been most evident has been a flight away from politics and towards simulacra of politics. And among those simulacra, two stand out: international law as the avenue to a new, general cosmopolitan peace – that is to say Kant's vision of perpetual peace expanded to include the world as a whole – and the militarized solidarity of humanitarian intervention.

Whether as expressed by the Bush administration or leading voices of European social democracy (and there is less separating these two groups ideologically than either likes to pretend: Freud's 'narcissism of small differences' is surely relevant here), the claims of both cosmopolitanism and solidarity have grown bolder. Bush insists that the instauration of a new world order based on freedom is not just feasible, it is to be America's project in the years to come. Meanwhile, in Brussels, the self-image of the European Union, if not necessarily its reality, is an exporter of democracy and human rights norms, not just to countries aspiring to EU membership – the right of any club, whether of persons or states – but to the entire world. (With the exception of China, that is, for China is the hard nut before which all this sentimentalizing pauses and doffs its cap.) To quote two sentences from Jürgen Habermas, which are astonishingly complacent even by the standards of his recent work, 'Even if we still have a long way to go before fully achieving it, the cosmopolitan condition is no longer merely a mirage. State citizenship and world citizenship form a continuum whose contours, at least, are already becoming visible.'

How the Frankfurt School moved from Adorno and Horkheimer's bedrock commitment to the melancholy project of calling things by their right names, whatever the political and cultural consequences, to Habermas's law-based utopian benevolence is a question with ramifications that go far beyond the arcane questions of whether historical materialism and Kantian (and now post-Kantian) notions of peaceful cosmopolitan order and the proper relation between morality and law can be reconciled.[1] But for our purposes, it is probably enough to remark that advocates of the new transnational order – of 'the power of norms versus the norms of power' as Thomas Risse has described it – share with those who continue to advocate the traditional Westphalian view of an international order based on state sovereignty that a commitment to justice and a commitment to the suppression of disorder are part and parcel of the same societal project.

Put somewhat differently, the challenge to the Westphalian order does not so much hold up another vision of the role of power – where is Foucault when we need him? – as it advocates a pooling of sovereignty in the context of supranational institutions. In a sense, this is the EU project writ large and imagined as something that can be transposed within either the UN context or that of less successful regional institutions like ASEAN or the African Union. Of course, the recent failure of the European draft constitution in France and the Netherlands suggests that the consensus for such supranational arrangements is not shared even among ordinary Europeans in 2005, let alone can be imagined as constituting a viable and legitimate framework for a post-Westphalian global order. Even the American position has been a kind of Hegelian insistence on the US as the instrument of history's 'march toward freedom', to use Bush's phrase. This ideology of revolution from above may explain why neo-conservatism has had such an extraordinary appeal for people who were Trotskyites in their youth, from Irving Kristol to Christopher Hitchens.

Obviously, few people in Europe, with the notable exception of Tony Blair, and, if we are being candid, certain intellectuals for whom the well-being of the state of Israel plays a disproportionate role in their thought, look at Bush and make the full Hegelian leap to the belief that they are seeing history on horseback (or in a humvee). But many share the view that although American power, at least when wielded unilaterally (there are those in the US, notably Samantha Power and Michael Ignatieff, whose view seems to be that while a 'unilateral' US may be the problem, a 'multilateral' US would be the solution), is the wrong answer, a worldwide cosmopolitan regime needs to be established and that, if this project is to be undertaken seriously, it must involve interventions to right human rights wrongs and stop the wars of ethnic cleansing that have become endemic in the post-Cold War world. Unsurprisingly, many who loathe American attempts to monopolize the use of force none the less are firm believers in the idea of a monopoly of force wielded in the interests of humanity.

This is perfectly logical. It is a commonplace of standard political analysis that one of the principal attributes of a functioning state (as opposed to a failed state) is its monopoly on the legitimate use of violence. The theorists of the new cosmopolitan global order, and of the pooling of sovereignty in supranational institutions, have tended to want to confer that legitimate attribute on the EU or other regional organizations, with the caveat that the legitimate use of force for any other purpose other than self-defence in principle requires UN sanction, even if Kosovo and Rwanda showed that this vision was not yet mature. On this account, stark in its legal formalism and troubling in its seeming equation of law and morality, a just war is a war the UN Security Council votes to authorize. Now how, in practice, the first Gulf War of 1991 is somehow 'more' just than, say, the war of independence being waged by the Polisario guerrillas in Western Sahara is hard to fathom except in purely UN-centred legal terms. In fairness, though, most advocates of the 'emerging global village' would argue that they are not principally concerned with the justice of wars as much as the necessity of protecting people from unjust or oppressive rulers. Indeed, the deep legitimacy and prestige of so-called humanitarian intervention derives from the fact that it is not thought of as war but as the enforcement of human rights norms.

Thus, Mary Kaldor of the London School of Economics, who was one of the staunchest advocates of interventions in the Balkans in the 1990s, has repeatedly said that she is not advocating war but rather a species of militarized police work. Even the language conventionally used to describe humanitarian interventions seems to go to great lengths to avoid the language of war. Hence, advocates normally speak of 'conflict resolution', 'preventive deployments', 'peacekeeping', 'peace enforcement', etc. Jan Eliasson, the former head of the UN's Department of Humanitarian Affairs and currently Sweden's ambassador to the UN, referred in a recent speech to such operations as the 'most civilized' use of military force. He might have added 'most legitimate', at least in the eyes of those people who, in the words of the American academics Carl Kaysen and George Rathjens believe that 'the UN, backed by regional organizations – what might be called the formal international system – offers the best instrument for achieving [a liberal world order], for only the formal international system has the political legitimacy to police the world.' A cynic might be tempted to suggest that the notion that the world can be policed in this way depends on either a nostalgia for empire (though those who suffer from that particular exercise in sentimental self-regard, like the British historian Niall Ferguson, tend to prefer *Pax Americana* to the blue flag of the UN) or, again, a kind of Fukuyama-like belief that the regulation of states to prevent them from abusing their own citizens is part of the establishment of that global liberal capitalist free market utopia that is eventually going to unite the world and make it prosperous and democratic. To say this may go too far in the sense that, self-evidently, many advocates of humanitarian intervention simply want a particular horror to end and believe that, at least sometimes, military deployment is the only viable alternative. But even those for whom these interventions are emblems of despair, not hope, seem to have little doubt about the moral worthiness of the enterprise – above all, when legitimized by the UN. Of course, this is the UN as its proponents wish it to be, not, as used to be said of the Soviet Union by dissident Marxists eager to salvage the Communist project, the 'actually existing' UN, which has never been able to reconcile institutionally its founders' hopes that it represent the best hopes of humanity and its identity as an inter-governmental body.

Now, human rights activists, civil society proponents persuaded that the moral task of contemporary times is the subduing of a selfish and parochial state sovereignty, and believers in Bernard Kouchner's *droit d'ingerence* and the militarized humanitarianism that accompanies it, put forward a UN empowered to guarantee international human rights and humanitarian norms by force of arms. The justification? Solidarity, humanity, justice. The goal? Cosmopolitan order, law-respecting peace, a just society. The enemy? All those beyond these norms, the rogue or outlaw states, those who would dare defy the normative consensus of the era. Here, we are on familiar ground. The same rationale that the Bush administration has given for refusing to apply to the Geneva Conventions to captured Taliban and al-Qaeda fighters, which is essentially that they are *gens hostis humanorum*, enemies of the human race, as the British considered pirates in the nineteenth century, is used by those who preach the gospel of humanitarian intervention. For them, states that kill their own citizens have forfeited their Westphalian prerogatives. They too are pirates; they too are illegitimate; and so attacking them, turning parts of their territory into protectorates, temporarily or permanently, *à la* East Timor or Kosovo, is morally and legally unimpeachable. And because, according to this argument, the principles and norms of global justice have already been enshrined in the UN Charter and its successor instruments, the Geneva Conventions, and in contemporary international law more generally, intervening to stop outlaw states from behaving like – well – the outlaws that they are poses no serious moral, ethical or political dilemmas for those who would do the intervening. Rather, as we are constantly instructed by panels of UN 'wise men' and commissions underwritten by social democratic governments like Sweden and Canada, the task is to find ways to translate these norms into realities. In short, individuals have universal rights that are inalienable and states that attempt to take them away must desist or, at least ideally, it should be regime change time. Why the United Nations, which is currently in the grips of a general crisis of unprecedented proportions, should be viewed as the vehicle for this new global dispensation is unclear. At best, that organization's future in a world of US hegemony in the immediate term, and of US rivalry with an equally nationalistic power, China, in the immediate to long term, is one of increasingly subaltern status. Presumably, the idea of the UN as global policeman derives its force from the fact that the UN Charter and subsequent UN instruments have the special legitimacy of having been signed on to by most of the governments of the world. At the very least, that would seem to make the human rights norms these documents enshrine more than just juridical constructs but instead manifestations of some sort of incontestable world spirit. Hegel again, in other words! Or perhaps it is the spirit of globalization, or, more accurately, its moral warrant. Thus, those who favour humanitarian intervention talk about rights – the right of outsiders to protect and the right of those whose human rights are being violated to be protected (except in China or Chechnya, that is). In any case, where else but the UN? It is important to be fair and not to pile it on. The current crisis of confidence in the United Nations is real. Within the Secretariat itself, most UN staff feel they are being attacked unfairly, and also both those states where it is felt the UN does too much and those where it is felt it does too little should not obscure the things that the world organization does well. Were it to become necessary, in the unlikely event that the UN dissolved or, as happened with the League of Nations, be confronted by true marginalization due to the formal withdrawal or simply the *de facto* non-participation of one or more important member states (the US, then as now, being the obvious candidate), to find a new 'stand-alone' international mandate for the Office of the UN High Commissioner for Refugees (UNHCR) or the World Health Organization (WHO) along the lines of that which establishes the legitimacy of the International Committee of the Red Cross (ICRC), the effectiveness of these UN specialized agencies would almost certainly be diminished. For however frayed the authority of the UN may be in the wake of the peacekeeping failures of Bosnia and Rwanda and of the Iraq imbroglio, its authority and special legitimacy in the eyes of most states is still an asset that one underestimates at one's peril. For while it is probably the case that the moral symbolism of the UN's blue flag with its map of the globe in the middle no longer engenders the same kind of admiration it did twenty years ago, the fact remains that governments would be even less likely to cooperate (above all, on refugee matters) with agencies that could not claim to be expressions of the will, enshrined in international law, of this 'world community' – no matter how easily debunked and how almost mythological in character that concept of 'world' or 'international' community may be. As Iraq demonstrated all too vividly, even a UN freed from the shackles of the superpower rivalry during the Cold War has proved unable to live up to the promise its founders believed it possessed as the world's premier peace and security institution. But in other arenas, it renders extraordinarily valuable service to a world in which altruism is in short supply. For anyone willing to examine without *parti pris* the work of the UN's specialized agencies in alleviating so-called humanitarian crises, looking after and serving as an advocate for refugees and the internally displaced, and intervening in public health emergencies, whether man-made (in the context of war and refugee emergency) or at least ostensibly natural (outbreaks of the ebola virus, the after-effects of the Asian tsunami, etc.), this should surely not be a matter of controversy. In much the way that the UN in the 1950s and 1960s served an essential function in what the late Sir Anthony Parsons called 'a decolonization machine', so the UN in our time has become, for all its faults, the sexual scandals associated with various peacekeeping operations, bad choices in appointments to senior positions (the trajectory in office of the former head of UNHCR, Ruud Lubbers, is a cautionary tale in and of itself), and a too often sclerotic and self-regarding bureaucracy, an extraordinarily important 'alleviation machine'. The world as a whole would be a lower place without it, but for the world's poor the further marginalization of the UN would have an effect so dire that it barely bears thinking about.

However, there is a fundamental difference between making this claim and arguing for an expansion of the UN's role as an intervener in what we rather misleadingly and self-servingly call humanitarian crises. Language is important here because, to put it starkly, there is nothing humanitarian about such crises at all. Usually, what is meant is a political crisis, often a civil war, and it is not the least of the problem with the term that it occludes this reality. As Rony Brauman has asked, was Auschwitz a humanitarian crisis? To which the answer must be: only in the most subaltern of senses. But if we can all smile in a superior way and agree that Auschwitz was the terrible culmination of Nazism, why then is the Rwandan genocide so often subsumed under a humanitarian rubric? Or why, during the war in Bosnia, did it seem licit (rather than obscene, which is what it really was) for the principal international response to be the dispatch of UN agencies that specialized not in politics but alleviation (UNHCR, WFP, UNICEF, etc.), UN 'peacekeepers' whose mission was to protect the humanitarians, and NGOs specializing in emergency relief? Why do most of us believe that, say, the French Revolution was part of an historical upheaval that was unavoidable, whatever its costs in what in contemporary times we would call 'humanitarian' terms, but that the Balkan Wars were exercises in sense-lessness that simply needed to be stopped by some outside force? It is really only through facing the political and moral implications posed by these questions that we can start to think seriously about the implications of UN intervention in so-called failed states, to alleviate humanitarian crises or right human rights wrongs. And it is not a comfortable exercise. First, it requires an almost endearingly naïve faith in the idea that the interveners know what to do when they intervene; in other words, that we know how to engineer decent societies, that agreement, at least on minima of what such a society looks like, has been agreed on. But of course, no such *compromesso 'storico* has taken place, as the vast gap in attitudes about gender relations between, say, the European Union and the Organization of Islamic countries demonstrates. Obviously, the sentimental attractions of the idea of righting wrongs under the aegis of that blue flag are undeniable. At first glance, at least, a humanitarian intervention under a UN mandate seems to put the hornets' nest of issues surrounding not just the legality but the legitimacy of such inter-ventions beyond discussion. The problem of individual state interest seems to disappear since it is not a particular state or alliance but rather the 'international community', however questionable or, at the very least, both intellectually and morally fragile and contestable that con-cept is, that has united to authorize such the intervention in question. The difference in the acquiescence, however grudging, at least by governments to the UN-backed 1991 Gulf War and the preponderance of opposition by states and populations to the UN-opposed Anglo-American invasion of Iraq in 2003 illustrates the point. And where humanitarian interventions are concerned – a context in which there is, in any case, less principled opposition to outside intervention – a UN warrant is virtually always determinative in securing public consent – at least (though certainly not only) in the West. A second, related point, is that, unlike Iraq in 2003, humanitarian interventions of the type put forward for Congo and Darfur in the past two years seem to have little or no commercial or geo-strategic 'hidden agendas' for the interveners. Above all, the idea that there is an almost Kantian categorical imperative, one that morally requires those in a position bring to an end horrific suf-fering in places like Darfur or Liberia, has proved compelling – especially to people with a commitment to cosmopolitan and internationalist ideas of what it means to be a citizen in contemporary times. These are people for whom solidarity is a bedrock principle. And if one feels this, then there can be no justification, say, for letting people in Darfur suffer and die while the world looks on, whether that inaction is motivated by the sense that one is more obliged to neighbours than to people far away, or that for Western powers to intervene (even under a blue flag and with a UN Security Council mandate) smacks dangerously of nineteenth-century imperialism, or out of a belief that war is an outmoded and counter-productive method of settling political disputes whether between or within states. That, too, is a suggestive feature of the rhetoric of the UN as sole legitimate leviathan (however divorced from the UN's sad reality): the unwillingness to take the history of military interventions, not to say of imperialism, as a cautionary tale relevant to the present age's moral aspiration to bring these rogues and outlaw states to heel. But the deepest problem revolves around the original intellectual sleight of hand: that conflation of law and morality, and the apparent concomitant belief that international law is now the central repository of the moral principles that should govern the world. That such a view, however simultaneously ahistorical, romantic and stipulative may make sense, instrumentally, for an organization that derives its principal legitimacy from the law (the International Committee of the Red Cross is the most obvious example). But it cannot be the basis for society as a whole, not least because the democratic deficit in a context where treaties are decided by what may technically be democratic institutions like the United Nations but in fact have little or no functioning methods for involving the peoples of the world as opposed to the governments of the world. That, of course, is the appeal of the NGOs for the UN, particularly 'progressive' NGOs (an NGO like the right-wing American National Rifle Association has little appeal to the UN secretariat for obvious reasons): they can claim to represent civil society in a way that the UN clearly cannot. Legitimacy is thus conferred, as it were, through the grace and favour of activism. Anyone doubting this has only to look at the role the relief group Oxfam now plays in consulting with the UN and Western governments on matters connected to debt relief and development. 'The first task of political thought,' John Gray has written, 'is to understand the present.' That would seem the minimum requirement. But therein lies the tragedy of cosmopolitan internationalism: no matter how admirable the world it posits may be, it puts forward a gravely distorted reading of our times – sentimental, self-regarding, suffering profoundly from delusions of grandeur, blind to any sense of the tragic or, indeed, any sense of limits. Poor Debord. He died so soon. For when he talked about the society of the spectacle, he had not taken in that most 'spectacular' of ideas, humanitarian intervention.

Note

1. Jürgen Habermas's *Between Facts and Norms*, the boldest elaboration of his theories of law-based democratic idealism, often seems conceived as an indirect rebuttal to Theodor Adorno's *Minima Moralia*. 'If defeatism were justified,' Habermas writes in the preface, 'I would have had to choose a different literary genre, for example, the diary of a Hellenistic writer who merely documents, for subsequent generations, the unfulfilled promises of his waning culture.' Of course, this is almost a perfect description of what *Minima Moralia* attempts to do.

10
Humanitarian Trends
Tony Vaux

Introduction

The key issue for Western aid agencies, especially in the US and UK, is the changing relationship with their own governments. Greater opportunities for intervention that followed the end of the Cold War, coupled with new concerns about global security, have made governments more active in humanitarian issues. More funds are available, but there is a strong tendency to distort humanitarianism towards Western security concerns. The critical problem is not so much that Western governments micro-manage humanitarian operations, but that they have a profound influence on where humanitarian operations are instigated and on what scale. Because non-government aid agencies allocate much of their private income to development, they are especially susceptible to pressure in their spending for relief and disasters.

This chapter suggests that the notion of 'human security' can be used to counter these tendencies and keep humanitarianism more closely aligned to the perspectives and interests of those in need.[1]

Humanitarianism after the Cold War

During the Cold War the superpowers avoided any action that might bring them into military confrontation with each other, and therefore in situations of conflict left a 'humanitarian space' for private agencies. But the issues causing conflict were generally locked into wider issues of superpower relationships and therefore not susceptible to the actions of aid agencies. Accordingly, techniques of conflict analysis and resolution were developed in isolation of wider political processes. Similarly, the focus on human rights was limited to a few isolated cases rather than on the political systems or forms of governance that produced them. The disciplines of humanitarian aid, development, conflict resolution and human rights protection were quite clearly demarcated. This enabled aid agencies to develop a 'pure' form of humanitarianism based on policies of detachment and reflected in the Red Cross principles of neutrality, impartiality and independence.

The picture was by no means consistent, least of all in Latin America where the direct involvement of the US provides a parallel with today's interventionism. Communism was regarded as an enemy in much the same way as terrorism is today. Any person or organization thus labelled was placed outside the protection of international norms. Many local organizations in Latin America espoused communism because it articulated a pro-poor philosophy. The American attack on communism sometimes took the form of an attack on poor people and their organizations. This led the aid agencies to adopt a 'solidarity' position and distance themselves from Western power. Humanitarian responses were deliberately sidelined by activists in aid agencies who regarded them, at best, as a diversion from the political struggle. But in Africa and Asia humanitarian responses developed in isolation from politics. Even the existence of war was obscured by a focus on human suffering and the concept of innocent victims. Humanitarianism became best known from its African variant and the 'Band Aid' solutions that were proposed.

With the end of the Cold War, Western governments became directly involved in the humanitarian response in Africa and at least in some parts of Asia. With the Soviet Union and its ideology gone, the West focused its attention on the general turbulence of the poorer parts of the world and their ability to generate unwelcome floods of refugees, economic migrants and asylum seekers. The aim was to create a *Pax Americana* in which global business could operate, supported by a belief that this was the best means of global development, as well as being good for the economy at home. They quickly realized that, especially in the case of conflict, they had the capacity to do much more than simply provide funds. They could apply political pressure and could now use their military forces without fear of reprisals. They could use humanitarian responses to achieve political objectives.

Western politicians had also noticed that wars could be popular, as in the case of the Falklands for the UK and the first Gulf War for the US. The American-led invasion of Somalia in 1991 caused greater circumspection. Throughout the 1990s the Western powers tested their strength in different situations. Reacting against the failures to respond early enough in Bosnia and Rwanda, by the late 1990s they had again become more willing to use military force. Politicians could use force to support their objectives, but they had to be careful to pick political winners. Kosovo was the political success that encouraged further ventures in Afghanistan and Iraq.

Underlying this greater awareness of Western military strength was a growing frustration with national governments, especially in Africa, and some disillusionment with the process of change through development. This created the view that a more interventionist style was not only possible but also necessary. The 1990s saw the emergence of aid conditionality around the concept of 'good governance'. The reverence for sovereign states that had been the basis of Cold War diplomacy was now set aside. By implication the UN Charter and the UN General Assembly were marginalized. The centre of global governance became the UN Security Council, dominated by the US. The US also retained tight control over key UN agencies.

Politicians had also discovered that humanitarian aid was popular, whereas development was not. Humanitarian aid could be rapidly shifted towards political priorities whereas development aid was limited by long and inflexible time scales. Aid budgets were increasingly directed towards high-profile disasters rather than development. They were also directed to private aid agencies rather than the UN.[2] Private aid agencies grew rapidly and proliferated in number. Competition became intense and agencies measured their success in relation to size. Threatened by the arrival of new (and often inefficient) rivals, the established agencies grouped themselves together around codes and standards. Success became associated with a close link to government funding, and following the interests of the donor public. Agencies followed the desires of the consumer, deciding that this meant the donor rather than the recipient of aid.

Technological advances in communication enabled the media to report on disaster responses as they happened. Journalists were under pressure to report every few hours and the more breathless and immediate their reports the better. But they could not move far from the centres of political activity for fear that other journalists might be there for the scoop. Journalists had little incentive to reach remote places or examine the issues in depth. It was easier simply to assemble a story around the activities of an aid agency, with the reporter standing in a refugee camp – or ideally a feeding centre for children. Such reports were often filed within minutes of arrival and the reporter then hurried back to the capital. Agencies working in locations accessible to the reporters and involved in the most photogenic activities became the centre of attention, with a positive impact on their fundraising.

The media became more susceptible to commercial pressures and aid agencies realized that media attention could be bought. In 1990, for the first time, an agency commissioned a TV crew to film its work and this was shown on prime-time TV. This duly brought a considerable increase in income and profile for that agency and a feeling that 'the gloves were off' among the others. By the late 1990s humanitarian missions were often accompanied by media advisers who acted as spokespersons, and agencies regularly sponsored visits by the media. Commercialism within the media made it increasingly easy to buy their time and interest.

But the biggest factor was that journalists needed to report on their country's political involvements. They focused on the places where their government was active, such as Afghanistan and Iraq, rather than those where there was greatest need, such as Angola and Congo. This became a loop back to the agencies. They could easily raise funds from governments and respond to public interest by going where the media went.

Changes in communication technology also meant that headquarters could now exert a stronger influence over field operations. Aid workers about to be interviewed by a journalist, but lacking a media adviser on the spot, could be briefed from headquarters. Senior managers were able to participate in every local discussion, and hence the weight of institutional concerns increased in relation to local analysis. Working through local partners became a problem: HQ wanted to see its own staff, showing the organizational logo and wearing the organizational T-shirt, baseball cap and multi-pocketed waistcoat. As the value of 'brand' increased the value of local partners declined.

The growth of business-oriented agencies, especially in the US, challenged the more traditional European agencies which had formerly seen themselves (rather idealistically perhaps) as purveyors of compassion and understanding rather than of money and products. With their clarity and efficiency, the business-oriented agencies easily impressed the officials in London and Brussels and began to take an increasing share of donor funding. The established British agencies began to adopt similar methods rather than lose 'market share'.

This process involved a great deal of doubt and soul-searching within the aid agencies, but the trend towards competitive behaviour was dominant. The European agencies had established a Code of Conduct in 1991[3] which imposed high standards for relationships with local partners and long-term support for local capacities. But although the majority of aid agencies had signed up to it, there was little commitment to its practical application (Slim and McConnan 1998). The Rwanda genocide of 1994 sent a serious shock through the humanitarian system. The subsequent evaluation (Borton, Brusset and Hallam 1996) revealed the shortcomings of the collective response, and a general sense of failure pervaded the aid establishment. Despite decades of experience in Rwanda, very few aid agencies had any idea of the impending crisis. The UN and US, which had received clear warnings, ignored them. It was the UN that took most of the blame (Melvern 2000).

Among the aid agencies there was much reflection. First, the unseemly scramble for a share of the response precipitated a sense of revulsion among aid workers. Second, agencies had taken on responsibilities that they could not fulfil, causing unnecessary suffering and deaths. Third, aid workers had found themselves supporting the perpetrators of the genocide who, by crossing a border, had become technically refugees and entitled to international support without any liability for their crimes. Neutrality and impartiality did not seem to be adequate principles for such a case.

One of the main outcomes of this reflection was the Sphere Project, leading to the publication of standards for humanitarian response. These were intended to ensure that aid agencies could not easily accept responsibilities and then fail to meet them. Standards for refugee care already existed in the UNHCR Handbook, but the new Sphere Standards (Sphere Project 2004) transferred the focus of responsibility from UNHCR to the agencies themselves – or to be exact, to a core group of the largest Western agencies. Thus they tended to marginalize not only local partners but also the UN.

The Sphere Standards assert the primacy of the professional and the specialist over the amateur and the generalist. In practice this can mean the primacy of expatriate over local staff. The Red Cross Code had been the basis for relating relief to development and for moderating the relationship between international NGOs and their partners. Although the Code is acknowledged in the Sphere Handbook, in practice it was superseded by Sphere. The emphasis in the Sphere Charter was on international humanitarian law rather than local partnership. This meant that instead of listening to the concerns and advice of local agencies a fixed set of rules was imposed. In the late 1990s aid agencies also became increasingly focused on a rights-based approach. But many of these 'rights' were expressed in global or Western terms rather than rights in relation to national government.

The message to non-Western peoples was that they had no responsibility for their own humanitarian problems. This added to the sensitivity and complex reactions that surround Western technological supremacy and military assertiveness. For some, there was a deep sense of failure in their own culture and political systems. Others might react angrily, especially if they saw double-standards and self-interest lurking behind the lofty Western language. In their view, Western agencies were dominant not because they were better but because they had money.

Aid agencies were scarcely aware of such perceptions. Radical discourse in poorer countries rarely found its way into Western countries except through the filter of Western academics. Western donors rarely funded local people to develop their own discourse or to overcome the technical limitations or rules of copyright that would enable them to spread their ideas. Instead, they funded Western academics to develop a discourse that reflected their own cultural and political dispositions.

In conclusion, humanitarianism came to be triangulated between the principles and standards generated by the aid agencies and the political spin of Western governments. The perspectives of people in need had always been difficult to perceive and even harder to incorporate, but they disappeared almost entirely when local partners were sidelined and Western security interests became paramount.

By the late 1990s humanitarianism had become closely linked to the Western security agenda. After 9/11 this agenda came to dominate all others and so humanitarianism moved to the centre stage in global politics. In Afghanistan and Iraq, the political, economic and security objectives of Western governments were ravelled together with humanitarian responses in an explicit and strategic manner. Aid agencies were contracted to play their part within a Strategic Framework. Many did so willingly and as a moral or patriotic obligation. The process was called 'coherence' by some and 'politicization' by others (Donini, Niland and Wermester 2004).

Accustomed to make public statements about the rights and wrongs of wars in which their own country was not involved, the aid agencies found it much more difficult to formulate public policy on Kosovo, Afghanistan and Iraq. Criticism of Western intervention, or even prioritizing humanitarian need, could easily be seen as involvement in politics. Their silence could easily lead others to conclude that they supported Western expansionism.

Relations between aid staff and the military became closer than ever. Photos of aid staff and soldiers working together regularly appeared in the press. Aid staff flew on military planes and worked alongside soldiers on humanitarian projects – something that they would not have considered as a possibility in relation to any armed forces but their own (Vaux 2001). Aid agencies found themselves supporting calls for military intervention, notably in Liberia, and at least toying with the idea in the case of Sudan. There was talk of a 'new humanitarianism' embracing humanitarianism within a political philosophy that linked global poverty and global security. Governments in countries that had got used to accepting humanitarianism as a gift without strings now began to wonder what they were letting themselves in for. Rumours of spying by aid workers began to spread.

Global humanitarian assistance

The Iraq War consolidated a trend towards greater distortions in the allocation of humanitarian aid. In 2002 Oxfam estimated that half of all the funds for the UN's 25 international appeals was being directed to Afghanistan. In 2003 the Global Humanitarian Assistance Report (Development Initiatives 2003) set out the trends as follows:

- Humanitarian aid has been growing over the long term both in overall volume and as a share of aid.
- There are large differences in how money is allocated to different emergency situations.
- Requests ranged from $38 to $304 per person. Contributions ranged from $20 to $177 per person.
- Taking the year in which spending was highest for each country, bilateral humanitarian aid for Bosnia was $116 per person compared to just $2 in Ethiopia.

Humanitarian aid to Iraq, where there have been no reported deaths from lack of aid, runs at $74 per person but for Congo, where deaths from the effects of war are estimated at over 2.5 million people, the level of humanitarian aid was just $17. In terms of general development all these figures are completely overshadowed by the $80 billion reported to have been allocated by the US for the rebuilding of Iraq. At the end of 2003 Britain's Department for International Development (DFID) termi-nated its ongoing programmes in middle-income countries in order to fund programmes in Iraq. It dipped deeply into the Contingency Fund that would otherwise have been used for other humanitarian crises around the world. In effect funds were being taken from the countries in greater need to finance Britain's political priorities. The British Foreign Office and the Ministry of Defence, together with DFID, pooled their resources relating to conflict into a single Global Conflict Prevention Fund. The idea was that the Prime Minister's Office would manage the process in order to ensure 'coherence'. In effect, this left DFID open to pressure from the 'senior' Ministries – the Foreign Office and Ministry of Defence – and arguably left it unable to comply with its obligation, under its Public Service Agreement, to base its allocations of aid on need.

Not so long ago aid agencies campaigned strenuously to support the independence of DFID but have not done so on this occasion. Agencies are well aware of the increasing discrepancies and politicization of humanitarian aid. Oxfam (2004), Christian Aid (2004) and ActionAid (Cosgrave 2004) have conducted similar analyses. But the issue has received surprisingly little public attention. None of the agencies has yet made it into a major campaign. Instead, the focus of attention has been on trade and debt where there is a much higher level of agreement with government.

Trends among the agencies

The effect of these trends on different agencies depends on where they balance themselves between government funding, general principle and religious values. Abby Stoddard (2003) divides the agencies into Wilsonian, Dunantist and faith-based categories. Although each agency may contain elements from each type, this is a useful point for understanding how agencies are affected by current trends.

The 'Wilsonian' tradition (following the American president Woodrow Wilson who deeply influenced the reshaping of Europe after the First World War) places NGOs in support of government in a collective enterprise. CARE was an example in its original form as Cooperative for American Relief Everywhere. By contrast, the Dunantist tradition follows the principles of impartiality, neutrality and independence that arose from Henri Dunant's sense of moral outrage at the Battle of Solferino. This led directly to the creation of the ICRC and indirectly to MSF. Similar motives led to the foundation of Save the Children in response to the First World War and Oxfam in relation to the Second World War. Such agencies tend to maintain a distance from governments, and try to define and follow a pure form of humanitarianism that is neither religious nor state-dominated.

The third group comprises those that are based on religious principles, such as Christian Aid, Islamic Relief and CAFOD. This group typically resolves issues by reference to religious principles rather than international humanitarian law or national interest. Arguably there is a fourth group that seeks to demonstrate 'solidarity' with partners, but this overlaps extensively with faith-based groups that, in effect, work in 'solidarity' with their partners of the same religion. Faith and partnership are inextricably linked.

All three types may take funds from governments and work with local partners. The system can remain in equilibrium provided that the national interests followed by Wilsonian agencies are not contentious from a Dunantist or religious perspective. But today this is a problem. Few agencies can claim to have taken a neutral, impartial and independent view in the case of Kosovo, Afghanistan and Iraq. They have been forced by Western political agendas to give those places much greater prominence than they deserve from a strictly humanitarian perspective. Some have compromised more than others, but this makes little difference in the eyes of observers around the world. Aid agencies are seen as a group, and as a group that increasingly represents the Western security agenda.

Aid workers may be willing to face such risks if they are absolutely certain about the justice of their (and their agency's) position. But they are understandably reluctant to put their lives at risk to ensure that Bush and Blair are re-elected or to support Western business interests in oil-rich states. Faced with criticism from local partners and people, and without clear information to the contrary, they may begin to wonder whether their own agency is interested in profile and market share rather than the needs of the people.

Perhaps the most sensitive problem for faith-based agencies is to determine whether the War on Terror contains a sub-plot against Islam. There is a widespread perception that current events reflect a 'clash of civilizations', Samuel Huntington's influential thesis in which Islam inevitably and eternally antagonizes Western values and institutions (Huntington 1993). It might have been expected that Islamic groups would strike back against Christians, but this does not seem to be the case. Extremist Islamic groups have targeted Western political power rather than religions, and they seem more concerned with atheism and materialism than with Christianity (Benthall 2003). Al-Qaeda seems to be particularly focused on political elites, especially in the US and Saudi Arabia.

The way is still open for communication between Christian and Islamic groups, but it may not stay open unless an effort is made to use it. Such dialogue is immediately necessary in parts of the world where Muslim–Christian relationships are tense. It is needed on a long-term basis in places where such confrontation has not yet occurred. There is now a greater risk that one side or the other will play the War on Terror card either by denouncing opponents as terrorists or by calling in real terrorists to take part in what could have remained a localized issue.

An aggrieved local cleric can quite easily bring down war on the heads of his neighbours, and exploit the clash of greater powers and principles to secure his own narrow interests. In Indonesia and Nigeria, for example, this has become a common pattern.

Moving forward

The major problem of humanitarianism is to align the allocation of funds more closely to need. The World Disasters Report (compiled by the Red Cross Federation) identifies this as a fundamental problem, suggesting that: 'There is an urgent priority to invest in credible, objective assessments of humanitarian needs across the globe, so that aid is allocated to those at greatest risk and need, not to those at the top of the strategic and media agenda' (Introduction 2003: 1).

But the problem is not simply the accuracy of the assessments. Donors do not need minute detail to know that the needs of Congo are greater than those of Iraq. The problem lies in the current process of politicization. Historically, donors have always favoured certain countries, often those with colonial links. The tendency was for such biases to even out over the various preferences of the international community. But if all the donors focus on one place, and the reason for doing so is 'global security', then the distortions will be much greater. If humanitarian agencies follow the 'global security' agenda, they will lose credibility in much of the world, and may face greater problems of their own security, access and ability to link with local partners.

In conclusion, the agencies have been reluctant to rock the boat in relation to the Western security agenda and its effects on humanitarianism. Public opinion in the UK has tended to be benign. As long as someone somewhere is receiving aid, and the totals are increasing, the public are satisfied. But there is less satisfaction among partners and there might be even less, if it could be measured, among people in need. The problem is that they lack influence on the way things are done. Their interests are not at the centre of the analysis.

How could aid agencies tackle this issue? They would do well to consider the concept of human security. Unfortunately the phrase has already been co-opted by those promoting the Western security agenda to mean little more than the extension of global security to the local level. But the term has quite different origins and could still be rescued for use by humanitarians. Potentially it reverses the polarity of thinking about security by placing the security of people in need at the centre of the analysis.

In 1994 the UNDP Human Development Report featured the concept of human security as an alternative to what had become, during the Cold War, an excessive international focus on the security of states. In those optimistic days it was thought that development and humanitarian aid could be separated from political interests and it would be possible to focus attention on the person in need. Human security was explicitly put forward as a means of combining concerns about physical security with general concepts of well-being. Amartya Sen became involved in the idea, helping to set up the Commission on Human Security. He described human security as 'Freedom from Fear' and 'Freedom from Want'.

The concept developed slowly until, after 9/11, the word 'security' became one of the most highly charged in the English language. All aspects of security were regrouped around the security of the American people. Human security became the means to secure American security through a global agenda. Mark Duffield (2001) believes that it is now little more than a conceptual device for extending Western security into the 'borderlands'. But this was certainly not the original intention, nor its actual meaning, and perhaps there is still time to rescue the concept.

The notion of 'human security' has three primary qualities. First, it is a bottom-up view of the world – it defines the problem as the minimal requirement of the person in need. Second, it draws no artificial boundaries between security and well-being. Third, it focuses the role for outsiders on what Sen calls 'downside risk' – everyone getting what they consider absolutely essential rather than general progress. A human security approach focuses on the threats or risks to a person's security. These may range from ill-health to war. It is not about getting richer but about staying the same – if that is acceptable. It has the great advantage of limiting the responsibility of the outsider to protecting a minimal existence rather than leading forward into an open-ended process of advance. It links relief and development. But it has the disadvantage that it does not fit well with numerical targets and bureaucratic systems. Human security is concerned with the minimum needs of each person rather than global progress or expanding markets.

Conclusion

The War on Terror has compounded the problems created by Western interventionism and the politicization of aid. This is not a new phenomenon, but the scale and focus are different. The dominant British discourse has been about principles, standards and norms, but these have a hollow ring to others around the world, and at worst may seem little more than a means to extend Western domination. The security interests of Western governments, reflected in the media, have seriously distorted the pattern of humanitarian response. Western aid agencies have not challenged this with sufficient vigour. Failure to distance themselves from the Western agenda has put a strain on relationships with partners, especially where the agencies expect them to take risks.

The dominance of the Western security agenda and the distortion of funding make this an appropriate time to reflect. Agencies should be more open and more challenging. With their government, they should be willing to state their position on any intervention, actual or potential, and maintain it even if there may be some loss of funding. They should develop policies which define when they will speak out as a matter of principle. At all times they should be open in commenting on the allocation of aid resources and be ready to challenge political distortions of global aid.

Agencies should consider taking a more proactive stance on issues relating to those who suffer negative stereotypes as a result of the War on Terror. It is common to hear politicians refer to the 'civilized world', leaving open the interpretation of what the opposite might be. Often it appears that the opposite includes poor people and Muslims. Such remarks should not pass unchallenged.

In practice the critical issue for aid agencies is the relationship with partners. Recent trends have put pressure on that relationship and opened the way for suspicion about institutional or national self-interest. There is also some suspicion that Western agencies have used technical standards and bureaucratic procedures to exert undue influence and reopen the way for expatriate leadership in humanitarian crises. These factors can lead to partners being unwilling to share risk in the crucial issue of speaking out. A preliminary step may be to reaffirm the importance of the Red Cross Code as a basis for partnership, debate it line by line with partners and agree specific details for specific countries.

There is also a need to develop the relationship with people in need. This can be done by pursuing the issue of international needs assessment and rooting out the political and institutional obstacles. Agencies should carefully consider using a human security perspective and developing appropriate tools and methodologies. This would enable them to base their programmes, strategies and public policies on the perspectives of poor people.

Notes

1. This chapter is based on a study conducted for CAFOD in 2004. The author would particularly like to thank Chris Bain, Amelia Brookstein, Matthew Carter, Clare Dixon, Beverley Jones, Rob Rees, Catherine Sexton and Jo Trask, all at CAFOD. Outside CAFOD I received special help from Andrew Clark, Antonio Donini, Mark Duffield, Atallah Fitzgibbon, Jonathan Goodhand, Brendan Gormley, Maurice Herson, Hossam Hussain, Randolph Kent, Joanna Macrae, John Magrath, John Mitchell, Michael Mosselmans, Jenny Pearce, Hugo Slim, Paul Smith-Lomas, Marcus Thompson, Peter Walker and Roger Yates.
2. Humanitarian aid as a proportion of total aid increased from 2.5 per cent in 1980 to 11.3 per cent in 1999. See Macrae (2002) for necessary cautions about such figures.
3. Code of Conduct for the International Red Cross and Red Crescent Movement and NGOs in Disaster Response Programmes. See www.ifrc.org.

References

Benthall, J. (2003) Humanitarianism and Islam after 11 September, in J Macrae and A. Harmer (eds.) *Humanitarian Action and the 'Global War on Terror': A Review of Trends and Issues*, HPG Report 14 (London: ODI).

Borton, J., E. Brusset and A. Hallam (1996) *Humanitarian Aid and its Effects Study 3: The International Response to Conflict and Genocide: Lessons from the Rwanda Experience* (Copenhagen).

Christian Aid (200) *The Politics of Poverty – Aid in the New Cold War* (London: Christian Aid).

Commission on Human Security (2003) *Human Security Now – Protecting and Empowering People* (New York: Commission on Human Security).

Cosgrave, J. (2004) *The Impact of the War on Terror on Aid Flows* (London: ActionAid).

Darcy, J. and C. Hofmann (2003) *According to Need? Needs Assessment and Decision-making in the Humanitarian Sector*, HPG Report 15 (London: ODI).

DEC (2001) *Independent Evaluation of the DEC Response to the Earthquake in Gujarat, January 2001* (London: DEC).

Development Initiatives (2003) *Global Humanitarian Assistance 2003*, www.globalhumanitarianassistance.org.

Donini, A., N. Niland and K. Wermester (eds.) (2004) *Nation-building Unraveled? Aid, Peace and Justice in Afghanistan* (West Hartford, CT: Kumarian Press).

Duffield, M. (2001) *Global Governance and the New Wars: The Merging of Development and Security* (London and New York: Zed Press).

Duffield, M. (2001a) Governing the Borderlands – Decoding the Power of Aid, *Disasters*, 25(4), December.

Duffield, M. *Carry on Killing – Global Governance, Humanitarianism and Terror*. Draft paper.

Feinstein International Famine Center, Tufts University (2004) *The Future of Humanitarian Action – Implications of Iraq and Other Recent Crises* (Medford: Tufts University).

Feinstein International Famine Center, Tufts University (2004a) *Ambiguity and Change: Humanitarian NGOs Prepare for the Future* (Medford: Tufts University).

Huntington, S. (1993) The Clash of Civilizations? *Foreign Affairs*, 72(3): 22–49.

Inter-Agency Standing Committee (2000) *Humanitarian Action in the 21st Century* (New York: IASC).

International Federation of Red Cross and Red Crescent Societies (2003) *World Disasters Report 2003* (Geneva: IFRC).

Macrae, J. (ed.) (2002) *The New Humanitarianisms: A Review of Trends in Global Humanitarian Action*, HPG Report 11 (London: ODI).

Macrae, J. and A. Harmer (eds.) (2003) *Humanitarian Action and the 'Global War on Terror': A Review of Trends and Issues*, HPG Report 14 (London: ODI).

Macrae, J. et al. (2002) *Uncertain Power: The Changing Role of Official Donors in Humanitarian Action*, HPG Report 12 (London: ODI).

Melvern, L. (2000) *A People Betrayed: The Role of the West in Rwanda's Genocide* (London: Zed Books).

OCHA (2004) *Addressing the Challenges to Humanitarian Security*. Discussion paper presented to High-level Humanitarian Forum, Geneva, 31 March.

Oxfam GB (2003) *Beyond the Headlines – An Agenda for Action to Protect Civilians in Neglected Conflicts* (Oxford: Oxfam Publications).

Reindorp, N. (2002) Trends and Challenges in the UN System, in J. Macrae (ed.) *The New Humanitarianisms: A Review of Trends in Global Humanitarian Action*, HPG Report 11 (London: ODI).

Rieff, D. (2002) *A Bed for the Night – Humanitarianism in Crisis* (New York: Vintage Books).

Slim, H. (2004) *A Call to Alms – Humanitarian Action and the Art of War*, HD Opinion Paper (Geneva: Centre for Humanitarian Dialogue).

Slim, H. and L. McConnan (1998) *A Swiss Prince, a Glass Slipper and the Feet of 15 British Agencies: A Study of DEC Agency Positions on Humanitarian Principles* (London: DEC).

Sphere Project (2004) *Humanitarian Charter and Minimum Standards in Disaster Response – Revised* (Oxford: Oxfam Publications and Sphere).

Stockton, N. (2004) *Afghanistan, War, Aid and International Order* in Donini, Niland and Wermester (eds.) *Nation-building Unraveled? Aid, Peace and Justice in Afghanistan* (Hartford, CT: Kumarian Press).

Stoddard, A. (2003) Humanitarian NGOs: Challenges and Trends, in Macrae and Harmer (eds.) *Humanitarian Action and the 'Global War on Terror': A Review of Trends and Issues*, HPG Report 14 (London: ODI).

United Nations. 2000. *Report of the Panel on UN Peace Keeping Operations* (New York: UN).

Vaux, T. (2001) *The Selfish Altruist – Relief Work in Famine and War* (London: Earthscan).

11
The Role of the Military in a Changing World – CIMIC: Military Stepping Stones on the Road to Civil Society

Gerhard J. Klose

At first it seems like a contradiction in terms. How could military activity contribute to the development of civil society? The point is, the German government, as well as other member states of the North Atlantic Treaty Organization (NATO) and the European Union (EU), want to develop their future military engagements precisely in this direction.

CIMIC, as these activities are called, stands for Civil–Military Cooperation and is, in principle, nothing new. From history examples can be drawn from the Roman Empire to Napoleonic France. When, for example, French forces under Napoleon conquered central and central-eastern Europe, their civil–military cooperation worked in more than logistic ways. France had a new idea to spread. The French army first brought feudalism to an end by military force and then established a new legal and administrative system and laid the foundations for a new democratic future in these countries. That could be interpreted as an early version of CIMIC: providing practical support to build civil society.

The most famous, and most successful, example of a CIMIC engagement was probably the reconstruction of Germany after the Second World War – a success largely accomplished by US involvement. From that time on, the US has kept large CIMIC forces as part of their reserve forces, and thus they were able to mobilize these forces at short notice during the Balkan Wars in the early 1990s. All other Western nations learned their CIMIC lessons there, from the US forces.

It was therefore astonishing that in 2003 the US made some fundamental mistakes in its application of CIMIC at the beginning of the second

Iraq War. In our view, for the US the business of CIMIC was more or less related to the politics of the Cold War. Even before the end of the Cold War, the Americans had started to refashion their armed forces as expedition corps for missions all over the world. At the same time, the focus was on consolidation of their unique technological superiority. In the meantime, the US's former CIMIC resources and capacities had become a third priority. However, with the negative results of the Iraq campaign having been analysed quite candidly, the US is again devoting a lot of attention to CIMIC-related issues.

During the reconstruction of Germany, no serious conflict was reported from the cooperation between the military and NGOs, a phenomenon that we cannot always observe today. These days conflicts often arise over the question of whether the military can also undertake activities that are beneficial to the general population, ranging from distribution of food to first steps in support of democratic structures and nation-building, or whether these activities should carried out by humanitarian NGOs only.

This conflict seems quite surprising, since the world's foremost international humanitarian aid organization, the International Committee of the Red Cross, would not have been founded if the military at the time had been willing to act in the way that is now set to become standard for military operations led by Western democracies. Today, planning a military operation will – in addition to traditional military aspects – always take the following civilian aspects into consideration:

1. Military forces are responsible for safeguarding the civilian population in occupied areas if no NGOs are available for that purpose.
2. Infrastructure vital for civilian life and the economy should not be destroyed.
3. A positive image of the armed forces in occupied/affected areas has to be taken into consideration. This should be assured in order to protect them from potential hostile acts by irregulars.
4. The civilian population should suffer as little as possible from military action, not only for general humanitarian reasons but also in view of the need for reconstruction and stabilization.
5. All activities designed to foster economic recovery and democratic stabilization of civil life have priority in order to allow own forces to withdraw as early and as completely as possible.

Why shouldn't NGOs back these developments? What is it that gives rise to tension between the military and humanitarian NGOs? Certainly, not every point on the list has become standard in the general military planning process. But for a number of reasons they will, and in part already have. One is legitimacy. In recent years the attitude of the public to military operations has changed significantly in many Western democracies. And this change seems to be a permanent. In the perception of the public, there is no threat of war among Western nations; national military engagements are no longer seen in terms of vital defence against an aggressor nation, a battle with combatants who have the same level of technology.

Today national and supranational military engagements are options. Decisions are made to go to war in support of the national interest – together with allied partners wherever this proves advantageous. But if national military engagements are seen as options, they need to win the approval of parliaments in democratic procedures. There are no decisions backed by emergency laws. All decisions about military action have to be legitimized by the representatives of citizens of the nations involved. For the majority of people in the West, economic reasons – a justification for so many wars in the past – are no longer sufficient. A more convincing, 'positive', aspect has to be added.

It is here that humanitarian aspects enter the scene – helping another nation rid itself of a dictator, preventing genocide, stopping the oppression of minorities, or at the least supporting the path to democracy. The best case occurs when more than one of these 'positive' elements apply.[1] Even arguments that support long-term international security, like stopping the proliferation of weapons of mass destruction, do not seem to provide sufficient grounds for intervention. It is becoming more and more evident that future military engagement will be legitimized only by humanitarian objectives. The war in Iraq can be taken as an example. In fact, in the view of Western democracies the use of military force is no longer legitimized without 'humanitarian' objectives in view.

When armed forces have to fight for such objectives, how they go about it will have to be quite different from the strategies of the past. Then, the main objective of a military engagement was to permanently neutralize the military power of the opponent – by defeating his forces and disarming them, and finally by securing the official monopoly on the use of force. Victory was granted to the military as soon as the capitulation of the opponent's forces was declared. Only the laws and logic of war were relevant. Reconstruction towards normal and stable living conditions for the defeated nation were not seen as a prime military responsibility. On the contrary, even after Second World War it was seen as normal to pay or receive reparations, a practice that always led to further instability. It was not unusual in the past for reparations to lead to subsequent wars.

Today, under the terms of humanitarian legitimacy, victory will be granted only if the hearts and minds of the opponent's population are won and the society seems to be on a assured path to stability and democracy. Forces will not be allowed to withdraw before that.

Disarming the enemy's forces is therefore not enough. Victory is conceded only when hearts and minds are won and stability is restored.

To achieve this goal, relevant considerations need to be included in the planning of military operations. This means that the military planning process has to include civil and political aspects, and not only tactical military aspects. Let us take an example: bridges, unless they are important for vital civil logistics, will not be permanently demolished for short-term tactical advantages, but will be temporarily blocked by other means. The same applies to radio stations, power plants and many other facilities essential to life and civilian society.

A catchword has been coined for this new type of operation: Effect-Based Operation. The Americans came up with it in consequence of their frank analysis of the problems they faced at the beginning of the Iraq campaign. They (re-)discovered that it is not enough to defeat and disarm the opponent; it is also necessary to integrate aspects of the defined goal of an intervention into military planning from the very beginning, and for the US army this constituted the rediscovery of the importance of CIMIC.

In short, the military needs to integrate humanitarian and civilian aspects into its planning from the very start.

Since the end of the Cold War, the military engagements of Western democracies have no longer been justified by the need to fight for home-land defence against neighbouring aggressors with the same level of culture and technology. We are now in a situation where we can choose whether we intervene or not. Only positive objectives can convince a Western parliament to vote in favour of military intervention. Neither economic nor long-term security threats will be sufficient to gain the backing of the public. The objectives of military operations have consequently changed. Military success is no longer the major focus. Rather, it is part of a combined political approach. The intention is to withdraw the military as early as possible and replace these forces with non-military actors like NGOs. Civil engagement is not only cheaper than military engagement, the former is also much more appropriate for the restoration of civilian life. In order to avoid a military operation that is counterproductive to the objectives of the political campaign, civilian aspects have to be integrated into military planning at all stages. This new and dominant influence of civilian aspects in military operations has found expression in CIMIC.

CIMIC has now become the main military tool used to bring civilian aspects into military planning and to organize military activities for humanitarian purposes and nation-building.

Within the military itself the changed nature of military engagement is made evident by the increased importance of CIMIC. This has not taken place without demur and criticism on the part of some army personnel. CIMIC is the official strategic and tactical element used to represent the new influence of all civilian actors and conditions on military operations. This could mean the civilian population in an occupied area as well as the activities of a local civilian government. It also includes the impact of the potential activities of all NGOs and/or non-military governmental organizations (GOs) within a given area of responsibility. CIMIC divisions have been established in all operational military headquarters of NATO and the national forces of the German *Bundeswehr*. At NATO's international headquarters there are the so-called J9 Division and G5 Division. They are responsible for advising the commanders about the potential role of all civilian players and aspects within a given military operation. Only open sources are used for information. On the other hand, CIMIC provides advice on the effects that military operations might have on the civilian environment. In addition to these staff elements, CIMIC field forces were established to do practical work, and doctrines were developed to give clear guidance. The present NATO doctrine[2] defines CIMIC as follows:

> CIMIC is the co-ordination and co-operation, in support of the mission, between the NATO Commander and civil actors, including national population and local authorities, as well as international, national and non-governmental organizations and agencies.

The definition of the respective doctrine for military missions of the EU[3] is similar:

> CIMIC is the co-operation and co-ordination, in support of the mission, between military components of EU-led Crisis Management operations and civil actors (external to the EU), including national population and local authorities, as well as international, national and non-governmental organizations and agencies.

These definitions make it clear that CIMIC is not independent. It does represent something like a military humanitarian corps, even though humanitarian disaster relief is within the scope of CIMIC staff responsibilities. CIMIC is an integral part of a given military operation, supporting the goals of the military objectives. But as these objectives begin to include more and more civilian aspects, CIMIC is also becoming more important for the planning and execution of military operations.

The present NATO doctrine, which is nearly identical to the doctrine of the German national armed forces, the European Union and the national doctrines of many other NATO countries, lists the following points as CIMIC's core functions:[4]

a) *Civil–Military Liaison.* The aim of civil–military liaison is to provide the co-ordination necessary to support the planning and conduct of operations. Such liaison early in the planning process and immediately following the deployment of forces provides the basis from which the other CIMIC functions develop. It will be a substantial part of the planning and development process of the other core CIMIC functions. Establishment of liaison on the political level by NATO is a precondition of success. Liaison with civil authorities and organizations is facilitated by, amongst other things, an appropriate public information policy. This will require adequate and timely dissemination of the achievements and progress made through civil–military co-operation, which will in turn help win the support of the population, IOs and NGOs.

b) *Support to the Civil Environment.* Support to the civil environment covers a wide spectrum of CIMIC activities. For this purposes support is provided to the civilian environment in accordance with a NATO military mission. Normally it is not support under the direction of civil authorities. It can involve a wide range of military resources: information, personnel, material, equipment, communications facilities, specialist expertise or training. It will generally take place only where and when it is required to create conditions necessary for the accomplishment of the military mission and/or because the appropriate civil authorities and agencies are unable to carry out these tasks. Decisions on depth, duration and extent of these support actions should be made at the highest appropriate level taking into account political as well as military and civil factors.

c) *Support to the Armed Forces.* NATO commanders, depending on the circumstances, will require significant civilian support from within their theatre of operations as well as co-ordination of efforts to minimize a disruption of the military operations. This means mainly controlling the population and civilian resources. So the military may be partly dependent on civilian sources. Commanders will also seek as much tacit civilian support for their operations as possible. CIMIC will play major role in all these areas.

There is yet another area of responsibility integrated into these core functions that falls under CIMIC and the responsibility of the J9 Division.

The official doctrine might give the impression that this task is optional. In fact, it is a legal obligation carried out as a result of the IV Geneva Convention.[5] This convention clearly states that occupying forces are obliged to guarantee a decent subsistence to the civil population within their area of occupation – if and as long as no civil organizations are available for that purpose.[6] And if (as in Iraq) the situation becomes too dangerous for NGOs and they have to leave the occupied area, the task will fall to the military.

So it was, for example, not only goodwill and a humanitarian attitude but a legal obligation when the military took over the running of the electrical power plant near Pristina during the first month of the NATO occupation. For the same reason the military could be obliged to provide food, drinking water, access to basic medical care or civil security. Military activities such as this would be planned and coordinated by CIMIC staff and executed by CIMIC forces.

As a consequence of the official doctrine discussed above, there should be no grounds for any tension with NGOs. The standard CIMIC activity will neither touch on nor influence the work of NGOs in any way. On the contrary, the doctrine does not elaborate any regular project organization for development or nation-building. Concerning humanitarian or development activities, the doctrine clearly states that, 'it will only take place if … the civil authorities and agencies are unable to carry out the task'.

Involving the military in humanitarian or development projects has officially to be viewed as an exception. But analysis of recent missions confirms that this exception has occurred quite frequently. An explanation can be seen in the refusal of humanitarian NGOs to accept any political coordination.

In theory, CIMIC mainly means a system of liaison with all civilian players in order to give advice to the military commander concerning the civilian influence on military operations. Conversely, CIMIC would provide information to the commander about the effects a military operation would have on the civilian environment. Though this is the key element of all CIMIC activities, it is not widely known, nor do politicians have a clear picture of CIMIC in all cases.

It is interesting to note that all the small beneficial actions that the military sometimes undertakes in its area of responsibility appear to be very attractive to the media. These are the actions best covered for public scrutiny. They are part of CIMIC activities, and they constitute a visible part of CIMIC activities. But compared to core actions they do nothing other than polish the image of the armed forces. Additionally, these activities provide the opportunity to come into contact with the local population and to get to know their problems and everyday life better. All in all, it can help to improve not only the image but also the security of own forces. This part of CIMIC therefore falls under the function of force protection. Such beneficial activities can range from putting a new roof on a school, providing school equipment, or distributing toys and sweets. These small projects are often financed by the soldiers themselves or by donations from communities and private individuals. They have (thus far) never been financed out of the public budgets.

But even though these activities are very small, symbolic acts, they do not get the approval, not to mention the sympathy, of NGOs. It simply does not fit their conception or expectations of the military. Their image of the armed forces seems to be influenced by negative experiences their activists have had in war-torn regions.[7]

NGOs claim to be the only party with the legitimacy to do humanitarian work. This attitude is common, particularly among German NGO workers. In addition, they express the opinion – supported by a large part of the German population and even parts of the political administration – that they are the only ones legitimized to spend taxpayers' money from the respective public budgets for humanitarian purposes. Consequently, they insist on their total independence from political control and consider this to be an essential point of their engagement.

Certainly, everybody can and will accept that NGOs are free to spend the money *they* have collected from donors as they see fit. But are they equally free to spend taxpayers' money? Normally, the largest share of the funds for humanitarian or development projects should be spent under the political and legal control of the public. But in reality, near-total independence for NGOs from public control is widely accepted in Germany. Where does this strong conviction derive from?

The specific situation of Cold War Germany may offer an answer. Over the last 50 years of this period an ideology of independence has developed and become quite self-contained. During this period influencing other countries' politics directly was a sensitive issue, especially outside the alliance. In order not to upset the delicate balance of power and/or antagonize ideological opponents, a projection of our long-term national interests had to be effected very cautiously, ideally 'under cover'. During the Cold War the work of humanitarian NGOs proved to be an excellent means – in many cases the only opportunity – for realizing political goals. Western values have been transmitted along these humanitarian lines and have initiated long-term political changes.

This could explain the broad acceptance of generous financial support for NGOs from taxpayers' money, even though very little control had been established over the effectiveness of how the money was spent. Effectiveness and efficiency were not important, and there were few alternatives.

The public demand for complete independence for NGOs also favoured political objectives. Furthermore, it helped to conceal political intentions. The pacifist attitude of the majority of Germans, especially after 1968, helped here. NGOs – many of them founded in the 1970s and 1980s – had defined their demands and standards during the Cold War years. They became accustomed to a generous system of financing, and finally took this as a given. All administrations responsible for public funding, regardless of their political leaning, publicly reaffirmed the independence of NGOs in order to ensure that their political intentions had a lower profile. But it has never been a legal obligation that the government should finance and support the activities of NGOs.

To sum up, during the Cold War 'humanitarian interventions' were the only viable option for transmitting the political interests of the West to the Communist sphere of influence and so were generously supported by Western governments. Many NGOs defined their goals and objectives during this period. No legal obligation was ever established to support the work of NGOs with public money.

The first major conflict between the German government, military and NGOs occurred in 1997. At the time the German government wanted to establish a home reconstruction programme in Bosnia-Herzegovina as a means of creating an incentive for refugees in Germany to return home. The idea was to have German NGOs accomplish this in a coordinated action, using funds from international organizations. A political programme manager, a member of the German parliament, was based in Sarajevo to coordinate the activities of the NGOs involved and to provide support in acquiring funds from international sources. But German NGOs emphatically – and successfully – refused to be coordinated by politics and politicians. They affirmed their total independence. They took this as an inviolable standard granted by the nature of their business. Finally, German armed forces were tasked with executing the government plan at very short notice. Even though they had never acted in this capacity before, the military was mobilized, and it successfully managed the programme in a short period. This became a starting point for German CIMIC project work and came to be seen as a model case for all subsequent CIMIC engagements.

Now German NGOs were on the alert. They organized massive political protests to influence political decision-making and prevent the armed forces from encroaching on what they perceived as their own area of responsibility: making use of those parts of the public budget that NGOs perceived as *their* budget. As one German newspaper wrote at that time, this was the starting point for new competition in the charities market.

The armed forces, on the other hand, could prove that they were working on behalf of the government, and in every single case they did their job. They had not been looking for a new role after the end of the Cold War, as NGO activists often insinuated. But the picture was frequently exaggerated: the armed forces received a negligible part of the respective 'humanitarian' budget hitherto reserved for NGOs. That is not surprising, since the German armed forces are operating in only a very few places abroad, compared to German NGOs, which work around the globe. This case initiated a conflict over principles.

In addition, many NGO representatives complained about insufficient media attention, while the small humanitarian engagements of the military were covered everywhere and in a positive light.

In this respect a special category of armed forces humanitarian engagement will be discussed separately, even though it is also managed by CIMIC: humanitarian disaster relief. Sometimes the armed forces are tasked by the government with accomplishing exactly such difficult work. The reason is that sometimes they are the only ones who have the necessary equipment, management structure and logistical power, or they are the only ones who can provide the desired international recognition of Germany's global responsibility. A recent example was the tsunami disaster in the Indian Ocean. The support provided by US forces from an aircraft carrier made quite visible what unique abilities and capabilities the armed forces can make available in a short time for immediate relief operations. The military structures and technical equipment of the armed forces are designed for much more complex and dangerous situations. That makes military response to civilian disasters very effective. But it is a very expensive tool and therefore the efficiency of such missions is always in question. Such actions should be limited to immediate assistance during the first few days or weeks following a disaster.

To make it clear, disaster relief is not a core military function. It is not accomplished in military style and is carried out unarmed. The NATO doctrine calls it 'Military *Assistance* in Humanitarian Emergencies'.[8] A supporting NATO document, MDCA,[9] clearly describes and delimits the scope of the use of 'Military and Civil Defence Assets'. CIMIC staff elements are responsible for planning such contingencies.

Even though the armed forces can become active in 'Military Assistance in Humanitarian Emergencies' only by direct order of the government, NGOs tend to attack military engagement in these cases. This conflict may have arisen on ideological grounds.

The opportunity to exert political influence in areas of national interest has changed substantially since the end of the Cold War. Since then there has no longer been a need to keep the projection of national interests abroad under cover. Now strategies and concepts can be discussed openly. Since then it has not been seen as legitimate to spend taxpayers' money inefficiently for such matters. Today, Western governments develop and make public political concepts concerning the best approaches to engagement in areas of national interest. Taxpayers have a right to know how their money is spent. Needless to say, it will take time for these changes to be fully understood and realized.

In Germany this process started later than in the other European countries, since Germans found themselves embroiled in German reunification. The first political issue concerning international engagement was Germany's long-term contribution to the reconstruction of Afghanistan.[10] An official government document illustrates the role played by the various actors involved. The German government, including the Ministries of Foreign Affairs, Defence, Development and the Interior in particular, was to contribute to the common goal of helping restore Afghanistan to stability and a democratic system. The newly established German provincial reconstruction teams (PRTs) can be seen as a small-scale test for this type of engagement in the future. Of course, this form of engagement draws its effectiveness only from the coordination of all efforts with a view to the desired objective. The German PRTs include a representative from the Ministry of Foreign Affairs who is responsible for such coordination. NGOs and their roles have been defined, but many German NGOs are still reluctant to cooperate. They are defending their independence and receiving strong support from the peace movement.

But are these NGOs fighting a battle that has already been lost? Most Western nations have irreversibly modified their approaches to intervention and the best ways to achieve their political interests.

A recent plan, the Action Plan for Civil Crisis Management, presented by the German government sheds light on this new political approach.[11] This concept gives full priority to civilian solutions for international conflicts and crisis management. Civilian actors and organizations are to be the main providers of aid. Task forces of policemen, administration specialists, civil servants, judges and detention experts for this reason will be trained and kept in readiness for missions with relevant international task forces.

The concept does not, of course, exclude military engagements. The latter continue to be the *ultima ratio* for certain situations. But even then, the central focus will be on civil means:

> An armed intervention cannot replace civil crisis management and efforts to combat the structural causes of a conflict. Experience from recent conflicts has proven that military means can be necessary as tools for crisis prevention and management, in order to prevent or stop violent execution of conflicts or to create the preconditions for further crisis management by civilian means. Crisis prevention often requires a close co-operation by military and civilian components within the framework of a general security concept that includes political, diplomatic, economic, humanitarian and military means.

The document clearly demonstrates the growing importance of the civil component, but with a high level of coordination among the various actors. It further illustrates that a stronger interface will be needed on the military side to take into account the growing importance of civil forces. Finally, this new concept clearly indicates a desire for coordination among the civilian elements.

The Barcelona Report[12] of September 2004 points in the same direction. The report, sponsored by the EU, develops a concept for future military engagements of the EU, the so-called 'battle group concept'. This type of intervention is characterized as an 'integrated mission'. Civil and military actors will be brought together to support a failed state back on its way to stability and democratic civil society. Under the heading of *Capabilities required*, the study notes: 'It will need an integrated set of civil-military capabilities that would be suited to carry out human security operations', and in the same chapter: 'The ultimate aim is to be able to deploy different packages of military-civilian capabilities according to the situation.' And under the heading 'Relations with NGOs and private corporations' it notes: 'NGOs could be registered as part of Human Security Volunteer Service, along with individuals. The service could provide a framework for contracts with NGOs that would involve vetting to ensure that they were reliable and effective.'

In the conclusion, the document states that the report 'has described the contours of a civil–military "Human Security Response Force" that would be equipped to act to protect and improve human security according to these principles'. This document provides clear evidence of the need for enhanced civil–military cooperation and the need to have the activities of NGOs coordinated.

The most recent change of policy for US forces goes in the same direction. The above-mentioned 'Effect-Based Operations' states that in the future civil objectives will be given higher priority than tactical ones, as we have seen during the second Iraq War.

All this points to the fact that since the end of the Cold War Western governments seem to have discovered more effective means to communicate their political interests and to manage crises. The EU has developed a concept paper entitled 'Integrated Missions', and the US forces have drafted a similar concept under the title 'Effect-Based Operations'.

All these concepts require effective coordination between armed forces and NGOs. All players will have to act out their roles and fulfil their tasks. The *primus inter pares* could be a representative of the Ministry of Foreign Affairs, as in the case of the German PRTs in Afghanistan. But in certain cases or phases of an intervention this might be a representative of the military or other government organization.

For humanitarian NGOs this new type of international engagement may be a problem. Their former independent status, impartiality and neutrality are no longer required by Western countries – at least not in conflict areas for which integrated concepts are to be developed and financed, whether with or without military participation. As in all cases where publicly funded budgets are used, these will be made available only if the new standards of cooperation are adhered to.

If NGOs want to have their share of work and money, they will have to make a choice: either change their ideology and take part in coordinated actions, or remain independent – but with the support of donor money only.

NGOs should understand that only few of them have been truly and fully independent all the time – Médicins Sans Frontières or Cap Anamur, for example, since they have always funded more than 80 per cent of their operations from donor money. But strictly speaking, even they are not as completely neutral as they imagine themselves to be, since nearly all Western NGOs inevitably communicate Western values, like humanitarianism itself, or the equality of men and women.

Sometimes this can be interpreted as a threat to non-Western cultures. This applies even more for NGOs with an overtly Christian background. They have never been seen as neutral. From the point of view of other religions, and especially in the eyes of Islamic fundamentalists, their help is always suspected of being missionary work. Antonio Donini brought up this point when he said in 2003 that NGOs need to understand 'that they don't have a humanitarian monopoly' and 'when the struggle between "Jihad and McWorld" becomes acute, humanitarian action is seen as part of McWorld'.[13] For many NGOs this is difficult to accept.

NGOs should bear in mind that future engagements in international conflict management will be different from those in the past. These operations will be dominated by civil objectives and civil management, not by classic military activities. That should help them to understand that political coordination has to be accepted, even for humanitarian concerns. Western states are in the process of changing the framework for their interventions. This applies to the work of the armed forces as well as to the engagement and philosophy of NGOs. Military operations will no longer be the focus of future complex integrated missions, rather only a part of them. Civil considerations and actors will be dominant.

As for the military, the increased dominance of civil aspects makes a stronger CIMIC function necessary. And the more NGOs refuse to be co-ordinated, the more CIMIC forces will be activated to take on the part provided for them in the concept. Military capabilities can always be made available and provide effective solutions at short notice. They are designed for action in a chaotic environment, and do what they are tasked to do. Furthermore, work for humanitarian purposes or development projects is very congenial to many soldiers, especially German soldiers. Most want strong political legitimacy. For them, as well as for many other Western soldiers, the humanitarian and civilian aspects of an intervention provide far better motivation than purely military action. But tasking the military with development programmes is a very expensive solution, even though – or because – in this case no overhead costs are taken into account. Civilian organizations especially designed for a given job can do that job more efficiently. But it always takes time to design and establish organizations, whereas military forces can be activated very quickly.

Within the military system, CIMIC is the interface used to represent the increased importance of civil aspects. CIMIC is also the tool used to plan and execute those humanitarian or development projects that will be given to the military – for whatever reason. CIMIC therefore represents a series of stepping stones that will later become part of the road to a stable civil society.

Notes

1. To put it in mathematical terms, these positive elements are necessary but not sufficient conditions for a military engagement. Military engagements will never be based on humanitarian reasons alone. The disasters in Rwanda and the Dafur region of Somalia can be taken as significant examples of that.

2. NATO Document Allied Joint Publication No. 9 (AJP 9), unclassified.
3. Council of the European Union, EUMC DOC 06/02, CIMIC Concept for EU-Led Crisis Management Operations, CCD-02–05–10/06 OPS-14/2001.
4. NATO, AJP 9, No. 109, 1.a.
5. Fourth Geneva Convention, Articles 55, 56, 59.
6. The consequences of this became very visible during the Iraq campaign. The allied forces did not like the idea, because they did not want to be perceived as occupiers, and thus be obliged to provide that service. It was not until an Iraqi government was established that the Allies were completely free of that obligation. That might have been the underlying reason for the very early establishment of a government.
7. Unfortunately (or naturally) most Western NGO activists have little or no experience with their own national forces. They are mainly pacifists and therefore reject military service.
8. Euro Atlantic Partnership Council, 'NATO Military Policy on Civil-Military Co-operation', 9 July 2001.
9. United Nations OCHA, Guidelines on the use of military and civil defence assets to support UN's humanitarian activities in complex emergencies, March 2003.
10. Government of Germany, Foreign Office (2003), Das Afghanistan-Konzept der Bundesregierung, 1 September 2003, Berlin, GE.
11. Deutsche Bundesregierung, 'Aktionsplan – Zivile Krisenprävention, Konfliktlösung und Friedenskonsolidierung', Berlin, 12 May 2004.
12. European Union, Study Group on Europe's Security Capabilities (2004) *A Human Security Doctrine for the EU, BARCELONA Report*, 15 September 2004, Brussels.
13. Antonio Donini (2004) 'Western Agencies Have No Moral Monopoly', *Humanitarian Affairs Review & Development News*, Autumn, Brussels.

References

Commission of the European Union (2004) Exchange of letters between UNOCHA und EU Commission, concerning their cooperation in the framework of disaster relief response, 24 October 2004, Brussels.

Council of the European Union (2003) *Civil–Military Coordination*, November, Brussels.

Council of the European Union (2003) *Suggestions for Coherent, Comprehensive EU Crisis Management*, 3 July, Brussels.

Council of the European Union (2002) *Civil–Military Co-operation Concept for EU-led Crisis Management Operations*, MC DOC 06/02, CCD-02-05-10/06 OPS-14/2001, Brussels.

Donini, Antonio (2004) Western Agencies Have No Moral Monopoly, *Humanitarian Affairs Review & Development News*, Autumn, Brussels.

European Union, Study Group on Europe's Security Capabilities (2004) *A Human Security Doctrine for EU, BARCELONA Report*, 15 September, Brussels.

Echterling, Jobst (2003) 'CIMIC – Zivil-Militärische Zusammenarbeit der Bundeswehr im Ausland', *Europäische Sicherheit*, October.

German Foreign Office (2003) *Das Afghanistan-Konzept der Bundesregierung*. 1 September, Berlin.

Government of Germany (2004) *Aktionsplan Zivile Krisenprävention, Konfliktlösung und Friedenskonsolidierung*, 12 May, Berlin.

Heinemann-Grüder, Andreas and Tobias Pietz (2004) Zivil-militärische Intervention – Militärs als Entwicklungshelfer, *Auszug aus dem Friedensgutachten 2004*, International Center for Conversion (BICC), Bonn.

Hütte, Michael (2003) Frieden schaffen nur mit Waffen? *Notfallvorsorge* 4/2003.

Liebetanz, Klaus (2003) VENRO-Papier Streitkräfte als humanitäre Helfer? Eine Entgegnung, *Magazin Notfallvorsorge* 3/2003.

Merrit, Giles (2004) Dutch Plans Link Peacekeeping to Development Policy, *Humanitarian Affairs Review & Development News*, Autumn, Brussels.

Ministry of Defence (2003) UK CIMIC Doctrine, 28 November.

Misereor, Brot für die Welt, EED (2003) *Entwicklungsdienst im Windschatten militärischer Intervention. Gemeinsames*, epd-Entwicklungspolitik 16/17/2003.

Münkler, Herfried (2002) *Die Neuen Kriege*, Rowohlt, September, Reinbek.

NATO International Military Staff (2004) *Review of NATO CIMIC Concepts and Capabilities*, 17 December, Brussels.

NATO Supreme Allied Command Transformation (2004) *NATO Network Enabled Capability Foundation Document*, 1 December, Norfolk, VA.

NATO's Strategic Commanders (2004) *Strategic Vision: The Military Challenge. An Estimate to Support the Future Transformation of Civil Military Cooperation*, 2004, Norfolk, VA.

NATO, *NATO Civil–Military Co-operation (CIMIC) Doctrine*, Allied Joint Publication No. 9 (AJP 9), 2002, Brussels.

Nachtwei, Winfried (2003) Kabul im August 2003 – Afg. Politik am Scheidewege, Reisebericht, August, Berlin.

Pro Press Publishing Group (2004) *Europe's Role in a New Security System*, Magazine for European Armed Forces, ED 04 Issue, 2 November, Bonn.

Rana, Raj (2004) Contemporary Challenges in the Civil–Military Relationship: Complementarity or Incompatibility, *IRRC Publication*, 86(855), September: 565–591.

RAND National Defence Research Institute (2004) *Men Make the City, Joint Urban Operations, Observations and Insights from AFG and IRAQ*, June.

Reinhardt, Dieter (2003) Privatisierung der Sicherheit, *Entwicklungspolitik* 16/17.

Save the Children (2004) *Provincial Reconstruction Teams and Humanitarian Military Relations in AFG*, London.

United Nations (2003) *The Use of Military Defense Assets to Support United Nations Humanitarian Activities in Complex Emergencies, MDCA Guidelines*, March 2003, New York.

VENRO (2003) *Streitkräfte als Humanitäre Helfer*, VENRO Positionspapier, May.

12
Is Universality under Threat? Humanitarian Aid and Intervention in the 2000s

Antonio Donini

On 21 August 2003 the humanitarian community had its own 9/11. A suicide bomber rammed a truckload of explosives into the Canal Hotel in Baghdad and killed the UN representative for Iraq and 21 of his colleagues. The dust has only started to settle on the significance of this event and of the continuing attacks against NGOs, the Red Cross movement and the UN. If shadowy belligerents in Iraq, Afghanistan, Chechnya and elsewhere consider aid workers to be legitimate targets, what does this mean for the future of humanitarian action? What does it say about the purported universality of humanitarianism?

The starting point of this chapter is the malaise in the humanitarian community arising from the compromises of humanitarian principle in Afghanistan and Iraq. It argues that instrumentalization of humanitarian action by the superpower and its allies has reached unprecedented heights. It then looks at some of the elements of the malaise and at the positions taken by different segments of the humanitarian community. This is followed by a more speculative discussion of variables likely to affect the shape of the humanitarian enterprise in the years to come as well as the universality – or not – of the humanitarian endeavour.[1]

The present context

The Iraq crisis has presented critical challenges to the humanitarian community. The very essence of humanitarianism has been thrown into disarray: How can aid agencies insulate or protect themselves from overt politicization? Why do the emblems of the UN, the Red Cross and NGOs no longer protect aid workers? Has something gone wrong in the way we are understood by the people we say we are there to help? What can be done to remedy this situation?

For the past two years, donors, UN agencies and NGOs have been agonizing over these questions and now the beginnings of an answer are taking shape. Most analysts would agree that the answer lies in the perception that humanitarian action has been compromised. Rightly or wrongly – the community is split on this issue – humanitarian action in Iraq and Afghanistan has been used as a tool for a political project. The deliberate targeting of aid workers is a reminder that taking sides, or simply the perception of taking sides, can have devastating consequences.

This is not the first time that aid workers have been attacked or that humanitarian action has been instrumentalized in pursuit of political or security objectives. What is new is the extent to which humanitarian action has been infiltrated and penetrated by political agendas that are at odds with humanitarian principles. In high-profile crises where the US is directly involved, it is unable to safeguard its neutrality. The 'you are for us or against us' rhetoric of the post-9/11 War on Terror is rapidly eroding the space for neutral, impartial and independent humanitarian action. In a sense, George W. Bush is the mirror image of Osama bin Laden. Independent and negotiated humanitarian space is being 'occupied' by military actors and their sub-contractees as well as by aid agencies who accept to be 'force multipliers' and are thus absorbed and managed directly by the military or by the latter's political masters.

Thus, humanitarian objectives – saving lives – are increasingly replaced by security objectives of 'world ordering' and of making countries 'safe for capital'. The Provincial Reconstruction Teams (PRTs)[2] in Afghanistan which aim to embed assistance within a politico-military strategy are a good example of what Mark Duffield calls the 'securitization' of aid (Duffield 2001: 22 ff). In Iraq, the conflation of political, security and humanitarian objectives is exacerbated by the fact that the chief belligerent is also by far the largest donor; this in turn affects the aid marketplace and agency survival imperatives leaving aid agencies with no option other than refusing belligerent funding or choosing not to be there.

Moreover, the functions performed by humanitarian agencies in the contexts of globalization and securitization have become suspect to many in the South who see these agencies as among the 'most powerful pacific weapons of the new world order' and as the 'mendicant orders of Empire' (Hardt and Negri 2001: 36) as well as to some in the North, for whom humanitarians 'maintain a secret solidarity with the very powers they ought to fight'.[3] In many settings the social contract establishing the 'acceptability' of humanitarian action can no longer be negotiated with belligerents. In fact, in the 'new' new wars where militant combatants do not necessarily seek to control territory or conquer political power, international humanitarian law (IHL) and the Geneva Conventions may no longer provide an adequate and sufficient template for humanitarians to operate. And, away from the limelight, forgotten emergencies (for example, the Democratic Republic of Congo) and silent ones (AIDS, malaria) continue to fester. The neglect of these crises further challenges the very universality of the humanitarian discourse.

Many in the South do not recognize the so-called universality of humanitarian values. Clearly, the gap in values and understanding is as significant as the gap in poverty and quality of life. Northern leaders, thinkers, aid agencies and donor institutions who fund and manage the bulk of what we call 'humanitarian assistance' may pay lip service to the importance of 'other' traditions and perspectives on universality, but discordant voices seldom get a hearing.

Across parts of the South, humanitarian action is viewed as the latest in a series of impositions of alien values, practices and lifestyles and when the struggle between 'Jihad and McWorld' becomes acute, humanitarian action is seen as part of McWorld. This polarization is made worse by the breakdown of the relationship that made humanitarian action acceptable or even desirable to belligerents. It is now becoming impossible to have a conversation, let alone a dialogue, with militant belligerents in places like Afghanistan and Iraq, with the price paid by aid workers increasingly high.

The future of humanitarianism as a philosophy, a movement, a profession and as a compassionate rescue endeavour for endangered populations may well hinge on the lessons that humanitarian agencies, individually and collectively, will draw from Iraq, Afghanistan and other crises where humanitarianism is under threat and on the institutional choices they make. Humanitarianism may well go the way of other 'isms' into the dust-covered filing cabinets of history. While the humanitarian community has never been a paragon of united respect of its stated universalist principles, positions have now become more polarized (Rieff 2002). If it does not re-establish its bona fides, the humanitarian community could fragment into different factions either intentionally or by default. A point could be reached where maintaining the fiction of humanitarianism as a single community of ideals and actors becomes counterproductive to the task of saving lives. Unable to coalesce around fundamental principles, or a common definition of what it is and does, the community could well splinter into its component parts: principled, pragmatic, rights-based, faith-based, 'solidarist', developmentalist, and the like.

Moreover, the Western monopoly on the humanitarian discourse is being challenged. Non-western humanitarian traditions – Islamic, in particular – are in the ascendant and may make further inroads into an already crowded field. Diversification should not necessarily be viewed as a bad thing, although there would be opportunity costs for agencies associated with the decision to break away from mainstream humanitarianism. Practical effectiveness – the quantum of suffering alleviated and rights protected – may well trump ideological consistency. In the brave new world of GWOT – the Global War on Terror – different situations may require new and inventive approaches to life-saving beyond what copyrighted humanitarians are accustomed to propagating.

And, further down the road, should one choose to look at humanitarianism from the angle of options available for the social transformation or modernization of populations living in extremis, it might be useful to start thinking outside the traditional humanitarian box. New tool-kits may well emerge whether embedded in globalization or angrily promoted by its discontents. In both cases these are unlikely to rely on the familiar components of the present-day humanitarian apparatus or on the concept of universality as we know it.

Not all observers share the bleak assessment of the maladies affecting humanitarianism. Most analysts would agree that Iraq has been bad for humanitarianism, but it has survived partisan political agendas in the past. Hugo Slim, for example, writes: 'Reports have emerged from Iraq, Afghanistan and the east coast of the United States which claim that "humanitarianism is in crisis." Rumours have reached me that humanitarians are enduring a demoralizing malaise and that humanitarianism is suffering a terrible and potentially fatal illness' (Slim 2004a). What is happening, his argument goes, is nothing new: the basic parameters of humanitarian action have not changed, it is always caught up in politics and humanitarians are adept at weathering such storms and navigating between the shoals. After this storm is over, humanitarians will be able to return to more predictable environments and accustomed behaviours. He adds, in another paper, that humanitarians should accept that the objectives (if not the means) of US-led interventions are, broadly speaking, in line with those of humanitarianism – the promotion of human rights, democracy and 'liberal peace' (Slim 2004b).

Leaving aside the issue of whether humanitarian action should promote anything other than the alleviation of suffering, there is no denying that humanitarian action is taking place in what is demonstrably an increasingly murky landscape beset by manipulations and tensions between policy choices that are complicated by divergent philosophies of humanitarianism (O'Brien 2004). A sense of powerlessness is also prevalent, reflecting the sheer intractability of some of the issues. GWOT casts a large shadow over the ability of humanitarians to be faithful to core universalist principles. The growing pressure to instrumentalize humanitarian action in the service of anti-terrorism and other non-humanitarian objectives is itself an ingredient in much more complex processes related to economic globalization, the privatization of the development aid regime, the weakening of nation-states (at both ends of the socio-economic spectrum), the lifting of inhibitions on matters of sovereignty – whether for 'ordering' interventions or in deference to the responsibility to protect – the flouting of international humanitarian law norms (Guantanamo, Chechnya), the blurring of the lines between military, civilians, mercenaries, private contractors and criminalized economic elements involved in internal conflict, and the like.

Politicization and its consequences

Have principles been overtaken by events? There is a widespread sense among practitioners that, after Afghanistan and Iraq, principles (and the emblems that identify the agencies committed to them) no longer command the respect from belligerents that they once enjoyed. What is the relevance of a commitment to neutrality when the institutional exemplar of that commitment, the ICRC, suffered attacks on its premises in Baghdad no less pinpointed or lethal than those that targeted the UN's sanctions-associated humanitarian presence itself? To some, the lesson is that even more scrupulous attention to principle and contextual savvy is required; to others, that traditional principles have outlived their usefulness and need to be revisited.[4]

It is instructive to look back at the Taliban era in Afghanistan. As humanitarians who were based in the region can attest, the relationship between the authorities and the aid community was extremely polarized. Aid agencies were seen as vectors of westernization bent on promoting an alien and inferior set of values. Yet, the Taliban (and their al-Qaeda 'guests' for that matter) never targeted foreign aid workers. When it came to saving lives, the social contract of acceptability worked: humanitarian space was not always respected and access to the most vulnerable sometimes denied, but, by and large, the UN and the NGOs were not harmed. Even if they would not admit to it openly, they accepted that aid agencies were relatively neutral and impartial and that they did not take their cues from their enemies, be they the sanctions-imposing UN Security Council or their opponents on the ground. The Taliban knew that the UN humanitarian wing was sometimes criticized by the UN political wing, or by the US, for being 'accommodationist' (Donini 2004: 117ff). They understood that humanitarian principles required the UN to speak and work with all sides, assess needs independently, and move across lines on occasion. Presumably, this was to their advantage as well.

The denigration of humanitarian principles in Iraq and in other high-profile conflicts has placed aid agencies in an ambiguous and dangerous position. The operating environment in Iraq and Afghanistan is now very different. Is there a direct link between the recent spate of attacks against the UN, ICRC, and NGOs in Iraq and Afghanistan and the perceived cooption of humanitarian actors into the Coalition's strategy? Would greater distance from the Coalition have created enhanced security? Similar questions can be asked in Darfur, Chechnya and the eastern DRC. We do not know the precise answers to these questions – it is difficult to go and conduct empirical research in the lion's den. What we do know is that in such contested environments harming aid workers is no longer taboo.

Not all principles are being eroded in the same way. Of the three core principles – neutrality, impartiality and independence – it is the first and the third that are in greatest jeopardy. Most organizations that see them-selves as 'humanitarian' remain solidly wedded to the principle of impartiality – assistance will be provided to all according to need.[5] Neutrality and independence, in contexts such as Iraq and Afghanistan, are much more difficult to uphold. This is where compromise has crept in. Some NGOs (and even parts of the UN) have acknowledged, more or less reluctantly, that they are not neutral. And of course, the acceptance of funding from a belligerent for activities that suit the belligerent's agenda is a sure sign that 'independence' is going if not gone. Similarly, the claims to neutrality and independence of agencies that receive an overwhelming proportion of their funds from bilateral government sources are doubtful at best even if such agencies are able to maintain a degree of operational impartiality.[6] The same applies to agencies that agree to become subcontractors to governments or belligerents.

In order to understand the challenges faced by humanitarian agencies, it is useful to look at the various positions in the community. Typologies are always arbitrary. Nevertheless four broad positions can be identified on matters of humanitarian principles and engagement with political agendas. These are not watertight separations as there is considerable overlap and the same organization may fall into one category in one situation and in a different one in another.

(a) *Principle-centred.* Some aid agencies and personnel, particularly those with a long history of operating in conflict settings and with deep roots in the 'Dunantist' tradition, affirm the continued relevance of principles. 'Neutrality remains as valid as ever,' concludes a review by a senior ICRC official following an examination of prevalent misunderstandings of this key tenet of ICRC work (Harroff-Tavel 2003). In fact, she observes, the more highly politicized the terrain, the more urgent is unswerving fidelity to core principles.

Some of those who share a continuing commitment to retaining the neutrality of humanitarian action caution against generalizing on the basis of events in Iraq, Afghanistan, and Kosovo. In many places such as the Occupied Palestine Territories, West Africa, southern Sudan and Colombia, agencies are still able to build trust with warring parties through their traditional practices of neutrality and impartiality. In general, the proponents of principle-centred action argue for a narrower definition of humanitarianism, which is limited to life-saving assistance, and protection of civilians, based on core principles of neutrality, impartiality, and independence. Many eschew engagement in more ostensibly political endeavours such as advocacy for human rights or reconstruction activities.

(b) *Pragmatist.* This perspective generally recognizes the importance of principles but is prepared to engage in highly politicized situations where principles are difficult to maintain rather than sitting on the sidelines. The pragmatist persuasion has many shades. It includes 'Wilsonian' agencies (Stoddard 2003) that broadly identify with the foreign policy objectives of the governments of the countries in which they are based, and whose funds they often seek. There are also of course a large number of NGOs driven by opportunistic and institutional survival imperatives that follow the cash rather than principle.

Many of the 'pragmatist' agencies agonized over whether or not to work in Iraq. Some were split down the middle, with the policy people on the side of principle and the fundraising staff concerned about institutional survival. After all, the latter would say, although collaborating with the Coalition or its member governments puts pressure on classical humanitarian norms, principles should not be an impediment to pragmatic action to save lives. Principles are not absolutes, they are 'for reference only'. Similar debates occurred in Afghanistan on whether or not to collaborate with the PRTs. The pragmatist view, which holds sway among some US NGOs and some UN agencies, is seen as troubling by others, in particular European NGOs, which by and large rely less on earmarked government funding than their US counterparts and can therefore position themselves more independently.

(c) *Solidarist.* A third path, embraced by some NGOs on both sides of the Atlantic, has evolved from the historical tradition of the Red Cross. Established humanitarian principles, their argument goes, are not enough. What is the point of applying a bandage to a festering sore, of providing a bed for the night in a crumbling edifice? Agencies that save lives are obliged also to address the root causes of conflict, which are political at the core. Solidarist agencies – Oxfam and CARE see themselves as examples – hold that it is necessary to engage in the political process, using justice and human rights as a template for action. Their agenda is much wider than the traditional humanitarian brief: an anti-poverty and social transformation agenda that mixes elements from humanitarian, human rights, and developmental world views, with heavy emphasis on advocacy. Solidarists do not view themselves first and foremost as humanitarian agencies but rather as rights-based agencies, though they may do humanitarian work in particularly fraught contexts where no other activity is possible.

Again, there are various hues of 'solidarism', ranging from agencies that take their ideological cues from recognized universal texts – the UN Charter, the Universal Declaration of Human Rights, the UN millennium development goals – and others with a more particularistic agenda who have no problems in taking sides politically (e.g. Norwegian People's Aid which often espouses solidarity with a particular cause and has no qualms in stating that it is independent but not neutral or impartial (Bjoreng 2003)).

(d) *Faith-based.* The fourth category cuts across the other three. The Christian tradition is the oldest and is based on the core values of compassion, charitable service and mission. It has its roots in the succour provided to the destitute and the sick by monastic orders in the Middle Ages and in their missionary work in the European colonies. Again there are variations on the religious theme. The largest and most reputable faith-based organizations do not directly engage in proselytizing, though religious values may well be at the core of their message. Some are directly linked to a particular church (e.g. Catholic Relief Services or Caritas) though they may not engage in evangelization per se. Others (for example, Shelter Now whose activities ran foul of the Taliban in Afghanistan) see evangelization as an integral part of their mission. Others still are 'non-' or 'trans-denominational' in the sense that they are not linked to an established church, work in partnership with secular and religious local groups and calibrate their religious message to the local context. A good example is World Vision in Afghanistan where most of its staff is Muslim and its programmes are indistinguishable from those of secular agencies (Stoddard 2003).

Another variant is constituted by Islamic NGOs. Although they are not part of the same tradition – and, in fact, are often shunned by official humanitarianism – they play an increasing if little recognized role. Some, like Islamic Relief, are modelled on Western NGOs and have similar standards of accountability; others, such as the plethora of NGOs in Somalia, are *sui generis* and have radically different standards of operation and accountability; others still are 'Islamist' or more militant in nature such as Hamas in Palestine which mixes a religious and irredentist message with the provision of NGO-type health and education services (Benthall 2003).

Except for the Islamic tradition, which is largely ignored or marginalized by mainstream humanitarianism, the philosophical, operational and corporate roots of the four groupings outlined above are inescapably Western and Northern. We will return to the question of how the humanitarian endeavour is perceived by 'the other' at the end of this chapter.

There is no convenient way of plotting the diversity of the humanitarian community on a simple chart. The variables are too numerous. One arbitrary way of conceptualizing a typology, focusing only on the funding/principles equation, would be the following:

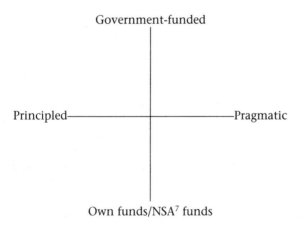

Government-funded

Principled————————————————Pragmatic

Own funds/NSA[7] funds

What are the implications of this extraordinary diversity for effective humanitarian action and for the universalist underpinnings of humanitarianism? On the one hand, given the current type of conflicts and the accompanying politicization of aid, the present diversity of approaches may be functional to the different types of situations that need to be addressed. The vastness of the humanitarian marketplace works against a common approach based on the same interpretation of principles. For some agencies, traditional principles remain important while others view them as an impediment to timely and effective action (or to expedient fundraising).

On the other hand, some argue that a clearer definition of what constitutes humanitarian action should be crafted and that the humanitarian 'label' be applied only to activities and organizations that would meet a set of verifiable criteria. It may be impractical to separate the principled humanitarian wheat from the multifaceted chaff, but the blurring of distinctions has its own set of consequences and security implications. In Afghanistan, for example, purists, pragmatists and solidarists operate in the same areas. Some work closely with the coalition or the PRTs, others shun them. Some – like USAID or other donor representatives – travel in military vehicles or with armed escorts. In large swathes of eastern, southern and western Afghanistan, UN staff travel with escorts provided by the government and armed with automatic weapons. Many NGOs do the same sort of projects as the UN but with very different security postures. In contested areas, NGOs tend to travel in unmarked vehicles and with no visible communications systems. The confusion of identities that inevitably arises can have serious security implications as the spate of attacks against aid workers has demonstrated.[8]

Perhaps a protected niche is required for agencies embracing core humanitarian principles with its own dedicated funding sources and modus operandi. Such agencies would be seen as 'copyrighted humanitarians' with transparent and visible characteristics different from those of other actors on the ground. Conversely, donors and humanitarian agencies themselves may come to recognize that there may be situations where life-saving assistance can only be provided by, or in conjunction with, the military. Such relief assistance may well be justified and legitimate (if, for example, authorized by the UN under chapter VII of the Charter) but not necessarily deserving of the humanitarian label.

An additional complicating factor is that the term 'humanitarian', as in humanitarian crisis, humanitarian emergency and humanitarian intervention, is often defined opportunistically – whether narrowly or elastically – according to the institutional and political needs of the moment. Is there a serious 'humanitarian crisis' in Iraq, Afghanistan or Haiti? Clearly there are significant numbers of civilians with urgent unmet needs and humanitarian agencies eager to step into the breach.

But crises are essentially political; it is the consequences that generate humanitarian need, including the need to intervene. The arbitrary use of the term 'humanitarian' for such crises is a useful fig leaf to justify 'humanitarian' interventions.

The increasing volume and complexity of activities related to the humanitarian sector has led to considerable hand-wringing among traditional humanitarian organizations. As indicated above, the ties that bind the humanitarian family have come under major pressure. Unilateral rather than coordinated action is still the preference of many. And this for two reasons: to safeguard the identity and promote the image of the individual organization and to distance the organization from the overt manipulation of humanitarian assistance under the banners of 'coherence' and 'integration'. Regrettably, the experience so far with integrated missions, as in Afghanistan, Liberia and, soon, the Sudan, has demonstrated the vulnerability of humanitarian action to political subordination. NGOs thus tend to be ambiguous *vis-à-vis* UN humanitarian coordination: they like it when it provides a buffer, as in Iraq, from political or military agendas; they hate it when it incorporates them in a strategy over which they have little influence. They also increasingly resent the UN's genetic inability to recognize the contribution of NGOs to the overall assistance effort. Partnership around an agreed agenda is still an idea whose time has not come in UN–NGO relations.

Does all this diversity matter to the victims? Does it matter who provides the bowl of rice? Is the WHO more important than the HOW? No doubt the US military will provide it differently from an Oxfam that works with communities, has a pre-existing relationship with them, is concerned about dependency, is sensitive to cultural issues and power relations within the community, etc. The fact is, however, that we simply do not know the answer to this question.[9] We know that the military are much more expensive than humanitarian agencies, but this is an under-researched area.[10] Similarly, there are no quick-fixes as to how to, and who could, regulate the alms bazaar when it is stricken by Klondike fever as in Goma or post-9/11 Kabul.

There may well be a process of natural selection that by and large ensures that agencies with reputable humanitarian credentials gravitate towards the contexts where one would expect to find them (e.g. ICRC and MSF in the midst of active conflict settings, Oxfam and CARE one step removed working in camps or in transition situations, etc.). It is unclear if this process can be assisted or if, on the contrary, it will lead to a more formal bifurcation in the humanitarian arena (a split between

'Dunantists' who will try to stick to a narrow set of principles and independent humanitarian action and those who will accept, or be forced, to become, 'force multipliers' for the superpower and its allies). As well, the fact that the term 'humanitarian' can cover many different realities challenges the very notion that humanitarianism is universal at its core especially since it excludes other realities – such as the work of Islamic charities – that are equally 'humanitarian' in the minds of others.

The evolution of the humanitarian 'rice bowl'

The entire aid industry is in turmoil, not just the humanitarian enterprise. The relatively slow movement of tectonic plates of the 1990s seems to be morphing into cyclones of devastating proportions. Fundamental changes are taking place in the profession, the industry and the marketplace. Some are dictated by the external environment; others relate to an internal process of evolutionary adaptation. It is either 'go with the flow' or 'gone with the wind'.

A number of contradictory forces are at play. I have already mentioned the hegemonic forces unleashed by the security agenda of the superpower and its allies and the politico-military occupation of humanitarian space accompanying it. At the same time, the nature of the North–South aid relationship has been deeply affected. The aspiration for social transformation inherent in the ideological mobilizing myth of development that characterized the Cold War era has collapsed. It has been replaced by the bronze law of the market and the managerial concepts that it has spawned: governance, privatization, accountability and the like. State-to-state North–South development assistance has been replaced by the mythologizing of civil society organizations. These organizations are increasingly tasked by northern states to provide state-like functions in weak states of the South thereby undermining the social contract between governments and their citizenry (while simultaneously providing employment for a multitude of expatriates who would otherwise be on the job market back home). The long-term effects of this transformation of the development enterprise are likely to surface in the coming decade. A violent backlash against expatriate aid workers, their values, and lifestyle cannot be excluded. Current attacks against humanitarian workers may well be harbingers of worse to come.

The erosion of the sovereignty of weak states is in turn accompanied by the banalization of superpower intervention whether for military, world ordering or 'shock into compliance' purposes. An example of the latter is the US arm-twisting of weak states to support the US position on the ICC. Another is the economic punishment threatened against countries reluctant to support the Coalition effort in Iraq. The UN, which used to have a role in defending or at least giving a hearing to Third World perspectives, is an impotent bystander. Multilateralism is in sharp decline, bilateralism in the ascendant and conditionality rampant. The manipulation of human rights instruments (at the UN and elsewhere), including the lofty objectives of human security and the 'responsibility to protect' further serves, opportunistically, to punish or reward weak states. Once again the promises of the UN Charter and of the Universal Declaration are manipulated to further the imperial designs of ordering and containing.

Closer to home, the humanitarian enterprise seems to be beset by two contradictory trends: 'act like a state' and 'act like a business'. On the one hand, large NGOs, particularly in the US, whether they act as subcontractors to the Occupying Power in Iraq or not, espouse Wilsonian foreign policy precepts which are reinforced by the interchange of personnel (including CEOs) between NGOs and government. NGOs propound values, jargon and behaviour that are virtually indistinguishable from those of public institutions (Braumann and Salignon 2004: 271). On the other, the same organizations, as well as many others, are engaged in a Darwinian struggle to survive and to increase their market share that is identical in its ruthlessness to unregulated competition in the private sector (Cooley and Ron 2002).

Moreover, as David Kennedy (2004) argues, the non-governmental sector whether it likes it or not has become an important part of 'governance'. NGOs, like the fourth estate, can wield considerable power, even if many would eschew formal recognition of this role. They are part of the way modern societies structure themselves. The distinctions between public and private seem to be vanishing, vindicating Karl Marx's analysis of the state as the executive board of the bourgeoisie!

The marketization of humanitarian action is accelerated by decisions taken by the NGOs themselves. Because humanitarianism is where the action is and because contracts, typically, are for very short (six months to a year) periods, NGOs are relying more and more on government contracts for institutional survival and development. Growth is rapid but risky. Agencies have to show results while they jockey for contracts and position. Supply chain pressure undermines accountability, sustainability and the development of local partnerships. Unintended effects or policy issues that do not fit with the contractors' political objectives go unreported. Limits are imposed, as in Iraq, for agencies under contract with the US government, on what NGOs can say out loud. The constant pressure to deliver government funds, goods and ideology makes a mockery of the purported independence of NGOs. Values and principles have been shredded by the conveyor belts of the supply chain.

Just to help matters, NGOs tend to devote their public funds to humanitarian activities while their shrinking proportion of privately raised funds goes to longer-term development or community-based activities.[11] This makes their humanitarian activities all the more vulnerable to political vagaries of donors and respect for principle more tenuous. Donor decision-making is far from consistent or impartial, pace the principles reaffirmed in the so-called good donorship initiative. High-profile and high-stake crises suck up the cash – and, in the case of the tsunami, the goodwill of public opinion – while forgotten, and often more deadly, crises fester and languish. Agencies that rely increasingly on public funds for humanitarian activities are rapidly losing any sort of cushion of NSA funds that would allow them to pick and choose where to work and to respond with some measure of independence and according to need. It would be interesting to contrast the policymaking choices and institutional survival behaviour of an agency that relies on the US government for 70 per cent of its funding (CARE) with World Vision where the proportions are exactly the reverse (Stoddard 2003). European NGOs are by and large in a better situation because their share of tied money from government is generally smaller. They rely also on EU money, which may be bilateral in origin but goes through a laundering process of sorts from which it emerges multilateralized and with less strings attached. The EU also sticks to a much narrower and more principled definition of 'humanitarian' than the US or Japan, for example.

The scramble in the NGO community is made worse by the increasing competition with commercial 'for profit' providers of assistance and the military, particularly, but not only, in Iraq. The trend was already present in Kosovo, East Timor and of course Afghanistan. The PRTs are the clearest example to date of the merging of security and assistance under a military umbrella.[12] This is presumably another growth area, as governments and militaries tire of the qualms and hesitations of NGOs. Privatization of aid goes hand in hand with the privatization of security. The prospect of private security companies providing 'humanitarian' assistance should not be ruled out. The spectre of militarized 'Mad Max' NGOs would be the logical next step. Given the implications of these trends for the survival of humanitarian action that retains a modicum of respect for principle, some urgent analysis is required of how the competition for the humanitarian rice bowl is playing itself out in an increasingly congested marketplace between NGOs, private contractors and the military in places like Afghanistan and Iraq.

Another trend needs to be highlighted: the increasingly oligopolisitic nature of the NGO marketplace. The NGO sector is the victim of its own success. More than 50 per cent of the global humanitarian assistance market is controlled by eight large consortia of transnational NGOs.[13] There are pluses and minuses to this evolution. On the plus side, consortia may be strong or diversified enough to resist extreme manipulation, unlike smaller or single-country NGOs. There is obviously strength in numbers as well as in the transnational nature of consortia. On the minus side, there is a risk that initiative, responsiveness and innovation – traditional NGO strong points – will be stifled through the homogenization of ideas and business practices. According to some, large transnational oligopolies tend to function in ways that are little different from their private multinational counterparts (Cooley and Ron 2002).

Real-time communications, teleconferencing, satellite and computer links with the remotest parts of the world breed added controls from agency HQ, standardization, pressures to fly the flag, plant the sign and don the cap, and less tolerance for innovation, responsiveness, attention to home grown perspectives and the like. Marketization may thus result in the direct opposite of what traditional NGOs, who like to see themselves as 'peoples' organizations', once stood for. Standards will replace principles (Vaux 2005). Managerial concepts and institutional isomorphism will thrive at the expense of innovation. Agencies will become more vertical, top-down and controlled by expatriates. The gap between international NGOs and local groups will widen and the mantras of community development and participation remain just that. Rather than working themselves out of a job, NGOs risk becoming self-perpetuating enterprises ever more linked into processes that are driven from the North.

If oligopolistic concentration reinforces the northern hold on the humanitarian enterprise, can this trend be countered or reversed through new forms of partnership with southern NGOs, local groups and state entities or other approaches that would cut across cultures and traditions? So far, alternatives to the current way of providing aid are few and far between. Especially in the humanitarian sector, top-down supply-driven approaches abound despite the rights-based rhetoric and the promises of accountability to beneficiaries. It may well be that there is an increasing disconnect between how social change and transformation are viewed in the North and the South. A pessimistic, perhaps realistic, scenario posits that the expansion of the NGO sector has reached a threshold beyond which it will breed opposition, and violence, from militant groups and alternative forms of social organization/ mobilization in the South.

As we have seen, humanitarianism in settings such as Iraq and Afghanistan has become subsidiary to a much larger and essentially political agenda that has to do with how the international community chooses to manage its overall response to crises. At the UN, the integration of political, humanitarian, and other responses has emerged as a standard template, particularly in high profile crises where the overall policy approach is driven by the Security Council or superpower interests. In lower profile crises, principled humanitarian action has a better chance of surviving. The post-Bonn UN mission in Afghanistan and UNMIL in Liberia have been the most 'coherent' and 'integrated' to date, but elements of integration are present in all recent UN missions from Kosovo to Iraq. The push for integration carries crucial policy and institutional implications for the humanitarian enterprise and the UN seems to be caught in the middle.

The choice confronting UN humanitarian entities is two-fold. One option involves full membership in the UN conflict management and resolution machinery, with a potential further loss of what remains of their independent humanitarian voice and the risk that they will be co-opted. The other option embraces some degree of separation, insulation, or independence of the UN humanitarian, and possibly human rights regimes from the conflict resolution machinery so as to nurture policy and partnerships in the wider humanitarian community. The latter option entails the risk of being less able to ensure that humanitarian concerns are given equal billing in the overall response. Indeed, the experience with 'equal billing' so far has been mixed at best. In Afghanistan, but also in Liberia and other African crises, experience has shown that the political UN does not see itself bound by humanitarian principles and has often limited appreciation for the value of the humanitarian endeavour in and of itself. Humanitarian action is always seen through political eyes that often look for tradeoffs rather than principles. Culturally and institutionally, there seems to be a reluctance to acknowledge that humanitarian action and human rights are valuable in their own right and also central to the quest for peace.

In some ways, increased insulation or independence of humanitarian action would constitute a return to the clearer institutional architecture of the Cold War era when humanitarian issues and human rights were in watertight compartments. A revived effort to insulate humanitarian action from adverse political agendas might also portend that a new

Cold War is in the offing, built around the global war on terror. One could envisage, for example, a return to ideology and polarization in international relations with a superpower-driven anti-terror camp pursuing an elusive enemy, and the emergence of a 'third force' composed of groups and nations concerned that the anti-terror agenda undermines the goal of attacking poverty and promoting justice. The risks for humanitarianism in such a scenario are significant, as are the implications for a UN coordination function.

Regardless of whether the integration issue is reopened, many humanitarian actors feel that efforts should be redoubled to influence decision-makers in the Security Council and elsewhere on humanitarian and protection issues. The objective should be to 'humanitarianize' politics without politicizing humanitarian action. Some feel that the success of such a strategy is dependent on a shift in US foreign policy towards more multilateral-friendly problem-solving, an unlikely prospect under the current administration. Others, seeing longer-term trends at play, doubt that much is likely to change in superpower-directed world ordering efforts even in the longer term. Nevertheless, advocacy with SC members and leveraging 'friendly' donors and other member states will undoubtedly remain high on the agenda of the ICRC, NGO consortia and other humanitarian players for the foreseeable future.

Little is to be expected in the short term on the issue of UN reform despite the serious predicament in which it finds itself post-Iraq and the current flurry of proposals. Caught between cooption and irrelevance and weakened by the Baghdad bombings and growing attacks against UN staff in Afghanistan – which have rendered the organization much more risk averse in crisis situations – it will take a while to recover. In the meantime, the centrality of its humanitarian functions – coordination, standard-setting – is in retreat. Many would argue that major surgery cannot be postponed any longer: a deep reform of the humanitarian system is necessary. As yet there is no apparent willingness to tackle such reform, whether in UN or in donor circles and this despite the Secretary General's own feeling, after Baghdad, that the UN was 'at a fundamental fork in the road'.

Is universality in jeopardy?

Given what has been discussed above, perhaps one should ask whether there is anything universal about what we call humanitarian action. Or is it that the concepts and the ideology still have some universal credentials but that the practice has drifted away from its universal moorings? An exercise to verify the existence of a consensus in the world's different cultures as to what constitutes 'humanitarianism' would probably yield interesting results. Luckily, for the mainstream humanitarian enterprise, this is not going to happen any time soon. Aid workers who have worked in fundamentalist Islamic contexts know the difficulties of getting local authorities to sign up to 'our' version of humanitarianism. In Afghanistan, for example, the UN tried unsuccessfully to convince the Taliban to agree to some 'humanitarian operational requirements' based on basic principles for the provision of aid – freedom of access and assessment of need, impartiality in distribution, non-discrimination, etc. The Taliban agreed … on condition that all the principles be qualified as 'acceptable as long as they did not contradict the policies of the Islamic Emirate of Afghanistan' (Donini 2005).[14] This led to frustrating discussions with each side claiming the superiority of its own set of ethical standpoints and to a predictable breakdown of communication.

As things stand now, while the principles may well be universal – or so professional humanitarians would like them to be – the reality is that humanitarian action, in addition to being challenged conceptually by other traditions of caring for the victims of war and disaster, is based on the 'restricted consensus' of the handful of donor states that finance the bulk of 'official' humanitarian aid. To be more precise, such action is also built upon the obfuscation of other realities, namely the contributions of non-traditional donors (such as Islamic countries and charities, remittances of diasporas and migrants, and of course the contributions of affected countries, communities, and families themselves). There are no hard and fast figures to pin on this parallel universe of humanitarian action – one might view it as the 'informal economy' of the humanitarian marketplace – but the scale of such untallied contributions is likely to be considerable, perhaps even equal in size to 'Western' humanitarian aid. And herein lies part of the rub.

The fact that humanitarian activities are funded by a small club of western donors and implemented prevalently by northern-based agencies reinforces the perception, which corresponds to the reality, that humanitarianism is 'of the North'. Unlike other forms of intervention in crisis countries – for example, UN mandated peacekeeping operations where all states participate in the debate and, nominally, in the action – the countries of the Third World have little visible stake in the policies and management of the humanitarian enterprise.

Self-regulation of the donor community can only go so far. The so-called 'good donorship' initiative has raised expectations, but it does not seem to have engaged donor bureaucracies at a high enough political level. Political decision-makers do not necessarily heed the message of their more principled and more alarmed humanitarian colleagues. Could the South, including affected countries, be more involved in the funding and decision-making related to UN humanitarian action? The obvious answer is assessed contributions. If such contributions can be made obligatory for UN peace operations, why not for UN-mandated humanitarian assistance? In all likelihood this would go a long way towards solidifying a more universal humanitarian consensus, in which all UN member countries would have a voice. If its universal credentials are re-established, in the UN for starters, perhaps this could help to dispel the widespread view within influential circles in the South that humanitarianism is a Western crusade aimed at imposing alien values with strong-arm tactics.[15] But the UN is only a small part of the humanitarian picture, and a shrinking one at that.

Much more will need to be done to bring other humanitarian traditions – the Islamic ones in the first instance, but others as well – centre stage.[16] A philosophical issue arises here: should this process of rapprochement between different cultures of caring for civilians in crisis and conflict be undertaken by advocacy built around existing tools – essentially IHL and the Geneva Conventions – or should everything be up for discussion? The dangers of succumbing to cultural relativism, or opening Pandora's box, would militate in favour of advocacy on the basis of existing doctrines. However, this will undoubtedly be seen as the imposition of 'northern terms'. Similar issues arise in the human rights arena. The problem of who sets the terms of the debate and how this is perceived in the South has no easy solution. Moreover, the 'rationalist' northern approach, steeped as it is in the values of the Enlightenment, may be ill-equipped to understand or even give a fair hearing to the views of groups who do not espouse clear distinctions between state, society, the individual and religion. It could well be that faith-based northern groups are in a better position to foster such a dialogue. It is not simply a matter of reaching out and working more closely with Islamic and other non-Western faith-based agencies. Fundamental behavioural changes are required to bridge the growing gulf between the outside assistance agency and those in need. Speeding around in big white vehicles or, worse, with armed escorts as UN assistance agencies are forced to do in Afghanistan, is unlikely to promote a better understanding. 'We' are not 'them', and we make little effort to be accountable to those we seek to help.

A final element of the universality issue is the relationship between humanitarian action and human rights. The end of the Cold War has thrust the humanitarian and human rights agendas into each other's arms or at least the actors to confront each other. The expanding definitions of humanitarianism that gained currency in the 1990s have resulted in considerable overlap and some friction between the two. The integration and coherence agendas have done likewise, often to the detriment of both humanitarian and human rights action. How will this relationship evolve in the future? Will there be more separation or convergence?

Much will depend on how 'sovereignty' is redefined in the years to come and/or how the rich world relates to the poor in the troubled borderlands. It is probably safe to assume that in many spheres of activity our perception of and attitude to sovereignty will continue to evolve significantly. This will affect attitudes in relation to the protection of civilians in conflict but also in relation to a wider set of threats that undermine the right of individuals to survive with a modicum of dignity.

In other words, the rich world may well continue to safeguard its way of life but it will be more aware that poverty, lawlessness, AIDS, illicit economies, the breakdown of state structures all pose threats to its own security and well-being. It is likely that measures to resist intensified northerly flows of migrants and asylum seekers will be coupled with more frequent, not necessarily high profile, interventions predicated on humanitarian and human rights justifications.

Reading the tea leaves

This chapter argues that the universalist claims of mainstream humanitarianism ring hollow at best. Humanitarian action is self-defined by those who practise it with little or no consideration for alternative approaches or traditions aimed at alleviating human suffering. Re-inventing a globally acceptable notion of 'humanitarianism' is therefore a tall order. As in the human rights arena, it is far from clear that reopening discussions on the foundations of the humanitarian discourse would actually advance the overall humanitarian cause. On the other hand, trying to universalize our own particularistic blend of humanitarianism, inextricably linked as it is with western history, thought and values, is unlikely to sway doubters and nay-sayers in the South.

One may therefore well ask: In the context of the global war on terror, is 'universality' a reachable goal or is it just an ideological and naive proposition? Humanitarian action has always been beset by political manipulation, it is inescapably of the North and acts as a conveyor for values and types of behaviour that are often alien if not hostile to its purported beneficiaries. If such is the case, would it not be logical to accept that the world is a messy place and that while the task of alleviating suffering is a just and urgent cause we have to accept reality, occasionally hold our nose, and get on with it? This is the road chosen by the pragmatist or 'Wilsonian' wing of the humanitarian enterprise and, as mentioned earlier in this paper, one of the possible outcomes of the current malaise in the humanitarian community is a more formal bifurcation between purists and pragmatists.

But even for purists the stakes are high. Eschewing military protection and affirming fidelity to core principles is no longer sufficient to guarantee the safety of staff working in fraught or hostile environments like Iraq, Chechnya and Afghanistan. In these areas, the social contract that made humanitarian action acceptable to belligerents no longer holds. Aid workers are seen as lucrative soft targets or vectors of an imperial crusade, or both. In certain contexts, it may no longer be possible to mend the relationship: shadowy insurgent forces no longer see advantages to maintaining a relationship with the likes of the ICRC or MSF, let alone the UN. Even proxies who know proxies are difficult to find. In such environments the only option is to continue to try to reach the most vulnerable through a deeper involvement with the local communities. The assumption is that even if communities are unable to protect aid workers now, if a solid relationship is established, it will be possible to do so later. This may require some unorthodox thinking, including a departure from current top-down, supply and ex-pat.-driven approaches and the tyranny of the project.

It may be useful as well to look at humanitarian assistance through the lens of local strategies for social transformation. Humanitarian action is first and foremost about saving lives, but it also brings the baggage of the foreigner with it. In the tribal areas of Afghanistan, for example, for many years the assistance provided by NGOs was the only window on the world available to local communities. Their views and expectations have been unavoidably transformed by this relationship. In some cases it has turned sour and NGOs have overstayed their welcome; in others it has created dependencies; in many it has worked to open up areas through a careful balancing of the old and the new. Even under the Taliban, in many rural areas girls were able to go to school because communities were able to understand 'from within' the value of education. In fact, according to one observer, never in the history of Afghanistan had so many girls gone to school in rural areas than during the Taliban years.[17] Today, the Tribal Liaison Office is able to develop partnerships with local communities using a similar approach even in the most insecure districts of the Afghan south-east. They rely on local elders to identify small-scale activities to be implemented directly by the tribal structures. Not even the Taliban would dare to touch local aid workers travelling with respected 'grey beards'. Similar home-grown approaches are burgeoning in Somalia where a range of social services are provided by hybrids – half-local NGO, half -private entrepreneurial endeavours – that run schools and clinics at a fraction of the costs of ex-pat. NGOs (Le Sage 2004). That they may occasionally receive seed money from the benevolent wings of shadowy Islamic groups and that their standards of accountability differ from what we are accustomed to does not detract from the fact that, like their Afghan counterparts, they perform useful, effective and socially 'transformative' functions. As Peter Berger noted, social processes tend to succeed only if they are 'illuminated from within' (Berger 1974).

'Until the lions have their historians, history will always be written by the hunters' goes the African proverb. Perhaps the time has come to give the lions, the gazelles and even the suffering grass a stake in the debate. In fact, testing the universality of the humanitarian impulse (and of its human rights cousin) at the grassroots level may be the way to go. Arguably, the caring for the war wounded, the protection of children and civilians in war zones are obligations recognized, in their own ways, in all cultures. This humanitarian substratum is undoubtedly universal. It is the behaviour of leaders and warlords which is problematic, not the dictates of cultures and religions. Hence, working with local groups and creating partnerships around common 'humanitarian' concerns may be a more productive way of promoting universality than a 'dialogue of (the deaf) civilizations' at the political level. Perhaps, also, northern humanitarians need bigger ears and smaller mouths.

Notes

1. This chapter builds on research conducted by the Feinstein International Famine Center (FIFC), Tufts University, on the implications of the conflicts in Iraq and Afghanistan for the future of humanitarian action (see famine.tufts.edu). Earlier work of the FIFC on these issues has appeared in the *Journal of Refugee Studies* and *Disasters* (Spring 2004) under the signatures of A. Donini, L. Minear and P. Walker.
2. On PRTs and the securitization of assistance in Afghanistan, see Donini et al. (2005).
3. G. Agamben, quoted in Duffield (2004).
4. For an ICRC perspective, see Haroff-Tavel (2003).
5. This may be true within a particular context, but, internationally, there are huge distortions in proportionality, e.g. in the allocations to the victims of the Tsunami vs. DRC.

6. The degree of independence and impartiality such agencies are able to maintain is likely to be inversely proportional to the political capital invested by the donor in the crisis, i.e. in forgotten emergencies it will be easier to maintain more principled approaches.

7. E.g. unallocated government multilateral funds with 'no strings attached'.

8. More than 50 national and international staff of NGOs and the UN have been killed in Afghanistan between January 2003 and May 2005. Data provided by the Afghanistan NGO Security Office (ANSO).

9. Data from the FIFC study on perceptions of security (Donini et al. 2005) indicates that local communities were more concerned by what and how assistance was provided rather than by who actually delivered it.

10. A recent study in Afghanistan has shown that mine clearance done by Coalition or ISAF forces is 20–30 times more expensive than 'humanitarian demining' done by national NGOs and coordinated by the UN.

11. Vaux in this volume and his paper for CAFOD, 2005.

12. This, quips an observer in Afghanistan, will be Coalition Forces commander General Barno's lasting contribution to US military history

13. APDOVE (Association of Protestant Development Organizations), CARE, CIDSE (Cooperation internationale pour le développement et la solidarité), Eurostep, MSF, Oxfam, Save the Children and World Vision, see P. J. Simmons, 'Learning to Live with NGOs', *Foreign Policy*, 112, Fall 1998, in Ron and Cooley, p. 12.

14. See Donini (2006).

15. This view does not apply only to the Islamic world. In India ICRC recently conducted a poll to see how it was perceived in Hindu fundamentalist circles. The were very surprised to learn that they were seen as a sect, which was promoting a book (the Geneva Conventions) and whose aim was proselytism and conversion ...

16. This is also an under-researched area; see Ilchmann and Katz (1998).

17. Carol le Duc, Swedish Committee for Afghanistan.

References

Benthall, Jonathan (2003) Humanitarianism and Islam after 11 September, in Macrae and Harmer, *Humanitarian Action and the Global War on Terror: A Review of Trends and Issues*, HPG Report 14 (London: ODI).

Berger, P. (1974) *Pyramids of Sacrifice: Political Ethics and Social Change* (New York).

Bjoreng, Eva (2003) Taking a Stand: Solidarity and Neutrality in Humanitarian Action, *Humanitarian Exchange* (London: ODI).

Braumann, R. and P. Salignon (2004), Iraq: in Search for a 'Humanitarian Crisis', in Fabrice Weissman (ed.) *In the Shadow of 'Just Wars'. Violence, Politics and Humanitarian Action* (Ithaca, NY: Cornell University Press).

Cooley, A. and J. Ron (2002) The NGO Scramble. Organizational Insecurity and the Political Economy of Transnational Action, *International Security*, 27(1), Summer.

Donini A. et al. (2005) *Mapping the Security Environment: Understanding the Perceptions of Local Communities, Peace Support Operations and Assistance Agencies*, FIFC, Tufts University, May 2005 (www.famine.tufts.edu).

Donini, Antonio (2004) Principles, Politics and Pragmatism in the International Response to the Afghan Crisis, in A. Donini, N. Niland and K. Wermester (eds.)

Nation-building Unraveled? Aid, Peace and Justice in Afghanistan (Bloomfield, CT: Kumarian Press).

Donini, Antonio (2006) Negotiating with the Taliban, in L. Minear and H. Smith (eds.) *Humanitarian Diplomacy* (Tokyo: UNU Press).

Duffield, Mark (2001) *Global Governance and the New Wars* (London: Zed Books).

Duffield, Mark (2004) Human Security: Reinstating the State, *Disasters*, Summer.

Hardt, Michael and Negri, Antonio (2001) *Empire* (Cambridge, MA and London: Harvard University Press).

Harroff-Tavel, M. (2003) Does it Still Make Sense to be Neutral? *Humanitarian Exchange*, 25, December: 2–4.

Ilchmann, W., S. Katz and S. Queen (eds.) (1998) *Philanthropy in the World's Traditions* (Bloomington, IN).

Kennedy, David (2004) *The Dark Side of Virtue. Reassessing International Humanitarianism* (Princeton, NJ and Oxford: Princeton University Press).

Le Sage, A. with K. Menkhaus (2004) The Rise of Islamic Charities in Somalia: An Assessment of Impact and Trends. Paper presented at the International Studies Association Convention, Montreal, March.

O'Brien, Paul (2004) Old Woods, New Paths and Diverging Choices for NGOs, in A. Donini, N. Niland and K. Wermester (eds.) *Nation-building Unraveled? Aid, Peace and Justice in Afghanistan* (Bloomfield, CT: Kumarian Press).

Rieff, David (2002) *A Bed for the Night. Humanitarianism in Crisis* (New York: Simon and Schuster).

Slim, Hugo (2004a) *A Call to Alms: Humanitarian Action and the Art of War* (Geneva: Centre for Humanitarian Dialogue).

Slim, Hugo (2004b) *With or Against?* (Geneva: Centre for Humanitarian Dialogue).

Stoddard, Abby (2003) Humanitarian NGOs, Challenges and Trends, in J. Macrae and A. Harmer (eds.) *Humanitarian Action and the Global War on Terror: A Review of Trends and Issues*, HPG Report 14 (London: ODI).

Vaux, Tony (2005) Humanitarian Trends. *Humanitarian Initiatives*. www.humanitarianinitiatives.org, February.

13

Transnational Humanitarian Action in the Eastern Democratic Republic of Congo: State Building and Citizenship

Dennis Dijkzeul

Introduction

The Democratic Republic of the Congo (DRC) is the quintessential failed state. Effective government has broken down in many parts of the country. The worst affected area is eastern DRC, which has known intense conflict, high mortality and great refugee and internally displaced people movements for more than a decade. Still, the DRC constitutes a silent emergency; relegated to small notices on the middle pages of newspapers, it receives relatively little international donor attention compared to such crises as the tsunami in South Asia, Afghanistan and Darfur. Nevertheless, many transnational humanitarian organizations have come in attempting to address aspects of the crisis.

This chapter looks at some of the practices, ideas and values concerning citizenship in eastern DRC, in particular the provinces of North and South Kivu, and assesses the influence of transnational humanitarian actors. It studies two paradoxes. The first is that the ongoing wars have fostered a greater sense of Congolese nationality, but little idea of what Congolese citizenship entails in terms of rights and responsibilities. At the same time, the wars have fostered social exclusion of some population groups. In this respect, the chapter examines local ideas of citizenship, in particular those relating to two very different groups, namely pygmies and Banyamulenge. The second paradox is that the transnational organizations (attempt to) save lives and try to do good, but are not perceived that way. This chapter also examines the impact of humanitarian organizations on the debates concerning citizenship and rebuilding civil society and the state. It thus assesses both the positive and negative roles of the humanitarian organizations and the local population in state-building and fostering a greater sense of citizenship.

The demise of the state

The defining characteristic of citizenship is membership of a political community, owing allegiance to it and possession of rights, in particular political participation. The community nowadays is normally a state. However, in the DRC the state has almost ceased to function, and issues of nationality have become divisive due to ethnic diversity and 'divide-and-rule' policies of different elites. In addition, allegiance has always been weak, because the population has known exploitation, exclusion and cycles of interlocking conflict since the days of the Arab slave trade. Understanding the demise of the state and concomitant weakening of civil society is important because it shows how concepts of citizenship have been undermined. It also determines the scope for action for transnational humanitarian organizations.

From breakdown to war

In the Congo the state began as a colonial construct. Full citizenship with all its advantages existed for the Belgian colonizers only. As a consequence, the Congolese state was weak at independence, and under Mobutu's rule, which was essentially based on patronage, it grew progressively weaker. The state as guarantor of people's rights and provider of services was broken down for the (temporary) benefit of those close to the president. To understand the current absence of 'citizenship' and the role of the humanitarian organizations, we need to understand these processes of state breakdown in more detail.

During the 1970s and 1980s, Mobutu 'nationalized' mining and agricultural companies in (what was then) Zaire and put his cronies in control. This weakened the economy and reduced the national tax base, which would otherwise have helped maintain public institutions. When he was unable to extract more resources from the agricultural and mining companies, he began to use the central bank to print money to pay off debts and keep his patronage system running. The negative effects of the ensuing hyperinflation were almost entirely borne by the majority of the population outside his patronage network (Wrong 2000: 126). Using official exchange rates set by the central bank also allowed the ruling elite to skim exchange rates (Terry 2002: 35–42). Finally, the central bank provided opportunities for money laundering at rates unheard of in the industrialized world. All these activities weakened the monetary monopoly of the state.

When, in the 1980s, Mobutu came under increasing pressure from the Bretton Woods institutions and donor governments to rein in the national budget deficit, he decided not to curtail his personal expenses and patronage system. Instead, he cut the budgets for health, education, infrastructure, security and other government services. As a consequence, service delivery systems deteriorated rapidly.

As his economic position weakened, Mobutu also created and exploited ethnic strife, which helped deflect criticism from his regime to weak ethnic groups, while providing looting opportunities for unpaid soldiers. When, in the early 1990s, the international community supported a Sovereign National Conference (SNC), which was to promote multi-party democracy, Mobutu promoted ethnic conflict between the Katangese and Kasai in Katanga (Shaba), partly because it was a cheap way to undermine support for Etienne Tshisekedi, an ethnic Kasai and Mobutu's main political opponent (Berkeley 2001: 188–229). Paradoxically, Mobutu was able to strengthen his authority in the short term, because he was asked to mediate between or offer protection to different groups.

Later, Mobutu exploited ethnic violence in North and South Kivu provinces, which border on Rwanda. These two provinces had a vibrant civil society, whose members participated actively in the Sovereign National Conference. Mobutu did not succeed in corrupting them as he did with many other representatives, because the Kivu representatives were strongly controlled by their local constituencies. He changed tactics by creating tensions between the Banyarwanda and local ethnic groups in the Kivus.[1] The Banyarwanda have been living in the eastern DRC since pre-colonial times, but their citizenship or Congolese status has never been fully accepted.[2] As a result, the participation of Banyarwanda in the SNC was disputed because they were not considered 'true' Zairians. In addition, Mobutu fostered violence between Hutus and the local minority ethnic group of the Bahunde on the Masisi plains in North Kivu. Simultaneously, these Hutus increasingly accepted the racist Hutu ideology from their Rwandan cousins and started to kill and drive out local Tutsis. The Zairian army supported these Hutus, and many Tutsis had to flee to Rwanda. Local groups, for example from the Bahunde minority, that wanted to fight the Hutus were shocked to find that the Zairian forces supported the Hutus instead of them.

In the end, attempts to institute democracy in the DRC failed because its leaders took Mobutu's threats of violence seriously and did not push their efforts further. Paradoxically, Mobutu's 'divide-and-rule' policies led to violence and chaos, while making it more difficult to dislodge him, as no viable alternative national leadership could emerge. Some observers even argue that Mobutu fostered the genocide in Rwanda (see Braeckman 1996: 167; Wrong 2000).

As a result of the Rwandan civil war and genocide in 1994, over a million Rwandan refugees passed through the towns and fields of eastern Zaire, which severely tested local capacities to deliver services to both refugees and the local population. The refugee crisis also caused serious environmental degradation and led to an influx of international humanitarian organizations. Initially, most members of the international community assumed that all Rwandans were *bona fide* refugees. However, the Hutu extremists responsible for the genocide had forced their Hutu compatriots to become refugees and hid among them. Later, they forced many refugees to remain in the camps. Within the camps they replicated their Rwandan power structure, so that they remained in charge. Neither Mobutu's regime nor international peacekeeping forces decided to disarm these Hutu combatants. Frequently, the extremists worked for the humanitarian organizations and the international military forces that had come in to support the refugees. Soon, the refugee camps were used as bases for rearmament and attacks on Rwandan soil (see Terry 2002: 155–215, 247–5). Many refugees wanted, or were said to want, to create a Hutu homeland on the Masisi plains in North Kivu, which further increased tensions with the local population, as well as with the Rwandan government.

In August 1996, the Zairian army attacked the Banyamulenge, a Tutsi group living in South Kivu. They, however, defended themselves more effectively than their counterparts from North Kivu. In reaction, several Banyamulenge leaders established close ties with the Tutsi-dominated government in Rwanda. Initially, many Banyamulenge felt ambivalent about these ties. While they acknowledged their ethnic bonds, they also perceived themselves as Congolese. In its turn, the Rwandan government built up and supported a rebel movement that wanted to fight Mobutu. This became the Alliance des Forces Démocratiques pour la Liberation du Congo (AFDL), which was led by Laurent Kabila. The rebel movement met with little organized resistance, which allowed the Rwandans to repatriate many refugees. Simultaneously, the *génocidaires* fled from the camps into the forests.

In May 1997, Kabila overthrew Mobutu with strong support from the Rwandan and Ugandan armies. Zaire became the Congo again. Over the next eighteen months, however, the alliance between Kabila and the

Rwandans broke down. Most Banyamulenge used to co-operate with Kabila, but now sided with the Rwandans. In August 1998, the Banyamulenge-dominated Rassemblement Congolais pour la Démocratie (RCD), with support from the Rwandan, Ugandan and Burundian armies, started another war to displace Kabila's regime. This war soon reached a stalemate. Kabila received support from Angola, Zimbabwe, Chad and Namibia, while Uganda and Rwanda grew apart over their differing economic interests and supported different rebel groups. As a result, the country was divided into roughly three parts.

The Front de Liberation de Congo (FLC) led by Jean Pierre Bemba, and supported by the Ugandans, occupied the north. Some of the people close to Bemba also had close ties to Mobutu. The RCD – supported by the Rwandans – maintained control over the eastern part, and the government forces controlled the west and south. In the meantime, the Interahamwe[3] continued to destabilize and loot parts of eastern DRC. The Mayi-Mayi – originally local self-defence groups or parts of local communities that fought against foreign occupation, increasingly turned into armed bandits that also raped and looted – were also active in RCD-and FLC-held territory.

Over time, the different warring factions and their international supporters became more interested in economic exploitation – for example, of diamonds and coltan – than in ending the war, so that it increasingly became unclear who was fighting whom (see United Nations, S/2001/357). Ugandans and Rwandans fought each other in Kisangani over their interests in, for example, diamonds. The relationship between the RCD and the Rwandans was also unstable.[4] Moreover, local ethnic conflicts – for example, the extremely deadly struggle between the Lendu and the Hema in Ituri – were spurred by Rwandan and Ugandan armaments. As a result, the Congolese war broke down into 'dozens of overlapping microwars … in which almost all the victims [were] civilians' (*Economist*, 4 July 2002). Economic activity deteriorated further and extreme poverty increased sharply. The eastern DRC became an 'unchecked incubation zone for diseases' and the mortality rate soared (Roberts 2000: 3).

At the national political level, progress was very slow. In 1999, the Lusaka agreements included the establishment of an unarmed UN peacekeeping force (MONUC) close to the frontline, and the warring factions partially withdrew, with the Namibian and Chadian forces pulling out completely. The Burundians remained for some time, but only to fight 'their' rebel forces across their border. The Ugandans withdrew some of their troops, but later returned, while the Zimbabweans and Rwandans did not pull back.

The death of President Laurent Kabila in January 2001, and the subsequent accession to office of his son, Joseph Kabila, led to renewed diplomatic interventions to implement the Lusaka agreements. These agreements included the withdrawal of foreign forces and political negotiations to establish a transitional government and a process towards multi-party elections. MONUC forces increased in size and firepower over time.

In the spring of 2002, the inter-Congolese dialogue between the main parties to the conflict in Sun City broke down, but the Kabila government and the FLC were able to reach an agreement, so that approximately 70 per cent of the country's territory came officially under control of the Kinshasa government. In July 2002, an agreement was reached with the Rwandans about their withdrawal in return for renewed efforts by the Congolese government to facilitate repatriation of ex-forces Armées Rwandaises (Rwandan Armed Forces – FAR) and Interahamwe irregular forces. By the end of 2002, most foreign forces had left the DRC, and this considerably facilitated the peace process.

In December 2002, the inter-Congolese dialogue led to the Global and Inclusive Accord 'between the government in Kinshasa and the RCD and the MLC rebel groups. This set out a framework for the establishment of [a] Transitional National Government (TNG)', with four vice-presidents representing the three warring factions and civil society (DFID 2003). The TNG was inaugurated in July 2003. It is an internally divided government, but the process of national reunification that it represents is highly popular in the Kivus.

Despite diplomatic progress, sporadic but intense violence continues especially in the eastern part of the country. In 2004, fighting between the Congolese Armed Forces (Forces Armées de la République Démocratique du Congo – FARDC) and troops of a renegade Banyamulenge general led to widespread looting and further gender-based violence in and around Bukavu. Such fighting by regular and irregular (proxy) warring factions may recur in the near future. According to the latest IRC mortality survey, 3.9 million people have died due to the war, with 40,000 excess deaths a month between January 2003 and July 2004 (Coghlan et al. 2004).

Due to the wars, 'the Kinshasa government cannot fulfill its mandate in the eastern provinces,' and the rebel groups (and their foreign supporters) 'that exercise de facto power have failed to adequately support services that address the population's basic needs' (IRC 2002: 4). The Congolese state does not control all its territory. Policy, regulatory, monitoring and coordination functions concerning national and international actors are either nonexistent or weak. Both the Weberian monopolies on force and monetary matters have broken down. In sum, the Congolese state does not possess the traditional attributes of a functioning state (IRC 2002).[5] Hence, it is unlikely that the TNG will be sufficiently effective soon. Its members are jockeying for position and are still lacking in policy capacities. Although the local population looks forward to the elections ('I am fifty and have never voted in my life and now, finally, I will able to cast my vote'[6]) many outside observers fear that they will lead to new rounds of violence.

Consequences for the population

The conflicts have had a profound impact on the everyday life of the Congolese population. First, they have caused considerable internal displacement and curtailed freedom of movement. Individuals and communities have been targeted by armed groups, as well as by police and military authorities, and subjected to various forms of torture, rape, extortion and looting. Consequently, people living close to the forests where the rebels are hiding do not dare tend their fields or fetch water. They either move away or spend the night in hiding, away from their homes, where they feel somewhat safer from looting and rape – but are then often exposed to the elements as well as to parasites. They frequently suffer from exhaustion and malnutrition. At the same time, those who were able to leave have gone and there has been a brain-drain to neighbouring countries and to the West. Many IDPs have moved to the major cities, which generally do not have the facilities to support such rapid population growth. In addition, many men have moved away from their families to take up illegal mining, for example of coltan.

Second, the conflict and accompanying economic decline curb the opportunities of the population to make a living. The DRC's long economic decline has diminished the role of plantations, mining, transport, trade, and industry. Instead, agriculture – including subsistence agriculture – which is primarily destined for domestic consumption, is the region's main source of income (ALNAP 2003: 34). Most of the population has also resorted to informal activities. Large numbers of the population suffer from malnutrition and chronic shortages of food. In addition, deforestation and desertification are hampering food production in some areas of the Kivus. City agriculture has become a common coping strategy. Finally, people who have joined the rebel groups rarely have alternative economic opportunities, making demobilization a difficult goal to achieve.

Third, marginal groups, such as the pygmies, women and street children, have been marginalized even further, while social cohesion has declined. Street children were uncommon only a few years ago, but since then many children have been abandoned by their parents or other caretakers. Many are killed, abused or accused of witchcraft. The latter accusations reflect widespread belief in – and associated fears of – black magic and the spiritual powers of certain individuals or other entities, such as animals. In addition, many women and children suffer from widespread sexual and gender-based violence. These forms of violence worsen the ongoing HIV/AIDS epidemic.

Fourth, the conflict hampers access to the countryside and leads to the destruction of infrastructure. Postal services, road infrastructure and telecommunications have either disappeared or function at a very low level. This has given rise to thriving mobile phone businesses, four-wheel drive imports and air traffic for those parts of the population (and international agencies) that can still afford them. However, problems in other social sectors cannot easily be circumvented. Water and sanitation, as well as gas, electricity and other infrastructure(s), can be replaced but only slowly. Currently, some rail and river links are being restored.

Fifth, when government services still function in the eastern DRC, their quality tends to be limited and they often fail to reach the most vulnerable. In particular, people living outside the big cities lack basic services such as health, education, water and sanitation. At the provincial or municipal level, some government institutions remain (sometimes to perform no more than a rubber stamping function). Government officials may still work, but they generally have received little or no pay in a long time. As a result, they have to take on second jobs, raise fees or take bribes in order to survive. Their skill base has also deteriorated. Despite all these difficulties, they still keep some services functioning at a low level.

Sixth, social service systems have broken down. After its abandonment by the central government, the health system generally used a fee system, requiring patients to pay for their own care. However, 'the underpaid, poorly trained, and demoralized staff … are incapable of operating their under-equipped, neglected, and often pillaged or damaged facilities in a manner that responds to the needs of the populations they serve' (IRC 2002: 4). In addition, people frequently lack the means to buy the remaining services, or they have access problems due to the insecurity and long distances involved. In the past, the weakened health system has insufficiently succeeded in addressing epidemics without international support. And it is struggling to address the new needs the wars have created, such as malnutrition or the consequences of sexual violence.

The quality of the education system has also declined considerably. It has grown dependent on contributions by parents and students. Often, teaching staff have other jobs on the side to make a living or give the same course at several institutes – they constitute the so-called *mercenariat pédagogique*. The lack of quality at the elementary level of education causes and aggravates quality problems at the higher levels. In addition, the professional training of teachers and research exchanges have come to a virtual standstill, unless the education institutions have close ties to either international donors or educational organizations, such as Belgium's Université Catholique de Louvain. As a result of the decline in education, people's capacities to perform services, create livelihoods, maintain their health and participate in social life have also diminished.

Finally, the underpaid and weakly controlled police and military, which ideally should play a key role in ensuring the security and protection of the population, are often identified as the perpetrators of violence or oppression in the areas they control. They are often unwilling or unable to withstand other forces, such as the Mayi-Mayi and Interahamwe. The population has thus lost most of its confidence in these institutions (IRC 2002: 4). Moreover, the legal system has almost ceased to function in many areas and is greatly affected by the – sometimes corrupt – influence of local authorities and some traditional leaders, leaving many, especially the poor, more disadvantaged than protected in legal processes and rendering the law, at best, ineffective in helping wronged civilians (IRC 2002: 4).

In sum, poverty, malnutrition and general vulnerability have increased. 'The gulf between the [tiny] wealthy minority, closely linked to those in power, and the vast majority of the population that struggles for survival on a daily basis, has widened' (IRC 2002: 4). A tiny elite, often with close ties to foreign players, has ruthlessly benefited from patronage and war. For most people, the struggle for daily survival (*se débrouiller*) takes precedence over building up or participating in public life. And the local population knows full well that at times it may be physically dangerous to play a role in public life.

As a corollary, the public sphere in the Congo has grown smaller and become fragmented. Different regions, as well as ethnic groups, have become increasingly isolated from each other. The Congolese lack a functioning and legitimate national body that looks after the common good, and their rights and obligations as citizens. They may identify with the remnants and symbols of the state if they choose to, but they rarely encounter a functioning – let alone accountable – state institution. The state as an overarching body that could foster joint interests and promote shared values across ethnic boundaries has been purposely broken down by patronage and war. The political economy of war, and the various international parties that benefit from it, as well as the slow and often halting peace process, do not offer much hope that this will be reversed soon. In the final analysis, personal well-being and progress in a system based on patronage and violence derive from personal favors by strongmen. Citizenship, as a concept of generalized rights and obligations valid for each individual, has no place in such a system. It may sound attractive, but it has become an increasingly esoteric concept.

Responses

Different types of organization have responded to the crises with activities at different levels of society: first, humanitarian organizations have moved in; second, civil society organization have attempted to rise to the challenge(s); and third, the local population has developed, or perhaps it is better to say retreated into, its own institutions.

Responses by humanitarian organizations

Many transnational humanitarian organizations came in during the Rwandan refugee crises but stayed to help the population once they realized how extremely dire the local situation was. Simultaneously, development agencies have either withdrawn or shifted their programmes into emergency mode. In fact, the reach of the central government in the Kivus had been limited for a long time, so that many transnational and local NGOs had come to play an important role in delivering services in areas such as health and education.[7]

The emergency interventions of the humanitarian organizations traditionally focused on short-term survival of the refugees and general population by bringing in resources for such activities as the provision of food, water, shelter, and medicine. If a previously insecure area opens up, the humanitarian organizations often attempt to move in. 'The criteria for effectiveness of [these] centrally managed, materials focused aid systems include speed, accountability to outside donors, and of course, receipt by individuals and groups deemed to be most needy. The role for local people – those seen as "victims" – to manage any aspect of this aid system is [often] minimal or nonexistent. Concentration on the delivery of things to these people, rather than on problem solving with them, places the beneficiaries of aid in a passive, accepting role' (Anderson 1998: 140). This traditional system of humanitarian assistance implicitly assumes that the humanitarian crisis will not last long and that other actors, in particular the national government, will be able to foster more regular development. Put differently, the state is supposed to take care of its citizens; the humanitarian organizations to take care of people in need.

Many of the organizations increasingly feel that this traditional *modus operandi* addresses the only symptoms of the chronic crisis. Even worse, it may actually cause dependency, provide resources that contribute to the continuation of conflict, and destroy local capacities. Therefore, they have started to look for ways to combine humanitarian and development work by creating more participatory programs and building local capacities. In so doing, they face several problems, namely:

- Considerable uncertainty exists concerning the best operational way(s) to make the transition(s) from relief to development.
- Maintaining the traditional humanitarian principles of neutrality, impartiality and independence becomes harder as these organizations are increasingly perceived as actors with their own agendas that become part of the local conflict context.
- Insufficient clarity exists on how and on which levels to negotiate with warring factions and their representatives about freedom of movement, access and staff security. Intimidations and violence seem to be increasing in frequency.
- Difficulties (methodological, cultural or otherwise) occur in assessing and addressing the needs of (diverse and divided) communities and the broader political context.
- Scaling up activities is expensive, while the regulatory framework that could facilitate or guide such expansion is often either underdeveloped or missing.

Even if the organizations successfully address the five issues above, they still face difficult security, policy and coordination problems that are customarily considered the state's purview. Yet the organizations cannot take on all state functions. The wider issues of (national) peace and security are simply too large for them, even though such peace would considerably facilitate their activities. Put differently, a state that functions well enough to take care of security, policy, and coordination issues would often considerably facilitate their work.

In addition, the different approaches used by donors and NGOs in working with local partners and selecting sectors for activities, as well as the competition between them, can lead to fragmented and unsustainable social service systems in different parts of the country, which can obstruct rebuilding and even hamper the post-war viability of the

Congolese state, for example, in the health system different NGOs use different guidelines, standards, monitoring and reporting systems. In addition, some support all health centres in 'their' health zones, whereas other organizations are more selective (Dijkzeul 2003: 183–99).

In general, expatriate humanitarian staff members stay only for a relatively short period of time, say six months to two years on average. As a result, they often do not know the local culture and capacities well enough.[8] In Bukavu, they sometimes miss out on cheap opportunities to support local institutions such as institutes of vocational training and higher education, which could create local capacities quickly and efficiently. At the same time, expats are often younger, with less experience, than many of the locals that they manage. Sometimes, this causes tensions among national and international staff.

Civil society

Whereas the state has broken down, the two Kivu provinces retain a relatively vibrant civil society, though one that has been weakened and become more isolated. Local organizations, such as community-based (women's) groups, churches or related organizations, medical or education professionals, and local human rights organizations attempt to respond to the unmet needs. In addition, local health committees, parent or alumni associations have frequently made an effort to improve health and education services or at least to keep them going. Although the local organizations provide an important social safety net, they often lack the financial means and managerial capabilities to address the multiple unmet needs in a sustainable manner. Nor are they able to scale up their services.

Currently, there are no strong labour unions or political parties that could constitute a countervailing power for state weakness. In its post-independence history, political parties in the DRC have often been used as vehicles for obtaining personal power and collecting spoils for certain individuals or ethnic groups. The churches, to some extent, fulfilled this role, especially in regard to providing social services in the areas of health and education, but they are neither strong enough nor well suited to take over other governmental tasks such as security and policy-making. In specific areas such as reproductive health, their positions are also frequently disputed by other actors. Nevertheless, many Congolese find solace in religion.

The local population

Strictly speaking, there is no such thing as the local population. As the following examples will show, the local population(s) are highly diverse and often internally divided.

In general, the eastern Congolese increasingly fend for themselves, and when possible resort to their ethnic groups, traditional chiefs or families, although these are also under strain. In some places, the conflict has even totally disrupted these institutions. For example, the tactics of the fighting forces that systematically pillage and gang rape have undermined families, when one or more family members were killed or forced to participate in rapes of other family members. Displacement has broken up local communities. Some traditional leaders have fostered conflict or have become corrupt, and so on. Two groups stand out as possible indicators for the difficult relationships among ethnic groups. One group is very weak, the pygmies. The other actually wields considerable power at the moment, despite its relatively small numbers, the Banyamulenge.

Pygmy citizens

The Pygmies are the original inhabitants of the Great Lakes region. Over the last two millennia they have been replaced by the Bantu. They have lost their own language(s) and nowadays speak Swahili. The Pygmies are especially vulnerable because their position as a minority was already weak, and their traditional way of life as hunter-gatherers has become impossible since they have been driven out of the forest. They still prefer to live close to the forest, but this makes them vulnerable to frequent attacks by rebel groups that hide there, such as the Interahamwe. Among the Pygmies, many adult males have been killed, so that only the young, old and infirm remain. Some rebels believe that having sex with a Pygmy woman makes them invincible. As a result, many women have been raped, causing great problems with sexually transmitted illnesses and unwanted pregnancies. In essence, a slow cultural genocide is taking place that may be followed by physical annihilation.

The Bantu population talks about the Pygmies in paternalistic terms. It is highly ironic that they repeat what the colonizers said about the Bantu population a century ago. 'The Pygmies are like children. They want their immediate needs to be satisfied and do not think about the long term. They are intellectually not capable of studying.'[9] The Bantu population essentially considers the Pygmies to be second-class people. If they work together, the Pygmies get paid less and receive less food. As one Pygmy replied about the attitudes of his Bantu neighbours: 'They do not hate us like they do the Banyamulenge, but they do not take us seriously, as they do the Banyamulenge.'

The Pygmies would consider it ideal if they were able to obtain their own (patch of) forest so that they could maintain their traditions and culture. Land pressure and their weak economic position make it unlikely that they will be able to achieve this without international support.

Banyamulenge citizens

In a very different way, the position of the Banyamulenge is also precarious. They arrived with their cattle in the Congo in the late eighteenth century and settled in the Mulenge hills. Unlike the pygmies, they are currently powerful. But they have become internally divided about their relationship with the Tutsi regime in Rwanda. Some Banyamulenge militias have taken part in violence, rape and looting. Despite the considerable political and military power of a few Banyamulenge leaders in the TNG at the moment, the widespread hatred towards this ethnic group may makes them vulnerable in the future. At the same time, their uncertain Congolese citizenship status has regularly brought them into conflict with other ethnic groups and their traditional leaders, for example concerning land entitlements (*securité foncière*). Traditionally, the *chefs coutumiers* of the original inhabitants decide about land rights, which can thus become an important exclusionary mechanism. In postcolonial times, citizenship status and landholding rights of the Banyamulenge, and Banyarwanda in the DRC in general, have been rescinded at the will of the national government. Mobutu changed course on this issue several times as part of his divide-and-rule policies. Solving the issue of land rights and national citizenship (so that the Banyamulenge can own land and obtain regular political functions) is crucial for their future.

The population is divided concerning the future role of the Banyamulenge in the eastern DRC. They generally acknowledge that the Banyamulenge have been in the Congo for a long time and that they have lived peacefully together for most of the time. Still, the Banyamulenge are also considered warmongers of foreign descent – 'even if a log lies in the river for a hundred years it does not become a crocodile'. Due to their ties with Rwanda (see more below), they are held co-responsible for the chronic crisis in the eastern DRC. Some Congolese state that the Banyamulenge, Interahamwe, and Rwandans are all the same and cooperate to exploit the eastern DRC and that they should leave. According to Lemarchand (2003: 29–69), the Banyamulenge are a genocide waiting to happen. Their citizenship status will be one of the major indicators for the strength of democratic values and ideals in eastern Congolese (civil) society. It may also be crucial for ending local conflicts.

Reactions to responses: local perceptions

While working in the eastern DRC, I am always surprised by the intensity and contents of local rumours concerning the wars, the role of the humanitarian organizations and the Banyamulenge, often akin to conspiracy theories, that the local population uses to explain their predicament. Turner (1998: 22–9; 2004: 227–47) states about Burundian Hutu refugees in Tanzanian camps that 'Living in uncertainty, having their symbolic order crumble due to violence and flight, they attempted to create some sort of order through rumours, and I found that many of these rumours circle around global issues'. Virtually the same could be said about the rumours I hear in Bukavu. These rumours explain the current political situation and allow some prognosis for the future. The core of the rumours explains the intentions of the different actors:

> The DRC is a large and rich country. If left alone it would be able to take care of itself very well. Rwanda is a small country. Hence, it can only gain and retain influence in the DRC because it receives international support, especially from the Americans. Otherwise, we would have already defeated them. 'If you see a dog in a tree, you know that there is somebody else behind it.'[10]

A related prejudice is that Tutsis, no matter where they hail from, are power-hungry and cunning, and that they will deceive others, including Western states, about their true intentions. In addition, it is sometimes stated that Tutsi women use their sexual prowess to entrap and weaken other men.

This way of reasoning shows how the eastern Congolese currently define themselves as not being Rwandans (or even Tutsi). Probably, the people of the Kivus nowadays feel more Congolese than ever before in their history. At the same time, this does not allow them to see the (possible) similarities they share with the Rwandans and look for alternative ways of cooperation or peace-building. It is remarkable that this explanation declares some Rwanda-related groups as outsiders, and imputes great powers to them, a fact which has served to strengthen national self-awareness, but only as victims. The local population groups have pinned great hopes on Kabila (himself originally a relative outsider) as a man capable of bringing about peace and democracy. While this way of reasoning explains the local situation, it does not lead to a critical self-assessment of Congolese strengths and weaknesses. Nor does it foster an open discussion on democratic ideals or the rights and obligations of citizenship.

This way of thinking also influences the perception of the transnational organizations. The local population often has a love/hate relationship with these humanitarian organizations. It has high expectations of the abilities of (white) foreigners. But as a result of these expectations, the population is often dissatisfied with the level of services and distrusts the intentions of the staff members working for the organizations. For example, are American organizations really there to help, or do they support the Rwandans? Have the international staff come here to help us, or do they look after their own benefits and interests more? Some local staff members will occasionally point out where they feel treated like second-class citizens. Humanitarian organizations are thus often seen as outsiders that are part of the larger international conspiracy.[11]

These organizations are relatively powerless to change this perception, because they perceive themselves in a very different light, doing good, stressing common humanity and being open to the populations' needs and concerns. They lack the tools to address these rumors. Often, they fail to see that their management and operations do not provide great examples of democratic, inclusive citizenship.

In sum, many Congolese expect the conflicts to be resolved by outsiders, in particular by the US. They often feel dependent on outside support, even though they mistrust this support. At the same time, they frequently distrust their local politicians and their own ability to influence them. In one discussion, a member of a local organization active in improving agriculture expressed surprise on learning how democracy and accountability could work. He smiled: It would be a nice idea, but it seemed so unlikely.

The Congolese thus perceive themselves as being caught up in a kind of international conspiracy, for which they easily find proofs. The downside of these explanations is that they place the Congolese in the position of dependent, passive victims. This does not provide an outlet for their traumas, except as ethnic hatred, and it does not lead to a focus on what Congolese can do for themselves together to organize for a better future. While some humanitarians and outside observers may argue that this victimization reflects strategic use by the locals of the humanitarian organizations, this explication alone takes insufficient account of the depth and prolonged nature of trauma.

Conclusion

In general, fighting patronage, building peace, strengthening civil society and establishing legitimate and accountable (state) institutions with and for the Congolese population will take time. Success is definitely not ensured and probably still a long way off. For most poor people, security services (police, military and judiciary) health, and education are the main contact points with the state (or what remains of it); if these function well, they can help in rebuilding so that the state may regain some legitimacy, which can contribute to maintaining peace. The challenge, however, is not just in rebuilding a state, but also in formulating a new, inclusive social contract on the rights and responsibilities of the Congolese towards one another and the state. This becomes highly visible with regards to the position of the pygmies and the Banyamulenge. Even if peace were to be established shortly, rumours, prejudices and distrust would still stand in the way of building a peaceful, inclusive society. No standard recipes exist to tackle this challenge.

Humanitarian organizations alone cannot and do not take on all societal challenges in the DRC. They do not offer a substitute for peace and cannot resolve the issues involved in rebuilding a state, land entitlement, political representation, or citizenship. These organizations need more support, both diplomatically and financially, to foster peace. And the examples the humanitarian organizations set through their activities, in particular through their very different treatment of international and national staff, is often not an inclusive, participatory one. At best, humanitarian organizations can play a supporting role by saving lives, integrating participatory development activities and promoting the ideals of democratic citizenship; but in all likelihood their role will be more marginal than they themselves realize. They should take local rumours and perceptions more seriously and use media and education to explain their activities and purpose better. But this means that they need better assessments of local perceptions of their work.

Hence, the role of transnational organizations is more limited than they tend to realize. A social contract may be established through a process of trial and error in which setbacks can easily erase earlier progress. The ongoing conflicts may have fostered a greater sense of Congolese identity (as not being Rwandan), but although this may facilitate the ongoing process of reunification, it may also lead to the exclusion and even extermination of some ethnic groups in the near future.

Notes

1. The term *Banyarwanda* encompasses both Hutu and Tutsi and means people of Rwanda.
2. Later the Belgians fostered immigration of Rwandans as labourers. Massacres in Burundi and Rwanda from the late 1950s onwards led to immigration of more refugees. Usually, Hutus and Tutsis, as well as local ethnic groups, coexisted peacefully in the eastern Congo.

3. *Interahamwe* literally means 'those who stand or attack together' in Kinyarwanda. The term officially referred to the youth wing of the former ruling party in Rwanda, the *Mouvement Républicain Nationale Démocratique* (MRND), but it came to describe all militia participating in the genocide regardless of party affiliation (HRW 2002: 8).

4. In 2002, the RCD cooperated with some *Mayi-Mayi* groups with which it used to clash, while continuing to fight other *Mayi-Mayi* groups.

5. In response, donors are currently looking into ways to strengthen the national government's functioning. With their help, the TNG is instituting a process of decentralization, which may in time improve administration in regions far from the centre, such as the Kivus and Katanga.

6. Field interview, October 2004.

7. The humanitarian NGOs are an example of transnationalization, or at least a process toward transnationalization, in the sense that they are non-state entities that usually operate in various localities – humanitarian crisis zones – in a decentralized manner. They execute their activities, in particular service delivery and advocacy, in, above, and between the traditional 'container spaces' of national societies. Nevertheless, they operate closely with the international organizations of the UN, such as WFP, MONUC and OCHA.

8. The ALNAP study on participation in the DRC (2003: 52), states: 'Certain local structures were disappointed by previous attempts to cooperate with international aid actors. They feel that they were "used" for particular tasks (such as supplying information or conducting activities that were compromised by poor security conditions or restricted access) without participating in others (such as defining funding priorities, general management and programme design).'

9. Field interviews, 2003 and 2004.

10. Field interviews, 2001, 2002, 2003, and 2004.

11. The operations of the UN peacekeeping force, MONUC, lie outside the scope of this chapter, because it is legally an international state-based – and not transnational – institution. However, its activities also influence the perception of the local population of other foreign organizations. In May 2004, MONUC withdrew when Banyamulenge militias entered Bukavu town. Later, the local population felt that MONUC protected the *Banyamulenge* militias when they were loosing their fight with the Congolese Army. In addition, MONUC staff have been involved in forced prostitution and even mass rape of Congolese women and children. Naturally, the ineffectiveness and scandals of MONUC have reflected badly on all foreign organizations (see Bitala 2005: 8).

References

ALNAP Global Study (2003) *Consultation and Participation in Humanitarian Action: Democratic Republic of Congo*, ALNAP (London: ODI).

Anderson, Mary (1998) 'You Save My Life Today, But for What Tomorrow?' Some Moral Dilemmas of Humanitarian Aid, in Jonathan Moore (ed.) *Hard Choices: Moral Dilemmas in Humanitarian Intervention* (Lanham: Rowman & Littlefield), pp. 137–156.

Berkeley, Bill (2001) *The Graves Are Not Yet Full: Race, Tribe and Power in the Heart of Africa* (New York: Basic Books).

Bitala, Michael (2005) UN Soldaten im Osten des Kongo: Wenn Blauhelme Nicht Mehr Blau Machen, *Süddeutsche Zeitung*, 51, 3 March: 8.

Braeckman, Colette (1996) *De Wortels van het Geweld: Burundi, Rwanda, Congo-Zaire* [*Terreur Africane*, transl. Coenegrachts, Ward and Jager, Tineke] (Berchem: EPO).

Coghlan, Ben, Rick Brennan, Pascal Ngoy, David Dofara, Brad Otto and Tony Stewart (2004) *Mortality in the Democratic Republic of Congo: Results from a Nationwide Survey – Conducted April–July 2004* (New York and Melbourne: IRC and Burnett Institute). Mimeo.

DFID (2004) *Democratic Republic of Congo: DFID Country Engagement Plan*. Mimeo, 18 September 2004.

Dijkzeul, D. (2003) Healing Governance? Four Health NGOs in War-Torn Eastern Congo, *Journal of International Affairs*, 57(1), Fall: 183–199.

Dijkzeul, D. (ed.) (2004) Between Force and Mercy: Military Action and Humanitarian Aid, *Bochumer Schriften zur Friedenssicherung und zum Humanitären Völkerrecht*, 50 (Berlin: Berliner Wissenschafts-Verlag).

Dijkzeul, D. (2005) *Models for Service Delivery in Conflict-affected Environments: Drawing Lessons from the Experience of the Ushirika/GBV Partnership Programmes in the eastern Democratic Republic of the Congo*, Consultancy report for the International Rescue Committee (IRC) and the UK Department for International Development (DFID). Mimeo.

Economist (2002) Africa's Great War, *The Economist*, 4 July.

HRW (2002) *La Guerre dans la guerre: violence sexuelle contre les femmes et les filles dans l'est du Congo*, June (New York: Human Rights Watch).

IRC DRC (2002) *Application for the Management of Survivors of Torture and Sexual and Gender-Based Violence Umbrella Grant Project for eastern DRC*. Mimeo. Bukavu.

Lemarchand, René (2003) 'The Democratic Republic of the Congo: From Failure to Potential Reconstruction', in Robert I. Rotberg, (ed.) *State Failure and State Weakness in a Time of Terror* (Cambridge: World Peace Foundation/ Washington, DC: Brookings Institution), pp. 29–69.

Moore, Jonathan (ed.) (1998) *Hard Choices: Moral Dilemmas in Humanitarian Intervention* (Lanham: Rowman & Littlefield).

Roberts, Les (2000) *Mortality in Eastern DRC: Results from Five Mortality Surveys*, Final Draft 2000 (New York: IRC Health Unit).

Rotberg, Robert I. (ed.) (2003) *State Failure and State Weakness in a Time of Terror* (Cambridge: World Peace Foundation/ Washington, DC: Brookings Institution).

Terry, Fiona (2002) *Condemned to Repeat? The Paradox of Humanitarian Action* (Ithaca, NY and London: Cornell University Press).

Turner, Simon (1998) Representing the Past in Exile: The Politics of National History among Burundian Refugees, *Refuge*, 17(6) (December): 22–29.

Turner, Simon (2004) Under the Gaze of the 'Big Nations': Refugees, Rumours and the International Community in Tanzania, *African Affairs*, 103: 227–247.

United Nations, S/2001/357, Report of the Panel of Experts on the Illegal Exploitation of Natural Resources and Other Forms of Wealth of the DRC, New York, 12 April 2001.

Wrong, Michela (2000) In the Footsteps of Mr. Kurtz: Living on the Brink of Disaster in Mobutu's Congo, Perennial/Harpers Collins Publishers, New York.

Index